THE BRINK

By the same author:

Thunder of the Captains

THE BRINK

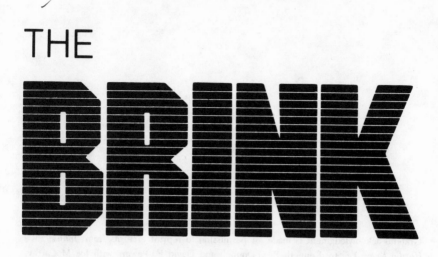

Cuban Missile Crisis, 1962

By DAVID DETZER

J. M. DENT & SONS LTD.

LONDON, MELBOURNE AND TORONTO

Grateful acknowledgment is made for permission to reprint excerpts from "*Johnny, We Hardly Knew Ye*" by Kenneth P. O'Donnell and David F. Powers with Joe McCarthy. Copyright © 1970, 1972 by Kenneth P. O'Donnell, David F. Powers and Joe McCarthy. Reprinted by permission of Little, Brown and Co.

First published in Great Britain 1980

Printed in the United States of America for J. M. Dent & Sons Ltd.

Designed by Sidney Feinberg

British Library Cataloguing in Publication Data

Detzer, David.
  The brink.
  1. Cuban Missile Crisis, Oct. 1962
  I. Title
  972.91′064   E841
  ISBN 0-460-04475-3

marta

Contents

Photographs appear on pages 117 to 124 and 215 to 222.

You have to take chances for peace, just as you must take chances in war. . . . If you run away from it, if you are scared to go to the brink, you are lost.

JOHN FOSTER DULLES (1956)

THE BRINK

Prologue

New York. September 18, 1960

Rain pattered on the runways at New York's Idlewild Airport. A crowd, standing all afternoon, their shoes growing soggy, seemed in good spirits despite the weather. The signs they carried were friendly: "Welcome Fidel"; "Venceremos" (we shall win). When the plane landed they clapped, and when its door opened and a young man of thirty-four emerged, they cheered. Unsure of their mood, he blinked uncertainly at the crowd; then apparently having assured himself they were friendly, he smiled slightly and waved. He walked to waiting microphones and spoke a few words: "I want to salute the people of the United States. My English, the same as last time, is not so good. All I have to say I will say to the United Nations." He turned and entered a waiting limousine.

Fidel Castro had come to address the opening session of the General Assembly. He was the first of more than a dozen world leaders to arrive. Others planning to attend included Wladyslaw Gomulka of Poland and Antonin Novotny of Czechoslovakia, Tito from Yugoslavia and Sukarno from Indonesia, Todor Zhivkov from Bulgaria and Janos Kadar from Hungary. From Russia would come Nikita Khrushchev.

(The police commissioner of the city, Stephen P. Kennedy, was concerned. He knew that demonstrators planned to be on hand during the week. Some of them might attack the dignitaries. Each foreign leader—especially Castro and Khrushchev—had avowed enemies in the city. The danger of assassination was real and Commissioner Kennedy took it seriously.)

Fidel, without incident, headed directly for the Shelburne Hotel, conveniently situated only half a mile from the United Nations. The Cubans had reserved twenty suites. Edward Spatz, the manager of the hotel, either from prejudice of one sort or another or out of fear of reprisals from anti-Castroites, had at first refused them rooms and had only relented after receiving a written request from the American government.

Perhaps Spatz had reason to be worried. By the time the Cubans arrived at the Shelburne, over a thousand anti-Castro demonstrators had gathered, yelling and pushing. Many carried placards, like the one which said: "Fidel Commie, Go Home!"

As he stepped from the car, Castro, obviously nervous, nodded grimly to newsmen and hurried inside.

A pro-Castro crowd arrived. Scuffles began among the demonstrators. Police broke up the fights, arrested some people, and dispersed most of the others; a few pro-Castroites remained. For the next two hours, in hopes the Cuban leader might speak to them, they stood in the rain, chanting, "Viva Fidel! Viva Fidel!" Finally he appeared on his third-floor balcony. He smiled and waved for about three minutes, then went back inside. The remnants of the crowd, apparently satisfied, drifted away.

Rumors spread throughout the week, and have never since died, that the Cuban delegation during its stay in New York acted feverishly rowdy and crude, pointing guns at outsiders on the slightest provocation, breaking hotel furniture in drunken destructiveness, and slaughtering chickens in their rooms. Such stories, while unproved, do not seem totally implausible. The Cubans, not surprisingly, felt a wary suspicion of Americans in general and New Yorkers in particular. Some of their number were a rather unsophisticated lot. This combination could explain much of their jumpiness. As to killing and plucking chickens, members of the delegation were convinced someone might try to poison Fidel and were therefore cooking some of their own food. Although ridiculed at the time, given what we now know about CIA machinations, such fears do not seem so outrageous. As to their reported rowdiness, one wonders how much of the rumors resulted from their appearance—beards, fatigues, and swarthy or black skins— and how much from a kind of anti-Latin, anti-Castro presentiment. The fact that the stories became so widespread is itself suspicious. In a city which had housed uncounted political gatherings and conventions of sales personnel, any Cuban noisiness, produced by less than fifty people, should have disappeared in midtown without a ripple, unnoticed. Any minor, uncouth acts committed by a handful of Cubans are not nearly so revealing as the shocked censorship of reproving New Yorkers.

The day after Fidel arrived a small drama occurred. Hotel manager Spatz asked for $10,000 as an immediate advance against bills and damage. This "unreasonable cash demand," Fidel said, was an insult, but he attempted to raise the money. He came up with $2,000, told Spatz he could possibly raise another $3,000, but the manager held out for the full amount.

Fidel's short-lived patience now snapped. He announced he would leave the Shelburne; he was willing to go anywhere, even Central Park. "We are mountain people," he stated with slight exaggeration. "We are used to sleeping in the open air." (One hesitates to imagine the scene of fifty Cuban Communists ensconced amid the muggers for a week in Central Park.)

At almost dusk Castro and seven aides rushed from the Shelburne and squeezed into an Oldsmobile. Following them through the door came the rest of the delegation who milled around outside, hailing taxicabs, while policemen scrambled to hold back pedestrians on the sidewalk. Cuban spokesmen announced to reporters they would stay no longer at the Shelburne; they were going to the UN until other accommodations could be found. Within minutes they were all gone.

Pro-Castro demonstrators rushed to the official Cuban residence, a small building not far away. Someone in the crowd pulled a fire alarm and a dozen pieces of fire equipment clanged to the scene. This activity attracted an even bigger crowd. It took police hours to disperse it.

Meanwhile, Dag Hammarskjöld, secretary general of the UN, had contacted a New York realtor. Together they made arrangements for Castro and his group to have free accommodations at another hotel. The Shelburne meanwhile phoned the UN and pleaded with the Cubans to return. Manager Spatz insisted there had really been "no cash problem involved." "We're not worried about money," he said. But that evening two station wagons arrived at his hotel. Cubans briskly entered and removed the baggage they had left behind.

At midnight Castro drove uptown into Harlem to the Theresa Hotel. (One wonders whether he had intended something like this from the beginning, for he loved dramatic gestures. His government, moreover, had been attempting to charm its own wary black population. Tweaking the white, capitalistic nose of America's hotel establishment, staying at one of the United States' most famous black landmarks, seems to have been intended as a public relations coup back in the island. Castro had actually begun discussions with the Theresa before his arrival in New York, during the period when he was having problems finding good accommodations in midtown, so the possibility of staying in Harlem had been in the back of his mind for some time.)

The Theresa, built in 1913 and named after the original hotelman's wife, was in the heart of Harlem at Seventh Avenue and 125th Street. Black musicians traveling through town often stopped there; black politicians planned their campaigns in its rooms and their rallies in front of it.

Its heyday, however, had now passed. Two elevators serviced its eleven floors, but only one worked. Its entranceway opened onto a small lobby; a coffee shop with a jukebox stood off to the side. The hotel operator, an aging gentleman from South Carolina named Love B. Woods, placed the Cubans on the sixth, seventh, eighth, and ninth floors. He gave them forty units including several suites. Whether it was their wounded pride over Spatz's insults or their government's propaganda which had brought them here, they paid dearly for it. The Hotel Commodore would have accepted them free; the Shelburne had charged them $400 a day. The Theresa Hotel, few of whose accommodations had private bathrooms, charged $840 a day—double its *own* usual price.

The Theresa's regular residents—200 of its 300 rooms were occupied by permanent guests—appeared a trifle grumpy at the invasion: The Cubans were everywhere, constantly expropriating the elevators and hoarding the bathrooms, disturbing the usual pattern, the tranquility, of the old hotel.

The Cubans in turn remained vigilant. On the ninth floor, not far from Castro's room, armed Cuban guards sat on folding chairs in the dimmed, littered corridor. When Castro ordered steak for lunch the first afternoon, three members of his entourage accompanied the order to the kitchen while the cooks prepared the meat.

Outside the hotel, crowds gathered. At first, many onlookers crowded the sidewalks; then, as the novelty wore off, their numbers dwindled. Most seemed friendly. They called out Fidel's name whenever they saw him. Some carried placards. Easily the most interesting sign read: "Man, like us cats dig Fidel the most. He knows what's hip and what bugs the squares."

This unlikely slogan, probably more spoof than politics, held much truth: Fidel indeed bugged the squares. Maybe it was his beard.

In the late 1950s most Americans looked on beards as at least an oddity, an eccentric means to cover a weak chin or an acned complexion, or a sign of moral or political extremism. Poets in Greenwich Village, "dope fiends," beatniks and the like (to say nothing of Kark Marx, Lenin, and unnumbered crazed anarchists) all wore beards. What Americans failed to realize was that when Castro and his followers came down out of the Sierra Maestra, almost all had sported full growths. Back in the mountains, they had not shaved out of necessity, since they had had little time for tonsorial concerns. Their beards had become their trademark, along with their wrinkled fatigues. They were *barbudos*, the bearded ones. When they had ridden into Havana in 1959 they had worn their beards with pride. To have whiskers was a medal of honor. But in Los Angeles, or DeKalb, Illinois, or Bradford, Pennsylvania, a beard drew stares and catcalls; those who wore them were sometimes called Commies or worse.

The day after Castro arrived at Idlewild, Nikita Khrushchev's ship, the *Baltika*, approached New York. As it drew slowly up the estuary, dozens of small craft carrying demonstrators and signs buzzed around it. One fishing boat, hired for the occasion, held seventy members of the longshoremen's union. "Khrushchev, Butcher of the Hungarian People," their huge sign read. Another boat, a Hudson River Day Liner, normally specializing in ferrying tourists up the river and back, carried one large banner.

Roses are red,
Violets are blue,
Stalin dropped dead—
Why don't you?

Two men in a tiny rowboat hoisted a sign, "End Arms Race Now." Closer into shore, a single demonstrator, paddling a green canoe, held up a poster pleading for: "World Citizens, World Disarmament, and Brotherhood." One banner, typifying that classic, tough New Yorker, stated simply: "Dear K! Drop Dead You Bum!" Khrushchev watched all this with wonder.

Meanwhile the *Baltika* pulled up to Pier 73, a sad, grim, dilapidated structure. The dock glowered like something from a nightmare, forboding and dark, its paint peeling, the stink of salt water and urine in the air. Its filthy skylight, cracked and broken, allowed rain to drip through, soaking the expensive, red oriental carpet and the small crowd of people awaiting the premier. The rain came harder now and fog drifted in, but the Russian leader, wearing a yellow raincoat over his dark suit, smiled merrily. As the ship docked, he leaned against its railing, waved at the crowd on the pier, and clasped his hands over his head. He then stomped jauntily down the gangplank followed by the rest of the East European leaders. Kadar of Hungary had never been far from home and had been seasick all the way across. As he stood on the pier, his face appeared pale and drawn. To make his misery complete, water now dripped through the roof onto his bald head. He stood stalwartly like the others while the Russian premier took silver-rimmed reading glasses from a leather case and read a prepared statement inviting President Eisenhower to a summit aimed at reducing world tensions. (Later that week, Secretary of State Christian Herter, when asked about Khrushchev's request, said he saw no prospect of any such summit meeting. Herter referred to the Communist leaders now arriving in New York as "trouble-makers.")

Khrushchev greeted eight little girls from the Russian Embassy who had been standing with anticipation all afternoon, waiting in their pretty white dresses, white ribbons tied around their pigtails, to hand gladiolas to the premier.

With the ceremonies over, the Soviet leader got into a shiny new Cadillac Fleetwood and left the pier. The other East Europeans brought up the rear.

Although Khrushchev was already a well-known international figure, he remained an enigma. His squat body, his melon head, the short white stubble sprouting sparsely on his scalp, the shrewd, impish, bad-boy light in his eyes, his gap-toothed smile, his theatrical anger, his fingers so broad his hands looked small, the thick heavy wrists of a peasant; all these—exterior things—were known. To Americans he sometimes seemed almost a comic figure, a lovable bear. The inner man remained unknown.

Khrushchev was born in a tiny peasant village about 300 miles south of Moscow in 1894. His childhood was very hard. His family lived in a dirt-floored, thatch-roofed hut. Little Nikita owned no boots. "I went about barefoot and in rags," he once said to some Western diplomats. "When you were in the nursery I was herding cows for two kopeks." His grandfather was a serf. His father was a failed farmer and occasional coalminer who treasured a lifelong— and unrequited—ambition to buy a horse. Nikita grew up a typical Russian peasant. His days were spent as a barefoot shepherd, his nights at home in the family *izba*, their drab hovel, spottily decorated with religious bric-a-brac. "When I think back to my childhood," he once recalled, "I can remember vividly the saints on the icons against the wall of our wooden hut, their faces darkened by fumes from the oil lamps."

In his teens the family moved to a squalid Ukrainian mining community. Nikita went down into the mines, apparently never as a miner but performing related tasks. Eventually he worked as a metal fitter, a job important enough that it kept him from being drafted during World War I.

His life remained unmercifully hard. His first wife apparently died of starvation during a famine. His autobiography, filled with a number of dubious contradictions, recalls a favorite schoolteacher and mentions political tracts read as an adolescent, but the truth would seem to be that he was illiterate into his mid-twenties when he started night school. "Life is a great school," he once told reporters. "It thrashes you and bangs you about and teaches you."

The Russian Revolution, beginning in 1917, changed his direction. With his peasant shrewdness, his natural vitality and ambition, his uncanny timing, he rose slowly through the ranks of the party. He developed into a remarkable politician, a sly wardheeler ingratiating himself with those in a position to help, instantly cutting himself off from others who might drag him down. Anyone succeeding in the deadly labyrinth of Stalinist politics showed acumen. Khrushchev, starting perhaps nearest the bottom, rose the farthest. On Stalin's death in 1953 he hovered just beneath the top few rungs. When those above him knocked each other off, Nikita Khrushchev in 1955 stood alone.

He was a remarkable leader, vibrant with energy, chattering incessantly in colorful vulgarity, his small, sly, porcine eyes glinting.

In Manhattan Khrushchev stayed at the Soviet Mission, a building on Park Avenue. On one side just across the street stood a police station, a fire station, and a synagogue. In another direction lay Hunter College. (At times the noise of fire engines, the sirens, and the demonstrators must have distracted those inside sitting on the overstuffed sofas.)

The day before Khrushchev docked, apparently in the mistaken belief that he was already in New York, about 2,000 demonstrators arrived at the UN, mostly Ukrainians demanding independence for their homeland. "God Bless America. God Free Ukraine," their signs read. A caravan of over sixty cars, a chartered bus, and several trucks circled the United Nations, their horns honking. One car carried on its roof a gallows and a hanging effigy with a sign that declared, "Kh—! This is Your Place!" A middle-aged couple chained themselves to a lamppost.

Yet on the day the Russian premier actually arrived in the city, although 1,200 policeman waited in the downpour at the UN, less than thirty demonstrators appeared, and these soon drifted away.

Only a few came to the Soviet Mission. A single station wagon prowled past, filled with Hungarians shouting, "Svinye!" (Pig!). And later on, one man drove slowly by, honking and yelling "Ubitel!" ("murderer" in Russian).

Khrushchev seemed unruffled by all this. Soon after his arrival, he went to a diplomatic reception at the Plaza Hotel. Since the time for this gathering had been announced in the newspapers, a crowd of several thousand was waiting outside the Soviet Mission to glimpse the premier. As he emerged from the building, many in the crowd shouted at him. He merely smiled and waved, saying to reporters standing nearby: "The American people are wonderful, they are good." At the Plaza, as he was getting into the elevator, several well-dressed ladies and gentlemen, clearly representatives of the bourgeois, capitalistic class, started to hiss at him. He turned, looked on them benignly, and, as he entered the elevator, pursed his lips in their direction and said, "Boo."

In truth Khrushchev found one aspect of his stay in the city quite trying. He was a hyperkinetic individual and felt trapped, cooped up in the Soviet Mission. He searched out ways to relieve his tension. He flitted here and there around the city.

The day after his arrival, he rushed out of the mission at noon. Reporters, whose assignment was to stand outside the Soviet building for just this sort of eventuality, hopped around on the sidewalk, calling plaintively to him (some in Russian), "Where are you going?" He leaned toward them from his seat in the back of the limousine. "We Communists don't tell our secrets," he said. "Watch for the newspapers. They will tell you where I'm bound." He sat back, pleased with his little joke, and signaled to the driver to go ahead. Policemen, unnotified about this sudden departure, scrambled toward their cars, reporters and security men following. Leading a motorcade, the Russian leader drove north into Harlem. At the Theresa he clambered out and went inside. For the next twenty-two minutes he and Castro parleyed in the Cuban's ninth-floor suite. By the time the two men emerged onto the sidewalk, a large crowd of Harlemites had gathered to observe whatever spectacle might be offered. Whole busloads of police had also pulled up. When the two leaders stepped from the door of the hotel, their arms around each other's shoulders, the crowd cheered. Khrushchev, smiling, got back into his car and left. On his return to the Soviet Mission he stopped outside a moment and said to reporters, "I salute Fidel Castro and wish him well. He is a brave lad [*molodets*]." He went inside to eat lunch.

Two hours later he was out again, this time to go to the UN. As he was sitting in the Soviet section conferring with some colleagues, a Cuban approached him. Khrushchev followed the emissary all the way back across the room. As everyone watched, he threw his chubby arms around Castro's heavy torso. He looked like a circus wrestler trying to lift a huge barrel much too big for him. He pressed his cheek upon Castro's chest, his bald head brushing against the much taller Cuban's shaggy beard. Castro, looking down, awkwardly pawed and pummeled the Russian's shoulders. Maybe they felt a trifle silly, for they both began to laugh. The moment seemed symbolic: Cuba and Russia linked together.

Later in the week Khrushchev stood talking to Tito at a party. He grumbled to the Yugoslav that security procedures would not let him go out much. "I have to take my walks on a balcony," he muttered.

Tito: "A balcony? So—do you give concerts there?"

Khrushchev (chuckling): "Yes. For free."

The two men were referring to the day before when the Soviet premier, restless from inactivity, had opened the doors to his balcony, stepped out on the stone balustrade, and peered down on the stunned reporters just 25 feet below. For the next fifty minutes he had offered onlookers a little show.

Seeing him, several Hunter College girls had defiantly begun to sing, "God Bless America." He had grinned maliciously, given a little fist salute to them, and had sung back the first few bars of the "Internationale": "Arise, ye prisoners of starvation."

Dressed in shirtsleeves, he had leaned against the ornate iron railing. Reporters, over forty of them, had shouted questions up at him. After a while he had gone back inside. Three hours later he had come out again and had held another bantering news conference. Nothing he had said on either occasion was of great significance; he was merely letting off excess energy. Some of his comments had included the following: When some male students hissed him from across the street, he told reporters that the young men did not represent the United States. A few cars had happened to pass at that moment, their passengers smiling and waving. Khrushchev said that these people more truly reflected the Americans. As to the student boys, Khrushchev had gestured disdainfully beneath some nearby mounted policemen. "They are what is below that horse over there," he had said; "horse dung."

Since he had previously been quoted widely as saying to Americans, "We will bury you," a reporter had asked him whether he still felt the same. The premier had become very serious, the Soviet flag flapping softly behind him. "No, I never said anything so foolish. Only a madman could say anything that foolish. A government might come to an end but the people always live on."

Because the presidential election of 1960 was in its final weeks, Nixon and Kennedy neck and neck, Khrushchev had been asked which of the two candidates he preferred. He had replied: "I don't see any difference in these two candidates or these two parties. Do you?"

Not far away, in Washington, D.C., at about that time, John F. Kennedy is asking a fund-raising dinner, "Can the world exist half-slave and half-free? . . . The enemy is lean and hungry," he says, "and the United States is the only sentinel at the gate. . . . Extraordinary efforts are called for by every American who knows the value of freedom."

Kennedy's campaign has recently been emphasizing his vigorous opposition to the Communist threat, and he has promised that, if elected, his youthful energies can meet it. He has been implying, without mentioning the name of the immensely popular old President, that Eisenhower's administration has been geriatrically soft on communism. America's lack of success in the space race, an apparent gap between Soviet missile capabilities and those of the United States, and the recent U-2 debacle have been among Kennedy's main campaign thrusts. Such "failures," he has indicated, seem to show weakness at the helm. "We must prove to a watching world," he has been telling audiences, "that we are the wave of the future." And, he promises, "a new generation of Americans is taking over in this country." In Sioux City, Iowa,

Kennedy has just lambasted Nixon and the Republicans for allowing Cuba to be taken over by Castro's "Communist regime," for permitting the creation "of a Communist satellite 90 miles off the coast of the United States."'

Kennedy is mistaken in many of his points. The United States is *not* really behind in the space race; there is *no* missile gap; the facts behind the U-2 affair are clouded in mystery; the Eisenhower administration has already approved secret plans to organize and equip an invasion of Cuba by exiles; and the CIA is plotting to assassinate Castro. (About the time Khrushchev went to the reception at the Plaza Hotel, elsewhere in the same building a meeting was taking place between a representative of America's intelligence agency and an unsavory underworld figure, John Roselli. The government agent was telling Roselli to go to Miami and make arrangements to kill Castro.)

Richard Nixon is in a quandary. He knows Kennedy's allegations are inaccurate. Nixon cannot, however, use his information, most of which is highly classified, to his own advantage. All he can do is feebly suggest that Kennedy's criticisms are naive and dangerous, that attacking Republicans at this crucial time encourages the enemy and therefore, as he says, might be "serving the cause of surrender."

Kennedy brushes aside such ineffectual Nixonian jabs. As he tells an audience in Washington, "I am not satisfied to have the Communists move 3,000 miles from East Berlin to our former good neighbor in Cuba."

A day or so later, campaigning in the Midwest, he says, "Those who say they will stand up to Mr. Khrushchev have demonstrated no ability to stand up to Mr. Castro."

John F. Kennedy promises he will stand up to both.

PART ONE

The United States is not a country to which peace
is necessary.

GROVER CLEVELAND

We cannot tell anyone to keep out of our
hemisphere unless our armaments and the people
behind those armaments are prepared to back up
the command, even to the ultimate point of
going to war.

JOHN F. KENNEDY,
Why England Slept
(1940)

1 *Cuba*

Cuba is a long, slender island, bigger than most outsiders think. In the early days of the Kennedy administration talk became common of invading the island. Some American officials claimed it would be easy to take it over. General David M. Shoup, commandant of the Marine Corps, was unimpressed by such suggestions. A tough, no-nonsense, compact, bull-necked, cigar-smoking leatherneck, Shoup had won the Congressional Medal of Honor in the bloody 1943 invasion of Tarawa. His vocabulary could be brutally direct and earthy; he had once been described as talking like "a Marine sergeant who had never passed the eighth grade." Yet he was an intelligent, sensitive man, and when he said something, others listened. On the matter of a Cuban invasion, he performed a simple audio-visual demonstration for a group of high-ranking officials. He took a map of the United States. On it he put an overlay of Cuba. To the surprise of many in his audience, the island stretched out much further than they had thought. Its 800-mile length lay from New York almost all the way to Chicago. Near the middle of the overlay stood a tiny dot.

"What's that?" someone said.

"That, gentlemen," Shoup replied, ending the lesson, "represents the size of the island of Tarawa."

15

A superficial history of Cuba might go like this: After it was discovered by Columbus in 1492, it became a major stopping-point for Spaniards on their way to and from the New World. The excellent harbor at Havana provided anchorage for great fleets as they prepared to cross the Atlantic, protecting them from hurricanes and British privateers. When their gold craze subsided, the Spanish discovered the value of tobacco and sugar, and Cuba took on an even greater importance. Plantations spread across the island. The Spanish brought in Africans as slaves.

The nineteenth century wrought changes, some of which came from the United States. During spasms of nationalism, Americans dreamed of expansion—and few regions offered choicer prospects. Americans always felt a highhanded disdain for Spain, home of the Inquisition and the Armada. It seemed only a simple matter—and a virtuous one—to seize this Caribbean plum just south of the Florida Keys. But in the years before 1860 other factors interfered and then the Civil War absorbed national attentions.

Eventually the Cubans revolted against Spain in two violent rebellions. By 1898, after two decades of intermittent bitter fighting, the rebels had nearly achieved their goal. Then, partly for economic reasons and partly out of a sense of Victorian decency, President William McKinley and the United States joined the fray—declaring war on Spain. Within a few months it was over. But the United States, rather than simply freeing Cuba, kept the island in a semi-colonial state. While the Cubans theoretically retained their independence, in fact the American government felt free to interfere in the island's internal affairs.

Gradually Cuba became partly Americanized. The island— already an odd amalgam of Hispanic, African, and Caribbean cultures—grew buttered over with the pseudomorphic styles of Miami. Perceptive observers called the process "Floridization."

Havana has always contained a disproportionate percentage of the Cuban population and a large fraction of its mercantile, industrial, and intellectual leaders. Most of the country's theaters, its restaurants and hotels were here, its psychiatrists and prostitutes, its poets, its bankers, even its murderers.

The heart of Havana beat near its docks, where for centuries visitors arrived first. In the 1950s this area, called the Old City, still hinted strongly of Europe, of sections of Naples, of Marseilles, of Barcelona. Ancient residences bordered narrow streets. Third-story, iron-railinged balconies overlooked courtyards through which gangs of ragged children darted. Anxious mothers leaned against the railings, peering out, hollering to their neighbors across the court. Tiny, unexpected restaurants served a variety of clientele: millionaire Texans, reeling Greek sailors, Cuban pimps, French essayists, honeymoon couples from Kansas City, gangsters from everywhere. Ernest Hemingway apparently became drunk all over town. He lived not far from the city's center and habituated several of its bars. Like remnants of the True Cross in the Holy Land, relics and legends still abound of how Hemingway *really* preferred this bistro or that. It is an odd and revealing fact about Cuba *today* that its most treasured house is not that of a politician or a general—nor even a Cuban. Even Castro's home is not so venerated by Cubans as that of this foreigner, this famous writer.

In this quarter of the city was also Chinatown. Chinese were brought here in the nineteenth century as coolie labor to supplement or replace high-priced African slaves. By the 1950s most of them had congregated in Havana. Chinatown became the unsavory core of Cuba's sexual underworld. Havana, originally created to service travelers on their way back and forth to the mainland, became a regional center for prostitution. Brothels flourished. A major industry grew up around them: Government officials received bribes, policemen collected protection money. Throughout the Old City, prostitutes could be seen standing in doorways, strolling the streets, or leaning from windows displaying their pneumatic wares. One report estimated that 11,500 of them worked their trade in Havana. Homosexuals also sauntered through the area, offering passing males five or ten pesos for the pleasure of their company.

In dives like the Shanghai Theater, one could watch grainy, generally soundless, blue movies. The typical plot: a bored house-wife, a door-to-door salesman or a delivery boy, and fornication—all the romance of dogs in heat.

The Old City also offered live entertainment. A man called El Chocolate became one of the city's most famous landmarks. He appeared all by himself, sitting center stage, naked and oiled. He could, by mere concentration, without moving a muscle, first create an erection, then achieve an orgasm. The audience, some of whom had brought opera glasses to see everything in detail, yelled encouragement. Women shrieked, "Come for me, El Chocolate!"

Havana also boasted the legendary Superman whose penis reached galactic proportions, who nightly performed an act with a variety of voluptuous women.

The city seemed permeated with sex. All over town partygoers might find themselves at *fiestas de percheros* (clothes-hanger parties). You entered, said a few pleasantries to your hostess, took off your clothes and put them on hangers, then spent the rest of the evening in orgiastic pleasures.

Not far from the Old City was Vedado. Originally an attractive suburb west of the harbor, it had become the site of Havana's newest hotels, constructed in a spurt in the 1950s. Each tall, glittering hostel tried to surpass the others: plush, deeply carpeted suites, sparkling swimming pools, glistening mirrors, polished bars where famous entertainers like Eartha Kitt and Nat King Cole sang throaty ballads—above all, casinos, their whirring roulette wheels and tuxedoed dealers, their gorgeous ladies in low-cut, expensive gowns, their waiters hurrying past with trays of daiquiris (first concocted across town at the red-velveted Floridita) and *cuba libres* (rum-and-Coca-Colas). Each seemed plucked from Miami, only a little over 100 miles away.

Beyond the outskirts of the capital, beyond the slot machines and the prostitutes, was one of the poorest—and most beautiful—countries in the Western world. In the other provinces of Cuba—in Pinar del Rio, Matanzas, Las Villas, Camaguey, and Oriente—Cuba displayed a different face. Small drab towns spotted the countryside, their flat-roofed, one-story houses flaking in the sun, their children with teeth rotting from too much sugar and too little attention, steeped in ignorance and sullen hopelessness. And beyond these depressing towns and ramshackle villages lay rural Cuban society, divided into two wings. On one hand were huge sugar plantations and the well-to-do folk who lived there. On the other were the hundreds of thousands of *bohíos*, those one or two-room peasant huts with dirt floors and thatched roofs, from whose doorways peered barefoot, illiterate, big-eyed youngsters. The life of those who lived in the *bohíos* was abominable. According to contemporary statistics of the Cuban government, only one out of twenty of the rural population *ever* ate meat and only one out of eight *ever* drank milk.

Between a third and a half of the Cuban population was black or mulatto. Although by the 1950s the island was not quite as rigidly segregated or racist as the United States, its society was permeated with prejudice—with the usual results. Blacks owned little of the rural land, less of the urban. In pockets throughout Cuba, tribal customs and voodoo superstition ruled the population.

Yet Cuba was not nearly so poor as Mexico or Haiti. She ranked in per capita income among the wealthier Latin American nations. She stood fifth in manufacturing, third in the distribution of telephones, second in radios, and far in the lead in per capita television sets. High-finned cars of the fifties jammed Cuba's roadways. The islanders owned vast numbers of the Edsels and wide-bodied Cadillacs. Each automobile seemed to sport a radio which blared Latin music into the streets. Havana itself offered listeners thirty-two different radio stations. Most Cubans, moreover, could hear Pat Boone or Elvis Presley over any number of Miami stations.

The island had a large, cosmopolitan, educated class. Some 53,000 Cubans possessed university degrees. Havana had eighteen daily newspapers. The country's writers—especially its poets—were prolific and talented.

The Cuban government combined corruption and inefficiency. During the twentieth century one leader after another entered the presidential palace with promises on his lips, to leave a few years later with money in his bags. Some of these men ran brutal regimes, others did not. But they all grew fat on bribes while their nation stagnated. The last of this unappetizing line was Fulgencio Batista.

Batista was not the worst of the lot. To be sure his administration practiced graft on a broad scale and his policemen and soldiers committed rape and torture. But so had previous regimes. Batista fell, not merely because he deserved it—and he certainly did. His government collapsed because of a combination of factors, not the least of which was the determination of his main adversary—Fidel Castro.

Castro is an extraordinary leader. People as different as Richard Nixon and George McGovern have been impressed by him.

Nixon first encountered him in 1959. "Castro was one of the most striking foreign officials I met during my eight years as Vice President," Nixon recalled. "As I told President Eisenhower later, he seemed to have that indefinable quality which, for good or evil, makes a leader of men. He had a compelling, intense voice, sparkling black eyes, and he radiated vitality. . . . He was intelligent, shrewd, at times eloquent."

McGovern met the Cuban seventeen years later, by which time Castro's wavy, chestnut hair had receded at the top and grayed at the sides, and his graceful, muscular body had turned tubby. Yet the American senator also found him appealing. McGovern remembers about their meeting: "In private conversation, at least in a diplomatic setting, he is soft-spoken, shy, sensitive, sometimes witty, sometimes slightly ill at ease. I frankly liked him."

Maybe an ability to mirror the best qualities in those around him accounts for Fidel's oft-described charisma. McGovern perceived wit and sensitivity; Nixon remembered the Cuban's intelligence and shrewdness—and even his "intense voice" (a quality Nixon himself had long tried to cultivate). All observers of Castro sensed a kind of pulsating humanity, undeniable charm and warmth.

Fidel was born in the far eastern corner of Cuba, deep in Oriente province, a harsh land of ignorance and poverty. His father, Angel Castro, a Spanish soldier, had arrived in Cuba during the days of the Spanish-American War. After the war Angel had worked briefly for the United Fruit Company, then had struck out on his own. He had hacked a vast estate, almost an agricultural empire, out of the Oriente forests. In a region where most people died poor, the ex-soldier's hacienda had spread across 10,000 acres and employed 500 men.

Angel Castro was a crude, rough man, large and strong, emotional but reticent, capable of violence—an archetype of all the planters and ranchers who subdued land in Australia and North and South America. While married to his first wife, he had five children by the family cook. Later, when he wanted to send his illegitimate offspring to a Catholic school, officials there insisted the children be baptized and confirmed. They also told him that since his first wife had passed away, he should now marry the cook. Angel did so. Fidel Castro was the second of her children.

At school Fidel fixed his mark upon his world, achieving local fame in both sports and politics. Always large for his age, he eventually grew to a brawny, broad-shouldered 6 feet 2 inches tall, weighing just under 200 pounds. He won Cuba's 1943–44 prize as the island's best school athlete. Later, at the University of Havana he was elected the law school's "class delegate," partly as a result of his athletic renown. .

Throughout his youth Fidel churned with impatient competitiveness. Within a week of his arrival at the university—proud, mercurial, quick-tempered, driving a new car given him by his father, a trifle out of his element in a society whose *habaneros* sneered at all ruralisms, in his own way, a classic bumpkin freshman—he challenged the president of the Student Federation to a fight. Other students, stunned at the audacity, gathered to watch. Observers do not recall who won the affair, but they remember the impetuosity of the boy. In another incident, merely to prove he had the willpower to do so, to indicate his machismo, he rode a bicycle straight into a wall.

His academic success was less notable. He was bright but not studious. His mind was quick and retentive, his speaking ability fluent, at times captivating. In his early years at Catholic schools his grades were good. Yet he maintained a wider reputation for rebelliousness and fighting than scholarship. At the university, as he himself later admitted, he "never went to lectures, never opened a book except just before examinations."

He felt nothing for the Law. The legal field, a typical Hispanic means of advancement for sons of the rural rich, was already overcrowded. Cubans, who loved their politics, assumed that legal training was a natural step toward a political career. And Fidel was ambitious. He wanted to become a leader of men. As he once said, "My desire to excel fed and inspired the character of my struggle."

Student government in Cuba meant more than clever argumentation. It included beatings and shootings and assassination. Groups of students schemed against and murdered each other. People then and later claimed that Castro was often involved. No clear proof exists.

In 1948 he married; the next year he had a son, Fidelito. He received his degree and went to work for a law firm. During this period he had little money and was often in debt. The electric company once shut off his lights, and his son went without milk. Political plotting remained his real interest.

On July 26, 1953, he and some 150 followers, outnumbered ten to one, with only a handful of rifles and a single old machine gun, attempted to capture an arsenal at the Moncada army barracks. The affair typified Castro: dramatic and brave, poorly organized and badly planned. Government soldiers easily captured most of his band, and, after a few days, Castro himself. But the savagery with which they treated their prisoners—they dragged three through the streets behind a jeep and tortured others—made the Moncada attack appear noble, especially when, at the trial, Fidel spoke so eloquently of his cause. He went to jail but his reputation grew.

Two years later the Cuban government, in a moment of generosity, freed all political prisoners, including Castro. A few weeks later he left for Mexico where he hoped to organize another attempt to overthrow his government.

In November 1956 he and eighty-one others set out from Mexico aboard a yacht, the *Granma*, bought from an American couple for $15,000. The next seven days at sea, often lost, seasick, and depressed, they searched for the coast of Cuba. When at last they arrived—at the wrong place—weakened by the trip, most were easy pickings for government troops. Only a few—including Fidel, his brother Raul, and an asthmatic Argentine named Ernesto (Che) Guevara—eluded capture and fled into the Sierra Maestra mountains. Twenty-five months later this handful of *compañeros* rode into Havana as victors. During these two years the majority of Cubans ignored both President Batista *and* Castro. Most merely coped with their daily existence. One man later recalled: "I had no idea what was going on in Cuba. I wasn't in favor of Batista but neither was I involved in the revolution. My aims were to go to the movies, to have money in my pocket, to dress well. I didn't give a thought to anything else."

Despite the attempts of later rhetoric to make the rebellion seem a poor man's revolt, in fact it was largely a bourgeois phenomenon, opposed by many of Cuba's blacks and apathetically watched by the great bulk of poverty-stricken rural masses. Of the 50,000 or more peasants living in the Sierra Maestra, perhaps no more than 500—1 out of 100—joined Castro's band; those who did, joined late, in the last months just before victory.

Afterward it seemed convenient to forget that Batista, a mulatto of lower class origins, was popular among the island's blacks. His army and police force were filled with blacks. When they occasionally captured one of Castro's few black supporters, they chastised him for following a white man like Fidel and turning away from his own kind.

Union members also remained quite loyal to Batista's government. They were generally well paid, and after six months on the job they could not be fired. Most urban insurgents came from the white middle class. These young people joined the underground for a complex of reasons, including a nationalistic anger at supposed American domination, at not enough high-status jobs for university-trained youths, and out of a principled distaste for the grossness of the government and the brutality of the army.

Batista's own weaknesses aided in his downfall. He had grown lazy. He ate hugely and bulged into corpulence. He became snobbish and ignored his roots. He grew entranced with canasta and spent countless hours at the game. His inefficiency and confusion eroded morale in the army. His soldiers damaged the reputation of the government with their atrocities. They committed horrible tortures in a notorious yellow Havana police station; they hanged defenseless children all over the island as "examples" and left the bodies dangling in the sun. Probably no image about Batista's regime remains as clear to Cubans today as those drooping bodies.

Yet such factors still do not account for Batista's downfall. His government had 40,000 comparatively well-armed troops. Castro even at the end had no more than a few thousand, armed mainly with captured hand guns. Throughout the entire rebellion, lasting over two years, Batista probably lost no more than 300 soldiers. One historian estimates that not more than 2,000 Cubans died during this period as a result of the civil war.

Batista would probably have fallen eventually, but a single act of the United States government accelerated his end. On March 14, 1958, Eisenhower's administration suspended arms shipments to Cuba. This action gave a body blow to Batista's reputation in Cuban ruling circles and within his army; it furthered the collapse of their morale. An implosion occurred. As the mood of the army decayed, Castro gained greater support which in turn caused the army's morale to decline further.

On New Year's Eve, 1958, as revelers in Havana drank toasts and sang "Auld Lang Syne," the bubble finally burst. Batista lost his last hold on the military. He fled, carrying millions of dollars with him on his plane. Castro, still in the hills, arrived several days later.

Castro's insurrection had closely followed Cuban traditions. Several times in the island's history, bands of rebels had mounted revolts in the eastern provinces. Like Castro, they had burned sugar cane and assaulted army garrisons; they had made alliances with Cuban insurrectionists; they had received support from exiles in Miami and New York. When they had at last taken charge, they, like Castro, had made broad, humanitarian promises. Most had even attacked Yankee imperialism. In other words, Castro's success was not unusual. He seemed much like his predecessors— perhaps only a touch better than they, with more integrity and energy.

On January 1, 1959, a Marxist regime in Cuba would have seemed farfetched. The island's Communist party had been wary of Castro—even contemptuous. To them, he appeared tempestuous, irresponsible, and unalterably bourgeois. Furthermore, they had long enjoyed a favorable position within the Cuban government. In 1943 Batista had appointed an avowed Communist to his Cabinet, the first such occasion in the history of the Western Hemisphere. Batista had used Communists as figurehead leaders over Cuba's labor unions.

As the dictator started to fail the Cuban Communists had gradually transferred their loyalties to Castro; by late 1958 they had unenthusiastically embraced his coalition. It hardly seemed a love match.

In a speech on December 1, 1961, Fidel declared himself to be a Marxist and said he had always been a revolutionary, even back in the early 1950s, but that he had covered it up so as not to lose popularity. He also made a fascinating admission for a supposedly devoted Marxist: "A little while ago," he said, "looking for some books on capitalism, I found what I had studied at one time, and I had read to page 370 in *Das Kapital*." He added: "I plan, when I have the time, to study *Das Kapital* of Karl Marx." (One may assume that he has not found the time since then, and that his copy of Marx's masterwork remains dogeared on page 370.) In the 50's Fidel would have made a poor Communist. He was too individualistic and hot-headed to become a disciplined party member. He had always felt a romantic desire to "aid the poor," but he would have found it intolerable to follow the dictates of a single philosophy, to say nothing of any rigid party lines. His humorless brother Raúl was no doubt a Marxist, but Raúl lacked Fidel's fire, his passion, his humanity. Even Che, who symbolized—and still does—a kind of lyric anarchism, was not a true Communist. Probably Fidel, an existential man defining his life's meaning by its flow, in the warp of his own actions, could never maintain a genuine life philosophy. A few American officials like Vice President Richard Nixon perceived in Cuba a part of the Red Menace, but most observers were not convinced.

At first a number of *batistianos* (followers of Batista) fled the island, but most Cubans idolized Fidel, supported his government, and at least accepted its measures. But by late in the year 1959 much of the property-owning middle class had lost their initial enthusiasm. The new government had reduced all rents on the island. This action satisfied tenants but made owners unhappy. A growing number of Communists began to carve out positions for themselves within the administration. They offered two things *fidelistas* lacked: organization and experience. (The relationship between Castro and the Communist party leadership, however, never did become warm; eventually Fidel would remove a number of them from his government.)

By the fall of 1960, as Cuba began moving to the left, the first trickle of exiles became a stream. Planes left Havana for Miami twice a day, filled with angry, unhappy people whom Castroites with disdain called *gusanos* (worms). The revolution accelerated into top speed. Cuban society had always lacked deep roots. Without a strong church structure, with few emotional ties to Europe (or even the United States), with few remnants of a landed tradition, Cuba had been ripe for change. It had only awaited a leadership, determined and disciplined and ruthless enough to grab and wrench it from its drift. In an amazingly short period, with remarkably little bloodshed, a new society began to form in Cuba.

The revolution (that is, just about everything that has occurred in Cuba since January 1, 1959) has had its negative side. By 1962 one could deplore the lack of civil liberties and the tens of thousands in prison. One could note a pervasive *burocratismo* (an officious governmental rigidity demanding countless forms in quintuplet). One could see soldiers and militiamen everywhere, over 250,000 of them; there was also a broad network of secret police. It must be noted, however, that the state was not so much Gestapo-like as it was "supervisory." Almost every city block had a headquarters of the local CDR (Committee for Defense of the Revolution). The duty of this citizens' organization was to oversee that block, to observe any strangers, to determine who was "gusano" in spirit (that is, who was not enthusiastic about the revolution). Loyal Cubans insisted that all this watchfulness was necessary because of the dangers of (1) an outside invasion from United States-supervised emigrés (obviously a justified fear); (2) internal guerrilla uprisings (quite common early in the revolution); and (3) widespread black marketeering which Cuban leaders called "counterrevolutionary activity," considering it one of their more severe problems.

Today, even after a generation of revolution, almost everyone, it seems, is involved in the black market. The reason is simple— Cuba does not have enough consumer goods. Cubans like to dress well but they find it hard to obtain good shoes and attractive slacks and blouses. Often the shoes they can find—and only on special occasions—are made of cardboard or cheap plastic. Also, Cubans constantly smoke cigarettes; two or three packs a day is common. But cigarettes are rationed. So one buys on the black market.

Officially, everything must be obtained with a *libreta*, a ration book. A Cuban novelist, Edmundo Desnoes, although loyal to the revolution, writes disdainfully about this situation. A character in one of his books wants a pocket comb but cannot buy one anywhere; all the stores have just run out of them. "Never, not then or ever after, could I have imagined how many insignificant things are necessary to keep a country running smoothly," the character thinks to himself. "For the past few weeks there hasn't been a soft drink to be had anywhere. I never thought that the manufacture of soft drinks could be paralyzed just because there was no cork for caps."

A common complaint about Cuba today is its drabness, its peeling paint from shabby buildings once dazzling in the Caribbean sun, its untended lawns, its empty store windows, its East European concrete prefabs, designed by builders accustomed to cold, gray afternoons. Havana, once one of the most exciting cities in the world, has become a second-rate, unattractive town.

When Cubans began to leave the island in 1959, the United States set up refugee centers to help them get settled. Of the total number registering from 1959 to 1963, a mere 3 percent came in 1959, and less than 17 percent in 1960. More came in 1961, and a deluge in 1962. It was not, therefore, Castro's takeover which caused the exodus: It was the Revolution. Approximately a tenth of the island's population eventually fled. More would have done so if the government had not first outlawed easy departures, then, when it actually allowed them, made them very difficult.

Only fatuous prejudice would consider all the exiles batistianos, whores, gangsters, or capitalists—or that those who remained on the island stayed out of devotion to the revolution. Despite the widespread contemptuous use of the word "gusano," perhaps a majority of Cubans have relatives in the United States.

On the other hand, despite its faults, the revolution has offered remarkable gains. Its leaders have been personally honest, show integrity, live modestly, and work hard. Moreover, the population knows it. While previous Cuban leaders enriched themselves from their position, the present administration seems to labor for the general good. While they might make mistakes, become irritating or tedious, they have not been grafters. In Cuban history that is . . . remarkable.

The revolution—although it has taken away most profit-producing properties, even down to small farms and rented houses—has provided a great many benefits. Cuba had previously had the highest unemployment rate in Latin America; now, to all intents and purposes, no one is "unemployed" (though a great many are employed beneath their capacities). The island used to have a large illiterate population. Gangs of children in the streets begged passersby for chewing gum and nickels. Now the island has universal schooling.

The government allows free dental and medical services to everyone; public health facilities are impressive; malaria and polio have been virtually eliminated.

Before the revolution, Cuba, like all Latin American countries, had sprawling urban slums. By the late 1970s these have been drastically decreased. The government has also pared away at rural poverty. It is impressive to wander through rural communes and see retired farmers living in respectable apartments with running water and electricity, and to remember that two generations ago much of even the United States lacked such facilities.

The revolution offers more subtle but equally important benefits. It has given vast numbers a sense of belonging, of worth. Despite Batista's reputation among the island's blacks, racial bigotry was the norm. It is now slowly fading. Peasants also feel less awkward and alienated than they did.

One senses an improved *national spirit* in Cuba. Gangs of armed toughs no longer shoot each other in the streets; American gangsters no longer corrupt government officials; whores and pimps and pornographers no longer openly peddle their wares to drunken foreigners; a spirit of inferiority no longer oppresses Cuban intellectuals. A sense of social openness, of equality, has spread everywhere: One of Castro's first acts was to open the private beaches to all. In places like the Hotel Riviera, where

gangsters and ladies in minks once gambled and frolicked, vacationing black Cuban workers and their families now stroll.

It is somewhat presumptuous for outsiders to judge the revolution. Cuba has come a long way since 1959. But she has had to give
up much to travel this road. The tragic stories of families divided
between Cuba and the United States are the measure of the
revolution.

2 *America vs. Castro*

The relationship between Cuba and the United States has never been simple. After 1898 America bestowed many benefits upon the island. The United States helped modernize Cuban industry, education, and medicine. Critics of American efforts have sneered that the United States acted only out of imperialist greed, that she bled Cuba and exploited her. Obviously such assertions are partly true, particularly in the early period, but over the years America's economic involvement in the island declined. United States investment in Cuban sugar resources dropped from 70 percent of the island's total in 1928 to about 35 percent in 1958. Of the two million workers in Cuba's 1958 labor force, American companies only employed 70,000. And Americans paid higher wages and provided for better working conditions than the rest of Cuban industry.

After World War II the United States focused its attention on Europe and Asia. Washington was little concerned with Latin America as a whole, to say nothing of Cuba. Between 1945 and 1960 America gave Yugoslavia—a Communist, East European country—more money than *all* of Latin America combined.

Despite such raw data, Cubans *felt* controlled by the United States. Cuban *dignidad*—its pride, its self-respect—suffered. Cubans still tell stories of degrading acts by Americans: of the drunken sailors who urinated in a famous fountain; or, the embassy official who drove through a stop light into police and announced, "I am a North American citizen and no authority of a country of Indians can detain me." Such tales of American vulgarity still infuriate Cubans. Yet in fairness one should note that sodden sailors of every nationality have acted obnoxious—and no doubt urinated publicly— in every seaport of the world. As for the embassy man, officials from all corners of the globe have broken New York City and Washington ordinances and have reeled away with impunity. When a foreigner behaves boorishly in the United States, Americans are naturally annoyed—when they hear about it—but they soon forget it. Cubans do not forgive such insults. Their nerves have been rubbed too raw.

One of the most important consequences of the revolution has been that it has severed ties between the United States and the island. Images of gangster hotels and corrupt officials are now only memories. Even though one can debate the general benefits of the revolution, the hiatus in Cuban-American relations seems to have been healthy. Cuba had been corrupted by the connection; now she seems clean.

At first Americans gave Castro a rather favorable assessment. Ed Sullivan flew to Havana to film an interview with the new Cuban leader. American editorial opinion ranged from neutral to enthusiastic.

But Eisenhower's government, firm in its anti-communism, wary about any Soviet success, remained suspicious. In January 1959, as Castro drove into Havana, Washington puzzled what to make of him. Was he, they wondered, influenced by the Communists in his entourage? Would he be able to hold power? Could he, they asked themselves, be dealt with?

The administration gradually made up its mind. American officials became disgusted by the trials of Batista's henchmen. These affairs were held in a stadium while thousands of Cubans sat in the stands shrieking, "Paredón, paredón" ("To the wall, to the wall"). Washington grew angry when the revolution expropriated American properties. Cuban exiles fled to the United States telling their bitter stories. Washington became enraged when Fidel's Cuban nationalism erupted in interminable speeches of increasingly strident anti-Americanism. The administration grew anxious

when Cuban officials in Havana became more receptive to Soviet
blandishments. Eisenhower himself became convinced that although Castro was probably not a Communist, he was following the
Kremlin's line.

In March 1960 the administration decided to arm and train
Cuban exiles. Eisenhower had been told that Castro was unpopular. A simple invasion by emigrés would, Eisenhower believed,
draw upon broad support in the island. Fidel's inefficient, unstable
government would collapse almost instantly. In 1954 Eisenhower's
administration had succeeded with a similar plan in Guatemala.

But Castro was both shrewder and more popular than the CIA
thought, and any American-sponsored attack would enrage most
Cubans and improve the position of the "maximum leader." As an
anti-Castro *habanero* said about this time: If the United States
invaded, "I would be forced to take up arms and defend my
country. People like me who hate this government will feel obliged
to defend it."

John Kennedy, soon after he became President, approved the
CIA plan, and the exiles landed disastrously at the Bay of Pigs.

The New Frontiersmen, realizing that another such invasion
would be foolish, turned to an ugly campaign of murder and terror,
of guerrilla warfare and economic pressure. Robert McNamara
later told a Senate committee: "We were hysterical about Castro at
the time of the Bay of Pigs and thereafter."

The Kennedys were patriots, brought up in a world where the
dangers of totalitarianism—both fascist and Communist—seemed
real and lurking. The regimes of Hitler and Stalin formed their
education. The Kennedy boys were decent men, philosophically
devoted to slow, "liberal" progress. Before the Cuban revolution,
John Kennedy had vacationed in the island and retained firm
memories of warm beaches and palm trees. The thought of this
pleasant land becoming "Stalinist" disturbed him, like seeing a
treasured childhood retreat decay into tawdry slumdom overrun by
rowdy toughs.

A few months after Kennedy took office he met Khrushchev in
Vienna. Afterward he told the columnist James Reston that the
Russian probably considered him foolish and immature for approv-
ing such a disorganized mess as the Bay of Pigs invasion; worse, the

Soviet leader apparently believed him weak for hesitating to follow it up, for refusing to send in American troops to finish the job. If Khrushchev thought him timid, Kennedy worried, Russia might become more aggressive. And if that happened, the United States might have to go to war. As with legendary gunfighters, so long as a President had a reputation for toughness, he might avoid serious conflict. The opposite also seemed to be true. His inaction during the Bay of Pigs, Kennedy thought, might lead to trouble. Somehow he had to rebuild his image, he had to become "credible." "That son of a bitch," he once said bitterly about Khrushchev, "won't pay any attention to words. He has to see you move."

Kennedy also worried about the political situation in the United States. While he could blame the fall of Batista on Eisenhower, as he had cheerfully done during his recent campaign, Fidel's continued success could only tarnish the New Frontier. The "Cuban problem" was growing. Eventually it might require surgery.

Kennedy and his administration had been humiliated at the Bay of Pigs. This rankled personally. Kennedys were famous for their competitive spirit: One didn't lose at touch football; one certainly shouldn't lose in cold war contests. Maybe John Kennedy's obsession with Castro reflected his father's upbringing. Or perhaps it exhibited that old Irish dictum common among Boston politicians: Don't get mad; get even.

Even as the Bay of Pigs invasion drew to a close, the young President publicly stated grimly: "Let the record show that our restraint is not inexhaustible." He also warned: "The complacent, the self-indulgent, soft societies are about to be swept away in the debris of history. We dare not fail to see the insidious nature of this new, deeper struggle." "We dare not," he added, "fail to grasp the new concept, the new tools, the new sense of urgency we will need to combat it, whether in Cuba or in South Vietnam." He meanwhile sent a secret letter to General Maxwell Taylor to join Robert Kennedy in an examination of America's para-military activity. The two men were to focus especially on Cuba.

Less than two months later they produced a report. "We have been struck" they said, "with the general feeling that there can be no long-term living with Castro as a neighbor."

In the autumn of 1961 the administration formulated a plan to destroy Castro, calling it Operation MONGOOSE. On November 30, 1961, President Kennedy sent a memo to Secretary of State Dean Rusk, okaying the project: He was willing to "use our available assets . . . to help Cuba overthrow the Communist regime." He formed a panel with the nondescript name, Special Group (Augmented), (the SGA), to oversee the operation. Its membership consisted of some of the most important officials of the government, including Attorney General Robert Kennedy, Maxwell Taylor, and occasionally Dean Rusk and Robert McNamara. They discussed such matters as the "liquidation" of certain Cuban leaders. Just a few weeks before the Cuban missile crisis, Robert Kennedy told SGA that his brother was "concerned about progress on the MONGOOSE program, and feels that more priority should be given to trying to mount sabotage operations." Bobby demanded "massive activity." On October 4, 1962, the attorney general took over the committee's chairmanship. Ten days later (the day before the missile crisis began), the group agreed to step up sabotage operations—or, as one of its memos said, that "all efforts should be made to develop new and imaginative approaches, with the possibility of getting rid of the Castro regime."

Meanwhile the Central Intelligence Agency had ordered one of its best agents, Theodore Shackley, back from Berlin. He was to prepare a "vulnerability and feasibility study" of the Castro government. In February 1962 Shackley, working out of Miami, began organizing a major anti-Castro operation. His headquarters stood on the South Campus of the University of Miami. Here, in a lovely white-clapboard-and-green-lawn setting, stood JM WAVE, code name for the Miami enterprise. JM WAVE had everything from machine guns to doctors to its own gas station. Its annual budget swelled to more than $50 million. Over 300 Americans and several thousand Cubans worked for it.

The CIA's (and presumably the New Frontier's) strategy of how to deal with Cuba was to weaken the reputation of Castro's regime. If existence in Cuba turned sour, they believed, Fidel's prestige would inevitably decline. Eventually dissatisfaction would increase to the point where a revolt would occur. Washington's objective, therefore, was to make life unpleasant in Cuba. It devised ingenious ways of doing so.

About the same time Ted Shackley flew to Miami to take over JM WAVE, President Kennedy announced an American embargo on all trade with Cuba (except for medical necessities). State Department officials urged NATO members to cease trading with the island. (In 1966 Washington cautioned Greece that if it continued trade relations with Cuba, the United States might halt all military and economic aid to Athens.) A second tactic in the economic warfare against the island involved acts of sabotage. CIA planners sometimes acted like sophomores plotting to sneak over and smear paint on the emblem of the rival school. Agents secretly put contaminants in Cuban sugar to discourage other countries from buying it. They opened boxes of machinery bound for the island and broke crucial small gears. They put additives in lubricating oils, so that Cuban engines would wear out faster. They sabotaged buses that the Cuban government had purchased in England. They persuaded a German ball-bearing manufacturer to produce ball bearings slightly off center. An agency official recalls: "We were doing almost everything you could dream up."

More malignantly, JM WAVE generated a series of guerrilla attacks on Cuba. The agency had already been organizing paramilitary missions in 1961. When Shackley took over, activity increased and became more destructive. (Not all such raids were sponsored by the agency. Even though Castro declared that every such act was perpetrated by the CIA, in fact many of them were the work of small independent bands of Cuban exiles.)

In Miami, within the quarter called Little Havana, lived almost 100,000 refugees. Along Southwest Eighth Street one could smell the odor of fried bananas and black beans, one could drink thick, rich *café cubano*, or speak and read nothing but Spanish. Here, in dozens of cafes, Cubans plotted. Miami contained as many as 200 exile organizations. Most were tiny splinter groups, not much larger than a single family or two. A few, however, became successful para-military outfits, retaining connections with secret underground operatives back on the island. These groups would have carried out raids no matter what the CIA did. One exile leader swore, "I would return to Cuba with a rock." JM WAVE merely provided such men with weapons and tried to coordinate activities.

American supervisors did accompany some missions. A few became famous among the Cubans—perhaps none more so than William Robertson.

"Rip" Robertson (the prototype of at least one adventure novel) was a bearlike man with a baseball cap on his head and a cigar between his teeth. Cubans on his team loved him. He hated Communists. He once told a commando, "I'll give you $50 to bring me back an ear." When the Cuban brought back two, he laughed and said, "You're crazy," and he paid him $100 and took the whole team home for turkey dinner.

Such commando outfits blew up sugar mills, dropped off weapons for local guerrillas, destroyed oil refineries and factories, and burned lumberyards and ships in harbor.

The most publicized semi-independent organization was Alpha 66, supposedly started by sixty-six men who had fought in the hills alongside Castro, but who had become disillusioned by his leftward slide. During 1962, Alpha 66 carried out many operations, including one accompanied by a reporter for *Life* magazine.

Of all the hundreds of raids, the most famous involved two dozen members of the Cuban Revolutionary Student Directorate (DRE). Their target was the Hotel Hornedo in the Miramar section of Havana. They had discovered through contacts in Cuba that every Friday evening at 9 o'clock foreign technicians—Russians, Czechs, Poles, and Chinese—held meetings in a particular empty theater. Fidel and other high-ranking Cubans often joined them. After a meeting they all would walk over to the nearby Hotel Hornedo for dinner and drinks. Its dining room, overlooking the waterfront, had large glass windows facing the sea. The DRE commandos prepared an attack. They bought two low-slung boats, capable of sliding under the Cuban radar net and fast enough to speed them safely out again. They purchased an old German 20-millimeter cannon, a mortar, a few rifles, and some pistols from a Mafia gun dealer in Miami.

At 10:30 in the evening, August 24, 1962, they brought their main attack boat within 200 to 300 yards of the hotel. Across the flat black waters, they could clearly make out uniforms passing back and forth in front of the lighted windows. They opened fire.

No one fired back, not so much as a pistol; no one even turned out the hotel's lights. After five minutes, the attackers started their boats and ran. They could not be sure how many they had killed. They later heard that Fidel had indeed been there that evening, and that afterwards he had gone into a rage. He reportedly had arrested several militiamen for throwing aside their guns and hiding when the attack started. Rumors said he had become so furious and humiliated he had even put hotel employees in prison for running away.

Such guerrilla assaults were dramatic but they could not bring down Castro. Nor, apparently, could America's economic offensive. The New Frontiersmen began to contemplate assassination. National Security Advisor McGeorge Bundy recollected, "We used to sit around the White House all the time thinking how nice it would be" if leaders like Castro "didn't exist." Even Secretary of Defense McNamara once openly proposed the assassination of the Cuban leader.

American pressure on Cuba increased throughout 1962: the embargo, the raids, the assassination attempts. It seemed as if the United States would stop at nothing.

Castro decided in the spring of 1962 that the United States, despite its promises, would soon invade. In January American representatives to a meeting of the Organization of American States (OAS) had declared Cuba anathema. On January 30, Kennedy had met privately with Khrushchev's son-in-law Aleksei Adzhubei and compared the situations of Cuba and Hungary. Exactly what he meant is unclear, but one cannot blame the Cuban leadership for fearing, as Castro later said, that Kennedy was reminding "the Russians that the U.S. had not interfered in Hungary [in 1956]." (The Kremlin may actually have reworded Kennedy's statement to frighten Castro.)

In April American Marines held extensive military maneuvers in the Caribbean. That same month Cuban exile leader Miró Cardona had a meeting at the White House. He returned to Miami and told friends that Castro would be overthrown soon. Little Havana rippled with exciting rumors that something was in the wind. There had not been this much electricity in the air since just before the Bay of Pigs. Fidel's friends in Florida kept him informed of all this.

On June 16, housewives in Cuba held food demonstrations in Cárdenas. Other demonstrations erupted at Santa Clara and El Cano. The Cuban revolution seemed shaky.

On July 26, Castro told a vast rally that an American attack was imminent. Unquestionably he believed it.

No doubt Castro turned to Moscow in his need. If the Soviet Union would supply him with weapons, he might save himself. He could use anything: planes, for instance, or torpedo boats—missiles of course would be nice.

Whether Castro first broached the subject of missiles with Moscow or they with him is unknown. He has given so many contradictory statements about it since then that the issue is befogged.

In fact, of course, it makes little difference. Since the Soviet Union owned the weapons, their motives, not Castro's fears, were the most important. Even if Fidel had not wanted Russian rockets, he would probably have accepted them if that would ensure that he got the weapons he did want.

3 *The Missiles*

Motivations are deceptive. Fears, desires, confusions interlace in intricate patterns. Beneath the surface lie eddies of forgotten childhood incidents, of psychic needs. Above hangs a fog of verbiage, of lies, misstatements, of faulty communications. It is hard to *know* why someone does something. To understand why a *group* of people act in a particular way becomes so asymptotically difficult as to be almost futile. Yet we do it all the time: "Germany wanted war," we say; or "Rome fell because her people became weak"; or, "Slavery was the cause of the Civil War." Such statements are not inane; they are not necessarily even wrong. But they are not answers; at most they provide a shorthand method of coming to grips with chaos. They are to the reality of events what stick figures are to human form. They do not define; they only indicate probabilities.

Deciphering Soviet motivation verges on mysticism. Kremlin rhetoric is sodden with cant. Its bureaucratic machinery and professional secrecy create Byzantine webs totally confusing to outsiders.

As far as the missile crisis is concerned, we are only sure of a few details.

On July 9, 1960, long before Cuba moved very far to the left, Khrushchev gave a speech. "It should be borne in mind," he said, "that the United States is not now at such an unattainable distance from the Soviet Union as formerly. *Figuratively* speaking," he said vaguely, "*if* need be," he added tentatively, "Soviet artillerymen *can* support the Cuban people [note merely the possibility, not the desire]." The statement, full of superficial bombast, was hardly binding. But just in case anyone misconstrued his meaning, several months later Khrushchev told a Cuban reporter, "I should like such statements to be really symbolic."

On April 18, 1961, at the time of the Bay of Pigs, the Soviet premier wrote President Kennedy threatening to give Cuba "all necessary assistance in beating back armed attack," but he only sent this message after the invasion had clearly failed.

One year later, apparently at a party Presidium meeting in late April 1962, Khrushchev raised the subject of placing missiles in Cuba. Subtle signs indicate that at least a handful of Soviet military leaders did not like Khrushchev's plan. Two high-ranking officers resigned about this time—General K. S. Moskalenko, commander in chief of strategic rockets and deputy minister of defense, and General S. I. Golikov, director of the main political administration of the armed forces. Both lost their jobs during the spring. Significantly, both received them back again in November—after the missile crisis was over. Evidently they (and perhaps others in the military) had opposed shipping rockets to Cuba. Perhaps they resented spending the money, especially for a proposal that would likely accomplish little or nothing. Perhaps they did not trust the Cubans: Sending highly technical and secret equipment far from Russia—something the Soviet Union had *never* done—particularly to a Caribbean country led by a volatile ex-guerrilla, would be potentially disastrous.

Khrushchev stated in his autobiography that the decision to send the missiles was still in doubt in May. While on a trip to Bulgaria, he wrote, "I paced back and forth, brooding over what to do. . . . After I returned to Moscow [on May 20] . . . we convened a meeting and I said I had some thoughts to go over on the subject of Cuba." If Khrushchev's autobiography is accurate on the subject (a debatable point, as it is so often inaccurate), and the two generals really were fired because of their strong disagreements, the scenario of events may have gone like this:

In April Khrushchev may have suggested sending the missiles. A few officials probably opposed the idea at the start, but they were removed or cowed. As Kremlin thinkers then began careful preliminary outlines of the plan, Khrushchev left on a diplomatic trip to Bulgaria. While there, his thoughts no doubt kept returning to his idea. By the time he returned, he was apparently convinced that it would work. At the next meeting of the Presidium the membership agreed to it.

Whether or not *this* is the way it happened, it is clear that before July 1962 the Soviet leadership did decide to send missiles to Cuba. Why did they come to this conclusion? One can only suggest a few possibilities, remembering that factors which might motivate one member of the Presidium might disinterest another. (Ron Nessen, President Gerald Ford's press secretary and before that a television reporter, once admitted that when covering the White House for NBC, he had felt satisfied giving viewers one or two reasons for a particular presidential act. When he went to work at the White House, "I realized that a complete TV report would require listing perhaps twenty reasons for a presidential decision." Furthermore, "A *really* complete report would require listing nineteen other reasons, considered and rejected for not making that decision.")

Apparently the main reason Moscow wanted missiles in Cuba was that in her military competition with the United States she was falling far behind.

At the end of World War II two isolated events occurred. As they converged over the next decade or so, they helped create the modern military world—and made America its leader.

The more important factor was the birth of the atomic bomb. Any nation possessing this weapon now had immense power.

The second element derived from the fact that a number of German rocket experts surrendered to the Allies. These scientists had helped develop the V-2. Pentagon thinkers understood the implications. A missile like the V-2, offering a delivery system for atomic bombs, had certain potential advantages. If it could be perfected, a rocket could prove cheaper and faster than planes, easier to maintain on the ground, and more difficult to destroy in the air. After the war the United States began Project MX-774 to develop just such a missile. The problem however did not seem pressing. In the years right after the war, most Americans felt confidence in their atomic shield. True, the Kremlin was proving intransigent in Eastern Europe, but there seemed little real need to worry. Even if a conflict arose with the Soviet Union, it could be solved from air bases in and around Europe. Missiles did not seem necessary.

Early missiles, moreover, were notoriously inaccurate. V-2 rockets aimed at London had often landed many miles away. Other than for random destructiveness or maniacal slaughter, to utilize a nuclear device effectively one must aim it with reasonable precision. Scientists developed a scale to determine a missile's accuracy which they called Circular Error Probability (CEP). The CEP of a rocket is calculated by measuring the circle within which fall half of the missiles fired at a target. If one shoots ten missiles at a target and five land within 2 miles of it, the CEP is 2 miles. An inaccurate rocket is *militarily* almost useless (beyond possible, but unpredictable, psychological effects). The farther one fires a missile, the less accurate it is. And the heavier the warhead, the more difficult it is to aim the missile with any exactness. To propel a 5-ton atomic warhead a few hundred miles requires a gigantic rocket, bigger than any possible in the years just after the war. Even if American scientists could develop such a monster, they had no good way to aim it. Guidance problems seemed prohibitively formidable. Planes loaded with several atomic bombs would be much more effective: If a wing of B-52s flew from England toward Moscow, most might be destroyed, but a few would get through and hit reasonably close to the target. On July 8, 1947, therefore, the government cancelled Project MX-774. Rocket scientists continued testing the V-2s they still had, but there was no sense of urgency. The question of rocket power seemed mainly theoretical.

Then the situation changed. The Cold War in Europe grew more bitter. Chiang Kai-shek fell to Mao. The Korean War began. The apparent struggle between the Free World and the Communist Menace grew frightening—particularly when, in September 1949, Harry S. Truman announced that the Soviet Union had just detonated an atomic device. The Allies no longer held their monopoly. The National Security Council suggested a drastic expansion of America's military forces. There was renewed interest in military experiments. The early fifties saw a spurt in the development of both strategic and military hardware.

In early 1951 the government reactivated Project MX-774. Once again they would try to produce an intercontinental ballistic missile (referred to in those days as an "IBM" until the company with the same initials forced scientists to call their weapon, ICBM). Missile experts were not optimistic; the problems of payload size and guidance systems dogged their efforts. Then, on November 1, 1952, the United States set off "Mike," the first thermonuclear device, an H-bomb. Suddenly an ICBM was possible. Since H-bombs provided giant explosions with smaller, lighter warheads, scientists could devise much more accurate rockets.

At RAND and some of the best universities, analysts formulated theories to go along with the new weapon. One of the most influential thinkers was Albert Wohlstetter, a mathematical logician trained in economics. Working quietly for RAND on the problem of where to locate overseas air bases, he asked himself a fundamental question: What would actually happen if the Russians attacked *first*, destroying American bombers on the ground? The Air Force was contemplating placing its strategic forces close to the Soviet Union in places like Turkey and England. Wohlstetter realized that these bases would equally be within easy reach of Soviet planes. Such overseas bases would be vulnerable, or, as they came to be called, "soft." Any weapons system vulnerable to Soviet attack (a "first strike") should be avoided, Wohlstetter thought. One of the main purposes of a nuclear arm was that it served as a "deterrent." But no matter how many megatons your bombers carried—and a B-52 could now deliver 24-ton explosives—if blown up on the runways they could accomplish nothing. Wohlstetter concluded, and he convinced the Air Force, that their planes should be based *inside* the United States, and that overseas bases should only be used for refueling and repairing. Air bases protected inside the United States were still not "hard," but they would certainly be safer (particularly if flight crews could be trained to get their planes into the air on a few minutes notice). America's strategic force would be protected by sheer distance, and with radar devices in Canada and Greenland (an early-warning system) the United States could prepare a defense and begin a counterattack before enemy planes had dropped their first bomb. As long as an enemy assumed it could not destroy all of America's *retaliatory* weapons, it would presumably not attack. To attain an ability to retaliate, a "second-strike capability" became the main goal of the United States military.

Wohlstetter was not finished. He then asked RAND's computers what might happen if Russian *missiles* could knock out America's air bases. He did not know how successful Soviet scientists were in their rocket studies, but he assumed they would eventually develop an ICBM. He recognized that when that happened, even SAC (Strategic Air Command) bases would be too soft. The United States, Wohlstetter decided, should build a missile system. It should produce hundreds of long-range missiles and disperse them widely, even concealing them in underground silos. These could be protected by other missiles in an interlocking web. The result could provide the United States with that "second-strike capability." If the Soviet Union attacked without warning and somehow destroyed all of SAC's air bases, America could still retaliate. This ability would presumably persuade the Russians not to attack.

Theories about strategic war became quite complicated. A nation would forge "ahead" if it could devise a missile guidance system which could guarantee destruction of an enemy's concealed silos. Or if it invented a better radar system, or a new jamming device . . . and so on. Planning became quite subtle.

While Wohlstetter was presenting his ideas to the Air Force, another RAND team was developing "game theory," sometimes called the "science of coercion." (Credit for creating game theory has gone to a man named John von Neumann who began work on it in World War II.)

War games undoubtedly go back to prehistoric men hovering in winter caves wondering what would happen if, in the spring, they tried this new tactic of throwing their stones with their fingers across the seams rather than parallel to them. The Chinese analyzed war; so did the Byzantines and the Romans. But all their theories, though often valid, were not *scientifically* applicable. Sun

Tzu might declare that a warrior should be crafty, but that does not solve the logistics of taking Alsace. In the eighteenth and nineteenth centuries French and German thinkers created modern military theorizing. The Germans especially studied war, and not merely in an abstract sense. Suppose, they asked themselves, they wished to attack Cologne with ten regiments? How much weight could they send across a specific crucial bridge during any single hour of the attack's first day? How much stress could the metal in the bridge's spans take? Moreover, what would the French do? If they did A, B, or C, how should the Germans deal with it? *Kriegspielung* ("wargaming"), as they called it, became intricate. Ornate miniature battlefields were created; tiny battalions attempted to duplicate presumed enemy behavior.

In the 1950s, American theorists took another step. They added two new elements. The computer speeded analysis, making it possible to solve ever-tinier problems, and certain RANDMEN added *political*-gaming as a sub-function of wargaming. Clausewitz's famous dictum about war being only an extension of politics has been often mentioned but seldom used. But in the 1950s analysts asked such questions as: How can we accomplish Goal XX? War might be one device to achieve that end, but war could be expensive and inefficient (and, at times, unpopular). Perhaps other means of coercion might be used. The analysts developed a whole "science" of game strategy. By the early 1960s their concepts were common knowledge among the New Frontiersmen, many of whom were specifically trained in its methods.

An important component of game theory is the necessity of reducing military and diplomatic incidents to neutral language. "Slaughter" is an ugly word; "population response," which means the same thing, is more palatable. "Megadeaths" sounds less horrifying than "millions of corpses." "Assassination" becomes "executive action." Game theory encompasses "multivariate analysis," "models," and "parameters." It works best when it deals with two simple sides, each acting rationally. By reducing human error, stupidity, and emotionalism to mathematical probabilities, it can indeed "solve" problems, certainly better than unscientific guesswork. Humanists are suspicious of the entire process, but the methodology, while not infallible, can work. It forms the basis of modern strategic thinking and provides the language of missile warfare.

In the mid-50's the United States began work on the Atlas, a missile which, when perfected, could carry a thermonuclear payload 6,000 miles or more and deposit it within a mile or two of a designated target. The initial Atlas launch required months of preparation and days of final countdown, and when the first rocket did go off slowly from Cape Canaveral, something went wrong inside its complex mechanism. It began to wobble out of control, then tumbled into the sea like a bird shot from the sky. This failure was followed by more checking, more planning. Finally in mid-1957 the Air Force successfully launched one. To those who saw it, the image remained indelible: sitting on its launch pad, tall and phallic, chill clouds of liquid oxygen swirling in the air, scores of technicians scurrying beneath it, dozens of engineers sitting inside the main building staring at computers.

During the five years after 1957 scientists improved the design. By 1962 the government had 126 Atlases of various types. Model F, no longer guided by men, using the stars and planets to position itself, was stored underground, protected behind reinforced concrete doors—a near-perfect "hard" site.

Before the Air Force completed Atlas, it began work on an even larger, more sophisticated rocket, the Titan. Titan I stood almost 100 feet tall and 25 feet around the base. Its massive engines could hurl a several-megaton warhead up to 9,000 miles. On a February morning in 1959, when the Air Force first tested it, its ugly snout rose calmly and perfectly, taking it precisely toward target. Titan II, fueled by a mixture of nitrogen tetroxide and hydrazine, could store its fuel in its engines. Unlike its predecessors, therefore, it could be fired relatively rapidly, within an hour or two.

The Air Force also developed the solid-fuel rocket, Minuteman. Fifty-four feet long, it was slim enough to fit inside a silo only 10 feet in diameter. No technicians or scientists needed to stay with it. Minuteman could lie quietly inside its dark, concrete hole, perhaps somewhere in an isolated three-acre field enclosed by barbed wire. An Air Force officer far away merely had to press a button. Minuteman's heavy door, 4 feet thick, would slide open, revealing the rocket's deadly pointed nose. Then, whoosh. . . .

The entire operation, sending a warhead 6,000 miles, would take only *thirty seconds*. By the 1960s hundreds of Minutemen dotted the Midwest.

But the United States would still have problems—like a wealthy man who has to buy guard dogs to protect his burglar alarms. Russia conceivably might send missiles to destroy the silos. If a one-megaton warhead detonated within two-thirds of a mile of a hardened site, the underground missile would likely be knocked out of action. The Air Force therefore developed a defensive system of huge radar installations and an anti-missile missile, Nike-Zeus.

About this time the Navy's Special Projects Office came up with the Polaris rocket. *A single Polaris submarine could carry more destructive power than all the bombs dropped during World War II.* Since a sub could move close to the Soviet Union, Polaris's rockets did not need to be very large. Moreover, they used solid fuel; they could be fired instantly. The submarine offered a further advantage: The sea itself formed a natural protective "silo." A sub constantly on the move would be almost impossible to detect and triangulate. Russian aiming devices could not lock onto it. A Polaris submarine was almost invulnerable to a surprise attack. It provided the kind of second-strike capability that Albert Wohlstetter had emphasized.

Atlas, Titan, Minuteman, Polaris—these (and others like Jupiter) threatened the Soviet Union with destruction.

Meanwhile, during the fifties the Kremlin placed its emphasis on huge booster rockets, capable of carrying extremely heavy payloads. Sputnik I, launched on October 4, 1957, was Russia's first dramatic success. Although the United States had successfully fired its Atlas several months earlier, to the uninitiated (as well as to many American experts who should have known better) the Soviet rocketeers seemed frighteningly ahead—not in some mystical "space race," but in the creation of ICBMs.

Despite appearances, however, Soviet missilemen were in a predicament. They could build single prototype rockets, but Russia's ability to produce high-precision equipment remained far behind America's. In the early sixties one high-ranking Russian admitted that their missile development had serious flaws. "Accidents and all sorts of troubles are daily occurrences," he said. "There have been many cases during the test launchings of missiles when they have hit inhabited areas, railroad tracks, etc., instead of the designated targets, after deviating several hundred miles from their prescribed course." Soviet military planners had made a stunning error. Their huge rockets were incredibly expensive and terribly inaccurate.

Russian planners therefore decided to stress weapons with short ranges: The medium-range ballistic missile (MRBM) and the intermediate-range ballistic missile (IRBM). Until 1960 these rockets fell under the jurisdiction of the artillery section of the army, and Soviet rocket experts graduated from Dzerzhinskiy Artillery Academy. Their primary task involved supporting troops in a war with Western Europe.

Then in 1960 this picture changed. Moscow's missiles had been placed above ground, not in silos (perhaps partly because of confidence in the KGB's ability to prevent spying, and partly because the great size of Soviet rockets made it difficult to conceal them underground). When Gary Powers' U-2 plane crashed in the Soviet Union, the Russians realized that America knew perfectly where the Russian missiles were. The Soviet Union might be able to prevent further U-2 flights but spy satellites might soon make these unnecessary. Then came a series of American moves which Soviet leaders interpreted as threatening. In 1961 the Kennedy administration announced that the "missile gap" (which presidential candidate Kennedy had spoken of so forcefully) did not exist. The United States, Kennedy now admitted, was way ahead. The Kremlin became aware that the Americans had discovered some way to *count* Soviet missiles. Suddenly Soviet rockets—locked on top of their "soft" pads—seemed very vulnerable, especially if the Americans decided on a first strike. In 1961, immediately after taking office, President Kennedy further accelerated America's missile programs, ordering the production of hundreds of Minutemen and a number of new Polaris submarines. He also emphasized the need for fallout shelters. In December 1961 the United States government published a pamphlet on how to prepare a family shelter and distributed it to the communications media. The following spring the Department of Defense began a widely heralded program to set up nuclear shelters for upwards of sixty million people. A suspicious Kremlin official might wonder what all this activity was about. Why worry so much about shelters unless you expected war?

In 1962 Secretary of Defense Robert McNamara announced that the United States would switch its missile targets from population centers to military installations. Some listeners might think this a humanitarian move. Others might see something much more sinister: Perhaps the Americans contemplated a surprise attack. Otherwise, why focus on missile sites? Apparently the United States might be moving from second-strike readiness to first-strike.

An ominous article appeared in the March 27, 1962 issue of the *Saturday Evening Post*. Written by a journalistic acquaintance of the President, Stewart Alsop, and entitled "Kennedy's Grand Strategy," it stated that the President told Alsop: "In some circumstances, we might have to take the initiative."

Khrushchev was in a delicate situation. The Soviet Union could gear up a drastic campaign of missile building, but this path contained certain weaknesses. Flaws in Soviet missile production could not be solved overnight. Even if all the wrinkles were ironed out, the Americans were far ahead and pulling away. Only a gigantic effort would enable Soviet scientists even to keep pace. To catch up would require an all-out, crash program—an incredibly expensive and unpopular prospect. Khrushchev's government was already facing serious difficulties. Soviet harvests had recently fallen well under expectations; public resentment over the lack of civilian commodities, especially housing, was growing; and Russia's uneasy friendship with China had crumbled, infecting Moscow's relations with a number of underdeveloped countries. In these circumstances, to spend billions of rubles on an ICBM system—particularly one that was potentially flawed and possibly already obsolete—seemed quixotic. Perhaps other ways might be found—at least to put off for a while such a massive endeavor. Eventually, weapons like Polaris-style submarines could probably catapult the Soviet Union back into the race. But developing such alternatives would take time. Khrushchev needed some stop-gap measure, a "quick-fix." Possibly Cuba could supply it.

If Russia put some of its available MRBMs and IRBMs on the Caribbean island, this single action might solve several problems at once. Even though Russian missiles had relatively poor CEP scores, from close to Florida they could do severe damage. Furthermore, Kremlin leaders knew that the United States radar network did not face south. Missiles in Cuba would point directly into what might be called America's soft underbelly. Placing only a few dozen of them there, moreover, instantly *doubled* Russia's first-strike capabilities. And medium-range rockets cost much less than ICBMs.

Certain problems remained. Since the missiles would have to be placed at easily detectable launching sites, and they were liquid-fueled (needing at least several hours to fire), they would be useless as second-strike weapons. To use them as part of a first strike, when half of any missile attack would come from the Soviet Union, would require absolute precision. Artillerymen normally try to avoid what they call a "ragged volley," in which a few guns fire before the others are ready. With missiles divided between Cuba and the Soviet Union, such a volley seemed inevitable. These difficulties did not mean that Cuban missiles would be ineffective, just less than perfect. They would still be a major improvement over the Soviet's present system. The Kremlin could use the interim to retool its whole missile program, replacing its obsolete giant rockets with a more sophisticated missile network like the United States had. Cuban missiles might give Russia the time she needed to accomplish her goal.

Another motive for putting missiles into Cuba was, apparently, Berlin.

In the vortex of European politics, the ancient conflict between Germans and Slavs has been history's bloodiest feud. Much of the Cold War is rooted in their rivalry. At the end of World War II Germany lay devastated and divided. The Soviet Union preferred to keep it that way; East Germany is partly an outgrowth of their desire to keep that area weak.

By the late fifties the Germans seemed once more on the rise. West Germany's economy had blossomed; its military power had followed suit. Although it did not have atomic weapons, its artillery and its air force (both encouraged by the United States) had nuclear capabilities. The creation of the Common Market in 1957 may have finally pushed Khrushchev into action. It raised the specter of Germany as the center of an economically vigorous and militarily aggressive alliance.

At first Khrushchev began a series of moves culminating in his demand that the Western Powers get out of Berlin. Secretary of State John Foster Dulles rejected Khrushchev's ultimatum. The Soviet premier then tried a different tack. He spoke warmly about the United States. In September 1959 he even came for a visit. He and Eisenhower held secret discussions at Camp David. The two men made progress towards some sort of European settlement. But during the following winter each seemingly thought better of the "Spirit of Camp David" and both sides returned to the attack.

When Kennedy came into office, he and Khrushchev agreed to hold a Vienna summit meeting in June 1961. By the time the young President arrived in Austria, the Bay of Pigs disaster had already occurred. Since Kennedy wondered whether the Soviet premier now doubted his toughness, he warned Khrushchev several times not to miscalculate America's will—particularly on the matter of Berlin. A few weeks later, as if to prove his point, Kennedy called up a large number of National Reserve troops. He also announced a 25 percent increase in America's military strength.

On August 13, workers began to build the Berlin Wall. This barrier immediately reduced the flood of German technicians moving toward better jobs in West Germany. It also stood as a symbol of Russian determination. Khrushchev may even have hoped it would halt Chinese criticism. (At a Warsaw Pact conference during the summer of 1961 an Albanian delegate—obviously speaking for Albania's Chinese friends—chastised Khrushchev and demanded that he solve the German situation.)

In February 1962 Walter Ulbricht, head of East Germany, came to Moscow. Undoubtedly, the subject of Berlin came up, and possibly Khrushchev promised him they would do *something*.

Several months later Arnold Smith, the Canadian ambassador to Moscow, heard a rumor. From snatches of information and gossip, he concluded that in November 1962 the Soviet Union would sign a treaty with East Germany. Soviet tanks would block all highways and railroads into Berlin. If any Allied aircraft attempted to bring supplies into the city, as they had in 1948, the Russian air force would shoot them down. Berlin would be sealed off. If the NATO Allies attempted to break the blockade, they would do so in an area where the Russians held all the military advantages. Unless Kennedy was willing to go all out and risk global war he would be beaten. Khrushchev would fly to New York and speak to the United Nations. He would offer a general peace agreement by which NATO troops would leave Berlin and create there "a free city." He would also propose a nuclear test ban treaty. The Canadian ambassador passed on his suspicions to Ottawa.

About the same time a conversation occurred between Anatoly S. Dobrynin, Soviet ambassador to the United States, and presidential aide Theodore Sorensen. The Soviet ambassador told Sorensen that Khrushchev had a special message for the President. The young aide recorded Dobrynin's exact words: "Nothing will be undertaken before the American congressional national elections that would complicate the international situation." The Soviet ambassador mentioned the subject of Berlin as an example. He also raised the possibility that Khrushchev might come and address the United Nations. But if he did so, Dobrynin said, "This would be possible only in the second half of November. The chairman does not wish to become involved in your internal political affairs."

Dobrynin's statements closely matched the story Arnold Smith sent to Ottawa. The Canadian's theories therefore may have been correct, particularly if one adds the crucial element Smith was unaware of—Soviet missiles in Cuba. One may speculate that Khrushchev hoped to use the Cuban missiles as leverage to gain his ends for Berlin.

A third reason Khrushchev may have placed missiles in Cuba was to forestall an American attack on the island. If the United States were really contemplating an invasion of Cuba, as Castro seemed to think, the missiles might deter it. Keeping a Communist regime in Cuba was important to Soviet prestige; to lose the island would be a public relations disaster. As Khrushchev said, "It would have been a terrible blow to Marxism-Leninism. It would gravely diminish our stature throughout the world, but especially in Latin

America." (Possibly the missile scheme also involved internal politics within the Kremlin. Khrushchev's power in the hierarchy may have been weakening, and he may have felt he needed some significant coup to buttress his position.)

But why did Moscow assume that it could succeed in its plans? It is easy to *want* things, as Khrushchev might want to win in Berlin or gain missile equality. Life is filled with countless yearnings. The Russians knew that the Americans sent U-2 flights over Cuba every few weeks; these would inevitably detect the missiles. Why did Soviet leaders believe that Washington would let Russia get away with it? Or at least that Kennedy's government would dawdle long enough for Khrushchev's plan to succeed?

Perhaps John Kennedy had been partly right in his statement to Reston that—for the moment at least—Khrushchev considered him irresolute and faint-hearted. But after Kennedy had told Reston about his concerns, the United States had acted firmly, even belligerently, during the Berlin crisis later that year. Any lingering Russian doubts about the toughness of the American President should have evaporated, though it is possible that Soviet leaders may have assumed that the United States would not take a *hard* stand about Cuba. Those in the Kremlin specializing in American analysis (perhaps they might be termed "Washingtonologists") would have noted several statements seeming to reflect the official stance.

On June 29, 1961, Senator J. William Fulbright (whom Kennedy had seriously considered appointing secretary of state) remarked to the Senate: "I suppose we would all be less comfortable if the Soviets did install missile bases in Cuba, but I am not sure that our national existence would be in substantially greater danger than is the case today." In January 1962 the State Department calmly told journalists that, "Bombers, naval craft, and possibly short-range tactical guided missiles might eventually be delivered to Cuba." On February 5, the department released an additional similar announcement.

The Kremlin, analyzing Washington's sentiment, may have concluded from such tepid remarks that the United States would do nothing if the Russians brought missiles to Cuba. The Kremlin may also have reasoned that even if Kennedy wanted to do something, several hurdles would stand in his way. The NATO allies would be reluctant to take a firm line, since they themselves had hunched beneath a nuclear threat for over a decade. Even if NATO did agree to act, getting them moving would take time. The same would be even truer of the OAS. Latin American countries normally resented United States power. Yankee-baiting had long been a diverting pastime south of the Rio Grande. Even within the United States, opposition might be strong enough to paralyze Washington—especially in an election year. Khrushchev, certainly inexperienced at democratic politics, always overestimated the significance of American elections. He may have thought that Kennedy would hesitate to act because of Republican opposition.

Whatever their reasons, the Russians miscalculated. But the fault was not entirely theirs. Kennedy should have made clear his total opposition to strategic weapons in Cuba. Had he taken an absolutely firm stance on the matter before the spring of 1962, the missile crisis probably could have been avoided.

4 The Kremlin Enterprise

Russians began coming to Cuba early in the revolution, some as political representatives, embassy types, others as "technicians," experts on agronomy and land irrigation, industrial techniques and building construction. They gave Cubans advice—generally ignored—on how to do certain things. Visitors from other Communist countries also came, especially Czechs, generally more relaxed and popular with Cubans. Russians had a tendency to remain aloof, to act a trifle like self-satisfied tourists. Most of them stayed in the hotels built by Americans before the revolution.

The novelist Edmundo Desnoes describes a scene. Some visitors from the Soviet Union are strolling through a Cuban museum: "A group of Russians walked in, more women then men, and discussed each painting; they would get up close to a canvas, lean back, study each detail." Desnoes makes an interesting comparison. "They are square, fat, but at the end of the last century Americans must have produced the same effect that Russians do now. A little coarse, clods of the earth." Cubans, a clean, fastidious people, shower frequently and prefer others to do the same. The novel's hero encounters a rather rank Russian, "a penetrating whiff, a hunk of life." "I looked him over carefully, at once attracted and repelled; he was blond, with an enormous face, like a buttock, with a small black camera hanging over his blue plaid shirt." Desnoes writes that Russians swagger around like emissaries of a "great world power down visiting their colonies." They are "humbler men than most Americans, true, and without any holdings in Cuba—but down deep their attitude is very much alike. Besides, what they can't take away in dollars they get out of us in propaganda."

They also got a place to put their missiles.

Russian "technicians" scrutinized Cuba very carefully in 1962. They examined port facilities to see which harbors were best and which had cranes capable of lifting great weights. They checked Cuba's railways and its roads. Heavy military equipment—like tanks and rockets—requires a good transportation system. Cuba's highways were adequate, but its country roads, to say nothing of the streets in some of its ports, needed improvement. The Soviet experts generally chose sites far away from towns. Each site needed to be mapped and surveyed. Electric wire and water lines had to be laid, forests had to be cut down, fields had to be leveled. This operation would require trucks and jeeps and mechanics to fix them. The vehicles would need gasoline and oil—and containers to put them in. Russia would have to protect the missiles from either a guerrilla attack by emigré refugees or a full-scale American invasion (or possibly even the Cuban government, which might try to grab them). The Russians would therefore want to bring heavy fences to encircle their bases and ground troops to guard them. These soldiers would need barracks, toilet facilities and toilet paper, barbers, prophylactics, tooth powder, mess halls and Russian food. To protect *them*, Moscow would have to send artillery and tanks and machine guns and rocket launchers—and of course ammunition. And then build warehouses to store all this. They would add anti-aircraft installations and fighter planes to keep the sites from being attacked. This would require airfields and hangars and storage buildings for replacement parts. These meant tractors and steamrollers and dump trucks. Much of Cuba is porous and parts of it are swampy. Some of these areas would have to be filled in. To do that, the Russians would need to bring drainage pipes and power shovels of all types. They would also want radar installations, partly to watch for air attacks and partly to pick up high-flying U-2s overhead. Moreover, to prevent these spy planes from figuring out what they were doing, they would set up ground-to-air missile sites. And to discourage an invasion by sea, they would bring in a small fleet of coast guard boats. These would need to be protected. Finally, the entire operation would have to be done in secret.

As huge amounts of matériel piled high on Cuba's docks, Moscow Radio stated that Russia was only giving Cuba "machine tools, wheat, and agricultural machinery"—and "some 7,000 tons of various fertilizers."

The first main body of Soviet troops to appear that summer were conspicuous. They wore khakis and white summer blouses, pretending to be civilians. But they were all young and strong, and observers noticed that they only brought two types of sport shirts. They hardly seemed tourists. One man said, "I could see them being moved across Havana, standing up in Russian and Czech light trucks as these were driven, often under Cuban police escort, through the streets." An American official described them as "primarily young, trim, physically fit, sun-tanned and disciplined." When they came off the ships, "they formed in ranks of fours on the docks and moved out in truck convoys." Yet these men, though probably in the army, were most likely construction workers, not infantry troops. Eventually fighting men did come, but later and with much more stealth. (The first arrivals may have been meant to test Washington's reaction: If the United States had made a major issue of it, the Russians could have withdrawn before becoming too committed.)

The port of Mariel serviced the province of Pinar del Rio. Its bay on Cuba's north coast, about 30 miles west of Havana, provided good anchorage—and relative obscurity. A quiet seafaring town, pretty, ringed by mountains, known mainly for its fish restaurants, Mariel had long been used by ships coming for sugar.

According to Cuban underground agents, on July 21, 1962, a Czechoslovakian technician named Stefan Padic demanded to see the mayor of Mariel. "You have," Padic announced to the mayor "two days to evacuate the houses within a mile of the waterfront." The population's sacrifice, he said, would constitute a patriotic act for the fatherland. They could look for housing elsewhere, perhaps in a local hospital, perhaps with friends in other towns.

On July 25, a heavy Russian freighter pulled slowly into the bay and docked at Pier 6. Soviet troops marched down its gangplanks while cranes hoisted military equipment from its decks. Other ships followed: the S/S *Latvia*, the S/S *Muritsky*, and the S/S *Aneckcahapobch*. During the following weeks similar events took place at five other ports around the island.

In the first half of 1962 only one Soviet passenger ship arrived in Cuba. Four arrived in July and six in August. The number of dry cargo ships jumped from about fifteen a month to thirty in July, thirty-seven in August, and sixty-six in September. So much matériel arrived in Havana it began to clog the streets. Soviet military vehicles sat fender to fender five across for several blocks along San Pedro Street. Russian troops were being billeted in camps all over the island. One former Cuban professor, after analyzing the reports, identified forty-seven separate locations. All foreign newsmen in Havana knew that Soviet soldiers had taken over a boys' reformatory not far from town. Curious journalists, trying to find out what was going on there, found themselves hustled rudely away. By October the Soviet Union had sent upward of 40,000 troops to Cuba. A partial list of the military equipment sent to Cuba would include: about 150 jet fighter planes, between 7,500 and 10,000 trucks, about 350 medium and heavy tanks, 40 ships, 1,300 pieces of field artillery and 700 anti-aircraft guns.

Later, after the crisis, some critics of the Kennedy administration demanded to know why Washington had been surprised by the missiles, why it had taken so long to discover them. In fact, however, in some ways it is remarkable the American government found out so soon.

Roberta Wohlstetter, a perceptive analyst of international affairs, has noted the difference between "signals" and "noise". A "signal" is a piece of evidence that accurately points to an action or motive; "noise" results from a jumble of confusing and contradictory data. One is surrounded all day by various sounds. One can usually pick out what is important—a child's scream of pain, for example. But when general noise increases, it deadens the senses. Surrounded by constant shrieking, one loses the ability to discriminate.

Intelligence work is the same. The more information pouring in, the more confused an intelligence officer becomes. Reports have to be read, translated, and sifted. There is a certain bureaucratic process that takes time. Someone has to type the reports. Someone else has to carry them from desk to desk. Additional people have to make decisions about what is classified and the type of classification. Then each report must be retyped (probably at least in triplicate) and collated and stapled and stamped and noted and filed. The more people involved in a process, the more time-consuming simple clerical factors become.

The amount of "noise" from Cuba grew deafening. Some reports arrived indirectly. A Greek ship captain told a friend about two military shipments on their way to Cuba. The friend then mentioned the story to *his* friend, Lincoln White, press officer at the State Department. White called Roger Hilsman, the department's director of intelligence. Hilsman added this scrap of information to hundreds of others. Tourists throughout the Caribbean, hearing tales of Russians moving into Cuba, were sending these along to Washington. Some information came openly from newspapers, some involved *private* reports from friendly newsmen assigned to Havana. Also, although the American Embassy in Cuba had closed down, a few Americans still remained on the island or visited it. Officials from foreign embassies forwarded interesting data. Latin Americans, for example, provided Washington with information. The CIA kept its own Cuban Intelligence Center at Opa-locka, Florida. Each week it interviewed Cubans filtering into Florida in small boats. It also kept close contact with the underground in Cuba through emigrés like members of the Student Directorate (DRE). Occasionally the CIA received secret messages radioed in code.

This tidal wave of information had major drawbacks. Secretary of Defense McNamara later said that the government received several thousand reports a month, each of which had to be analyzed and evaluated.

Most reports were exaggerated or imaginary. Washington had a file five inches thick devoted to missiles in Cuba, *three years before the Russians sent them.* Some reports were so outrageous they were laughable and made all the others suspect. There were tales of African troops with rings in their noses and stories of lurking Mongolians. "I can remember one report I read in the past few days," Roger Hilsman told reporters in August 1962, "which is about a Cuban who says, 'My cousin Joe, you see, was up at such-and-such a point and he saw Chinese Communist troops.' . . . The last line of the report says, 'Of course, knowing my cousin Joe, I guess maybe it's only 1,000.' " (The reporters laughed but possibly "Joe" had seen a regiment of Soviet troops from the Uzbek region.)

On August 7, 1962, Salvador Lew, a well-known Cuban exile, spoke over Miami's Spanish-language radio station WMIE. He described the arrival in Cuba of *uniformed* Soviet soldiers. Señor Lew's announcement may have been accurate, or at least partly so. At 8:15 that very morning, Soviet troops had docked at Havana— but they were wearing *civilian clothes.* Lew's apparent slip (or exaggeration) was the kind of thing that made Washington suspicious of Cuban sources. Intelligence officers want absolute accuracy. If an agent in the field sent a report to headquarters that he had just observed marching men "with guns," he would be harshly reprimanded. A "gun" could be a pistol or a cannon, and the difference is crucial. Misinformation casts doubt on the dependability of the person making the report.

Cuban refugee informants seemed suspect because they had a vested interest in American antagonism toward Castro. Many of them hoped that if the situation in Cuba became (or appeared) unacceptable, the United States would intervene; they could then go home. Castro's own double agents even occasionally contributed counterfeit reports.

Inaccurate information had helped lead Washington in 1961 to the Bay of Pigs. Cuban refugees had wanted so strongly to believe Castro's regime was shaky and unpopular they had been able to convince the CIA. When that invasion had failed, the agency's reputation had declined. No one in high-ranking position, either in the CIA or elsewhere, put much faith any longer in Cuban informants.

Washington also had other sources. The Air Force and the Navy kept constant surveillance of Soviet ships and photographed those heading for Cuba. The Mediterranean Fleet watched shipping lanes out of the Black Sea, and the Atlantic Fleet watched the flow coming from the Baltic. The National Security Agency used its huge antennae to intercept messages from Soviet shipping. ITT, which had originally built Cuba's communications network and which secretly retained an electronic tie-in, intercepted information and relayed it to the United States.

Washington was well aware of Russian activity on the island. All signs pointed toward some major military buildup there. On August 24, Roger Hilsman, representing the State Department, briefed reporters that at least twenty to thirty Soviet ships (not counting those flying other flags) were bringing in "large quantities of transportation, electronic and construction equipment" including radar vans, generator units, and anti-aircraft machine guns. Hilsman described all this as "the sort of stuff you would use to strengthen your coastal and air defense systems."

John A. McCone, director of the CIA, became the first high-ranking official to suspect missiles.

McCone personified the mid-twentieth century executive. Born in San Francisco in 1902, he had gone to Berkeley and studied engineering. He had risen rapidly in steel and construction businesses on the West Coast. He was a careful, ambitious man. When he married the first time at thirty-six, he was already president of his own fast-growing Los Angeles engineering firm. During World War II he entered shipbuilding. He cultivated friends in Washington and learned the intricacies of government contracts. On the surface he seemed amiable, but underneath a sociable exterior lay a tough, calculating, highly organized mind.

After the war America's economic growth overseas seemed threatened by the spread of communism. McCone's seat on the board of directors of ITT introduced him to world politics. He grew dissatisfied with business. His natural patriotism, his ambitions, his contacts, and his abilities led him toward government. Although a conservative Republican, he was chosen by Harry Truman in 1947 to be a member of his Air Policy Commission, studying the effects of air warfare. The following year he became deputy to Secretary of Defense George C. Marshall. Then, during the early days of the Korean War, Truman made him undersecretary of the Air Force. When he resigned in 1951, his timing was impeccable. The political-military situation had turned ugly during the Truman-McCarthy controversy, and Senator Joe McCarthy was beginning to make things uncomfortable for government officials.

When Dwight D. Eisenhower became President, McCone may have expected a high position. He was a Republican businessman, expert on military-administrative affairs. Exactly why Eisenhower failed to pick him for anything is unclear. Maybe McCone could not get along with some member of the administration—perhaps John Foster Dulles or Eisenhower himself. It was not until 1958 that he returned to the capital, this time as chairman of the Atomic Energy Commission.

In November 1961 Kennedy chose John McCone to take over the agency. The new director was a handsome white-haired man with glasses, a multimillionaire, and a passionate hater of communism.

CIA headquarters lies 20 miles south of Washington in Langley, Virginia. Nestled in the woods of Fairfax County, amidst hundreds of acres of trees and rolling hills stands the main structure—a huge, rather ugly building, gray in color, several stories high with small windows near the ground barred and covered by heavy mesh screen. Set in the lobby's marble floor is a huge seal, the eagle's-head symbol of the agency.

On the top floor sits the large, somewhat cold office of the director. Here, in early August 1962, John McCone became convinced the Russians were about to install long-range missiles in Cuba. He had put together dozens of separate details, tiny shards of information about Soviet ships docking in Cuba. He developed a gut feeling: Something sinister was happening down there, something much more ominous than tanks and torpedo boats. He knew that Russia had already this year sent military aid to Iraq, Syria, and Indonesia; and that for the first time in history the Soviets were using military personnel in secret combat roles—as bomber crews in Yemen and submariners in Indonesia. McCone found the Cuban situation menacing. From the few pieces of data his mind leaped to rockets. The reports from the island were still inconclusive. He talked to his friend, P. L. Thyraud de Vosjoli. Vosjoli, head of French intelligence in Washington, did not know what was going on there, but in early August he flew to Cuba to unearth it. The Frenchman created a network of Cuban informants and sent their conclusions to his headquarters in Paris, and also to McCone in Washington.

The director sent a memo to the President on August 10, warning Kennedy about the possibility of missiles in Cuba, stating that "something new and different" was happening on the island. The Russians, among other things, seemed to be preparing to install surface-to-air missiles (SAMs). If so, he reasoned, they would probably bring in long-range missiles. Why else would they need SAMs?

On August 17, McCone brought his concern to a high-level meeting. Two days earlier he had ordered CIA U-2 planes to photograph certain suspected sectors of the island, but he felt these flights would be insufficient. He wanted the Air Force, he said, to make low-level observation missions over the island. Kennedy was not present at the meeting, but both Rusk and McNamara were there. McNamara successfully argued against McCone's proposal. Washington had no evidence the Soviets were installing missiles, and if the United States conducted provocative flights, the Cubans or Russians might fire at the American planes—especially now that the island had anti-aircraft guns. Unless McCone could provide specifics, the gamble hardly seemed worth it. McCone's virulent anti-communism had worked against his case. His colleagues had discounted his warnings as almost the product of paranoia. (In fact the Soviets had *not* yet brought long-range rockets to Cuba; these would not arrive for a month. Nor was there a single missile pad on the island. So McNamara was right.)

Apparently, and here reports are contradictory, on August 22, McCone personally stated his concerns to President Kennedy, once in a meeting and once privately. According to his recollections, he told the President: "The only construction I can put on the matériel going into Cuba is that the Russians are preparing to introduce offensive missiles. I question the value of SAMs, except as a means of making possible the introduction of offensive missiles."

The day after he talked to the President, McCone flew to Seattle to be married. He had instructed his staff to keep him up-to-date on the Cuban situation, so they compiled and sent him daily reports. As his nuptials approached, he grew increasingly apprehensive about Cuban missiles. He sent a stream of coded telegrams to Washington and frequently talked to his headquarters over a scrambled telephone. In late August he married a lovely Seattle widow, and they sailed from New York on a honeymoon cruise to Europe. But only a week later, in Paris, the day after his boat arrived, he met with Roswell Gilpatric, deputy secretary of defense, and told him his suspicions. During the next few days, although theoretically vacationing at Cap Ferrat on the French Riviera, he contacted the agency at least five times, recommending they write up strong statements about the missiles and continuing to plead for low-level flights over the island. (One wonders what his bride made of all this.)

The first hard confirmation of McCone's fears came on August 29 when a U-2 photographed clear evidence of SAM installations going up near Artemisa, about 60 miles from the town of San Cristóbal, not far from Mariel. Since SAMs could not shoot down planes flying *below* 10,000 feet, these anti-aircraft missiles could not interfere with an American invasion. Presumably, they would only be useful to knock down U-2 planes.

Meanwhile the congressional election campaign began heating up. By late August Republicans around the country were lambasting their Democratic opponents for the usual heinous crimes: overspending, inefficiency, and governmental meddling. In addition Republicans increasingly mentioned Cuba. Their 1962 handbook for Republican candidates advised them to hammer at Kennedy's difficulties with Castro. Homer Capehart, a Republican running in Indiana for reelection to the Senate, insisted that the United States invade Cuba immediately. Newspapers headlined Capehart's demands.

Public opinion polls indicated a general decline in Kennedy's popularity and a problem for Democrats. No one ever *knows* what a nation "feels." One can tabulate its responses to a specific question and determine that "43 percent of the respondents stated they were moderately concerned about . . . " But pollsters in 1962 would have admitted that their techniques remained rather unscientific, that they had not achieved real precision. Polls could not yet truly test depth of feelings, primal emotions. Republicans had no way of *knowing* that the subject of Cuba interested voters, but they assumed so, they hoped so. Their local contacts, their friendly editors, their private polls indicated that a lot of Americans felt angry about Castro—about his executions in 1959, about his Yanqui-baiting, about his attempts to gouge the United States out of millions of dollars before he would free his Bay of Pigs prisoners. America is not a patient nation; it does not swallow anger easily nor turn its other cheek.

For seven weeks, beginning on August 31, 1962, Kenneth Keating, a Republican senator from New York, vigorously attacked Kennedy's Cuban policy. Keating's motives are hard to analyze. He himself was not up for reelection for two more years. Perhaps he hoped to make a greater name for himself that would carry him through his 1964 campaign. Maybe he just wanted to help his fellow Republicans. Possibly he genuinely felt angry at the administration.

The thing that made his attacks so significant, particularly in retrospect, was that he emphasized the recent military buildup in Cuba. No one else—either Republican or Democrat—talked much about it. By his own count he gave twenty-five public statements on the subject.

Early in September John Kennedy decided to speak openly about Cuba. He may have been attempting partly to stem the rising tide of Republican attacks, to cut the ground from under adversaries like Senator Keating. He also seems to have wanted to give Moscow a clear warning, especially after the discovery of the SAMs. Moreover, on September 2, the Kremlin had issued a joint communique with Cuba stating that, in view of recent American threats, the Soviet Union had agreed to send weapons and technical advisors to Cuba. This was the first time Moscow had admitted sending armaments. Kennedy apparently felt it necessary—especially in light of the election campaign—to offer his reaction immediately.

On September 4, the White House released a statement. It opened with an announcement that the United States had spotted SAM installations and several Russian torpedo boats in Cuba, plus Soviet technicians to run them. Although the United States had "no evidence of any organized combat force . . . of offensive ground-to-ground missiles, or of other significant offensive capability . . . were it to be otherwise *the gravest issues would arise.*" The statement further warned that Kennedy's government would not tolerate any attempt by Cuba "to export its aggressive purposes." To prevent that from happening, the United States would use "whatever means may be necessary."

One should note that when Kennedy mentioned Cuba's potential "offensive capability," he was referring to the possibility that Castro might utilize such weapons "to export" communism. The White House only seemed concerned that Cuba might use "offensive" weapons against *other Latin American countries.* (Cuban-based guerrillas had recently been trying to foment revolts in places like Haiti, Honduras, and Nicaragua.) The statement does not indicate any anxiety that Cuba might use "offensive" weapons against the United States itself.

On September 11, Tass declared that armaments arriving in Cuba were "designed exclusively for defensive purposes." Russia, Tass bragged, owned such powerful rockets that it had no need to place missiles outside the Soviet Union.

In a press conference two days later, Kennedy reiterated his government's position. He said that, so far as he knew, the arms being shipped to Cuba were not offensive. If Cuba, however, ever attempted "to export its aggressive purposes by force or the threat of force," the United States would "do whatever must be done to protect its own security and that of its Allies." Kennedy specified certain regions: (1) "our base at Guantanamo"; (2) "our passage to the Panama Canal"; (3) "our missile and space activity at Cape Canaveral" (possibly threatened by some radio-jamming device or even the SAMs); (4) "or the lives of American citizens in this country" (a vague but not particularly serious catchall). Kennedy still could not imagine that Cuba might actually dare to threaten America herself. But he had placed the reputation of his administration (in an election year) squarely on this issue: He would not allow "offensive weapons" in Cuba. (It should be noted that Khrushchev presumably had placed *his* Kremlin reputation on putting missiles into Cuba. Since the equipment was already at sea by the time Kennedy spoke, it would have been politically almost impossible for the Soviet Union to have stopped the operation— even had Khrushchev wanted to. Kennedy's statement was too late.)

To avoid any semblance of seeming squishy soft on Castroism, the Democratically controlled Congress overwhelmingly passed a joint resolution proclaiming its determination to prevent the extension of Cuban communism and to oppose any Cuban act "endangering the security of the United States."

5 *Pumping Steel*

Late August 1962

They called her *Omsk*. She was a fine ship, new and gleaming and proud. Built in Osa, Japan only months before, she carried every modern device—radar and gyrocompasses and echo-sounding instruments. She was over 500 feet long, and from her belly to the tip of her antennae she was as tall as a ten-story building. Her bow was reinforced, so she could plow through the ice-jammed winter waters of the Baltic. Her port of registry said Vladivostok but she sailed all oceans. On her decks bristled the weapons of modern warfare—including guided missile launchers to keep other ships from becoming too inquisitive. Inside her hull were eight giant compartments, each over 60 feet from side to side, each as high as a house. Her hatches had been built particularly large, reportedly to carry timber, but they could also accommodate other cargos, large objects of almost any kind.

In the Soviet Union late in August, the *Omsk* lay huddled against a pier. Outside on the dock men strode purposefully, preparing her to leave. Hard-eyed agents of the Soviet secret police watched everything. Deep in the holds, lashed firmly into place, lay a sinister cargo. In the dimness, far from the busy workers outside, were missiles. They were a dull burnished gray, cold to the touch, patiently quiet.

68

September 8

By the time Kennedy gave his September 4th speech, warning Khrushchev not to put "offensive weapons in Cuba," the *Omsk* was nearing the island.

KGB agents, responsible for guarding and transporting all Soviet nuclear weapons, stood on deck. In the harbor other Soviet agents kept watch. All Cubans, even militiamen, had been barred from the area. This operation was to be absolutely secret. When the ship docked, gigantic cranes began their work, tenderly, delicately lifting the deadly cargo from the wide-mouthed hatches. Hundreds of other objects began to be stacked up on the dock, all the paraphernalia necessary to prepare a missile for launching.

September 9

On the other side of the world a U-2 plane, flown from Taiwan under the auspices of Chiang Kai-shek's government, was shot down over China. American officials became worried. Apparently the Russians had set up SAMs in China. Unless the United States proceeded very carefully, its spy planes might cause a diplomatic furor which in turn would force the administration to ground them indefinitely. With the Soviet Union becoming more aggressive in Indonesia and the Near East, to say nothing of Cuba, the United States needed all her intelligence sources.

September 10

COMOR (the Committee on Overhead Reconnaissance) held a meeting in McGeorge Bundy's office at the White House. COMOR had been created to advise the President on the use of the U-2, where it should fly and when. Kennedy wanted no repetitions of the Gary Powers incident, especially just before an election. COMOR had to approve each flight.

Mac Bundy presided over the meeting. Dean Rusk, representing the State Department, expressed his concern—especially in light of the recent discovery of Cuban SAM installations—about international repercussions if a U-2 were shot down over the island. He suggested some alternatives. Instead of flying the entire 800-mile length of Cuba, the planes could cross the island from side to side and, at least for a while, cover only the eastern end of the island. As far as the western side was concerned, they could fly around the edge of the island, outside the 3-mile limit, and photograph at an oblique angle. Almost the whole island could be covered this way—except sections like the central part of Pinar del Rio near the town of San Cristóbal.

A U-2 flight, scheduled to cover the eastern part of the island on September 6 and delayed due to cloud cover, was rescheduled for September 17. The plane took pictures but clouds obscured almost everything. The same thing happened again on September 26 and 29.

Intelligence did suspect something extraordinary was happening in Cuba. Among their concerns was the possibility that the Russians might be constructing for themselves a large port facility. Cuba straddles all major Caribbean shipping lanes. And her shadow leans across the Panama Canal. American naval experts did not like the prospect of a Russian fleet within striking distance of anywhere in the Caribbean, including American waters. On the eastern side of the island were several possible sites for submarine bases. COMOR's decision to order U-2s to fly the eastern side, therefore, was neither foolish nor timorous.

September 12

A headline covered the front page of Cuba's *Revolución:* "Rockets will blast the United States if it invades Cuba." CIA readers in Washington paid little attention. The words seemed mere braggadocio. Cuba's newspapers under Castro had become simultaneously florid and dull. They seldom said anything of importance.

That same night an intelligence operative west of Havana spotted a truck convoy rumbling quietly through the darkness. Some trucks pulled trailers more than 60 feet long with large oblong loads covered by canvas. The agent decided the loads were missiles—not SAMs which measured less than 34 feet or other short-range missiles: something bigger. This September 12 observation did not arrive in Washington until the 21st. It may have come by way of an escaping Cuban refugee.

Another agent (though possibly the same one), espying the tail of a large missile, estimated its circumference and drew a rough picture. This sketch also wended its way north through a network of intelligence operatives.

Other agents saw or heard things. One learned that the Russians were building a large missile site not far from the town of San Cristóbal. This report started slowly toward Washington.

September 15

Exactly one week after the *Omsk* landed, *Poltava* arrived in Cuba. She too was brand new, just built at the Nosenko shipyard in the Soviet Union. She too had huge hatches, large enough to accept unusually large cargoes. On her decks she carried trucks and vans, but she rode high out of the water—as if her cargo consumed much space but weighed rather little.

Mid-September

Across the island rolled lines of Soviet vehicles. Often they moved secretly at night; sometimes, however, their trips took so long they stayed overnight in roadside bivouacs. They moved toward four sites: Remedios and Sagua la Grande, east of Havana; Guanajay and San Cristóbal, west of the city. The Kremlin was placing one set of MRBMs and one set of IRBMs on each side of the island.

An IRBM site required much construction work. Land had to be cleared and roads laid. A special facility to mix concrete had to be built. The construction crew had to erect walls and bunkers. They also had to make four launch pads, each with a launch ring and flame deflector in the center. They had to erect buildings 114 feet long and 60 feet wide to store warheads. They had to surround the entire operation, including the tent area they lived in, with a perimeter fence apparently almost 6 miles long. (The Russians used heavily armed combat troops to guard each site.)

An MRBM installation was much less complicated. These

medium-range ballistic missiles were essentially mobile. They were designed to be used in combat by ground troops, and the Russian military looked on them as artillery. Most Soviet MRBMs had a range of only about 200 miles. Even at that distance their CEP scores were mediocre. Their chief advantage was that they needed neither fixed installations nor launching pads. All they required was to be brought by a long trailer to a level spot. Technicians would then attach nose cones to them and tune them. Each missile would be hauled by a special erector to an upright position, filled with oxidizers and propellants, and be ready to fire. Although an MRBM site normally needed missiles, trailers, erectors, fuel trucks, a generator, various pipes and cables, tent facilities for both missiles and men, and a long fence around the perimeter, a single installation *could* be built in a matter of days. Since the Russians, however, were placing four widely dispersed launching installations at each site, it took them a full month to finish each one. Also, they seemed in no great hurry. They worked only during the daylight hours.

They were moving slowly . . . but they were progressing.

American intelligence later declared that the range of the Soviet MRBMs was enough to reach New York and Washington. A CIA memorandum from October 26 states that a "low level photograph clearly indicates that the MRBM sites are for the SS-4 (Sandal) 1,200-nautical mile ballistic missile system."

Other sources do not agree. *Aviation Week and Space Technology,* perhaps the major journal in the field, questioned Washington's figures, pointing out that Soviet MRBMs had never been credited with more than a 500-mile range. Even this estimate, *Aviation Week* said, was optimistic. On October 27, the *New York Times* stated that, in the past, experts had declared that such missiles could only go 400 to 600 miles. The *Times* referred to the missile as a T-1, not an SS-4 (Sandal) as the CIA called it. The most prestigious work in the field is the biennial volume, *Jane's All the World's Aircraft.* Its 1963-64 edition, published after the crisis, refers to a new Soviet MRBM, designated as T-1, with a NATO code name of "Sandal." *Jane's* was unsure of its range but estimated it as more than 220 miles. A recent query to the editor of *Jane's* elicited the following response: "To the best of my knowledge the missiles emplaced in Cuba were SS-4 Sandals. These can best be thought of as 'Super V-2s' with a length of about 68 feet 10 inches." (According to the Department of Defense, however, the length of the Cuban MRBMs was 73.3 feet.) The editor of *Jane's* has concluded: "The missiles could have reached the targets in the U.S.A. that were mentioned by Washington." Considering the contradictions in these various responses, the matter remains in doubt. The San Cristóbal missiles could certainly have reached Miami, but whether they could go much north of that—particularly with any accuracy—is open to serious question.

The CIA's calculations about IRBM ranges are equally questionable. *Jane's* estimated 1,300 miles and the American government said 2,200 miles, or enough to hit every part of the United States but the far Northwest. (*Aviation Week* cynically wondered whether Washington's figures were meant to frighten voters throughout the country just before the election.)

Another riddle involves the explosive power of the missiles. Any missile is dangerous, of course, but much of the October crisis would stem from the assumption that Russia had put *nuclear* weapons in Cuba. *But there is no concrete evidence they did so.* American aerial photographs merely show missiles, related equipment, and bunkers designed apparently to store warheads. But *no* warheads. McNamara later admitted that he only *believed* that Soviets had brought nuclear weapons to Cuba, he could not be positive.

One wonders, given Russian reluctance to move nuclear weapons from Soviet soil, if in fact they merely sent rockets and *non-nuclear* warheads. If the Kremlin's purpose was essentially political (for example, Berlin), all they needed to do was give the *appearance* of nuclear capability. Moreover, sending atomic warheads to Cuba offered certain disadvantages. Something might go wrong—such as a ship sinking, or a misfire, or even the Cuban government grabbing them. It seems at least possible that the Russians were bluffing.

September 17

A U-2 plane flew over eastern Cuba, looking for a submarine base. It saw nothing out of the ordinary.

September 19

The Board of Estimates met in Washington to determine what the Soviet Union was doing in Cuba and to draw up a "National Intelligence Estimate." Representatives of every major American intelligence organization sat on the board: one each from the CIA, FBI, Army, Navy, Air Force, Atomic Energy Commission, National Security Agency, and the Departments of State and Defense. They received additional advice about Soviet motives from the two most knowledgeable men in the State Department, Charles E. (Chip) Bohlen and Llewellyn E. Thompson. They examined all the available data. (None of the really decisive eyewitness reports had yet arrived in Washington. The U-2 photographs showed nothing beyond the known SAM sites and a base for torpedo boats.)

The board admitted that Russia might bring missiles to Cuba, either to awe the Latin American states, or to use them as a bargaining chip against Berlin. But the board doubted it. The Russians had always been cautious with their missiles. Putting them far away in Cuba under Castro's unstable and perhaps unreliable regime would seem foolhardy. Especially since such an act might goad the United States into some violent action.

September 26

Another U-2 flight was made over Cuba's eastern side. Nothing.

September 27

The sketch of a missile's tail assembly arrived at CIA headquarters. The agency considered it interesting.

Other reports came in. Someone had heard Castro's own pilot boasting drunkenly that his country no longer needed to fear the United States. Cuba, the pilot said, now had great power of its own. "We will fight to the death, and perhaps we can win because we have everything, including atomic weapons."

A bearded Cuban got into an argument with an American. When the American said the United States might some day feel forced to invade, the enraged Cuban replied, "But we now have missiles. We can defend ourselves."

"What do you mean by missiles?" the American demanded. "I thought you only had missiles that were anti-aircraft missiles with a range of fifty miles."

"Oh, no," the Cuban replied smugly, "we could hit Florida."

Colonel John R. Wright, Jr. and his colleagues in the Department of Defense's intelligence section had been studying U-2 photographs. He kept staring at closeups of the SAM installations near San Cristóbal. There was something familiar about them. Construction, he noticed, was being done in an unusual trapezoidal arrangement. He remembered seeing this same pattern before . . . in the Soviet Union . . . guarding long-range missile sites. He suggested to his superiors that the next U-2 flight should take another look at San Cristóbal.

An article (dated October 1, 1962) appeared in *Aviation Week*. Datelined "Washington," it said: "Pentagon strategists consider the present arms buildup in Cuba the first step toward eventual construction of the intermediate-range ballistic missile emplacements." According to the author, these "Pentagon strategists" had noted that the SAMs were "aimed at preventing aerial photograph reconnaissance."

One wonders who the "Pentagon" source was. Could it have been McCone, who had just returned from his honeymoon? He was, of course, not from the Pentagon, but that label could have been journalistic camouflage. The article also stated that another "informed defense source" remained unconcerned about the Cuban situation. The military buildup only seemed great, this latter person is quoted, "because Cuba had little to begin with." The real danger was Berlin. (Apparently someone in the Pentagon had accepted with relative equanimity the possibility of Cuban missiles. In the light of the later, opposite reaction of the Kennedy administration, this is surprising.)

September 28

The Soviet ship *Kasimov* approached Cuban waters. Ten huge crates, each about 60 feet long, sat on its decks. An American plane, flying overhead, took pictures. Intelligence experts, analyz-

ing the photos, pondered the size of the crates and their shape.
They compared the pictures with others taken of various Soviet
crates all over the world. The analysts were methodical; they
wanted to be sure.

September 29

The CIA, after examining the evidence, marked the San
Cristóbal area "suspicious."
A U-2 flew over the Isle of Pines on the southern side of the
island and a section on the southwestern tip; it saw nothing.

October 2

Senator Keating made a speech in the Senate. He described
"crates that are so large that special unloading machinery is
required." Obviously someone had been feeding him information.
The fact that he used the word "crates" may indicate that his source
was not a Cuban refugee, as was often surmised, but someone in
intelligence, someone who had recently seen the September 28
report about the *Kasimov* cargo.

October 3

A story arrived in Washington of "unusual activity" in the
western province of Pinar del Rio.
The CIA decided that San Cristóbal should now be marked
"Top Priority."

October 4

The CIA received one of mid-September's eyewitness reports
about long-trailer truck convoys.
COMOR met to plan the next U-2 flight. This time McCone
was determined. He laid out all his evidence. The other intelligence men on the committee concurred that the Russians
might be placing missiles in Pinar del Rio, but the committee was
not convinced that a U-2 flight was the best device to check it out.

The danger from SAMs remained. Possibly other, less risky measures could be found, maybe remote-controlled, unmanned planes or balloons. Nothing could be done right now, anyway, because the weather over that part of the island was bad. U-2 photography needed rather clear skies, and a hurricane was presently hammering the island. COMOR agreed to check out other alternatives.

Roger Hilsman now urged the administration to draft a contingency plan in case they did discover strategic missiles in Cuba. Considering that the possibility, even the probability of missiles there had become common knowledge among America's various intelligence agencies, it is almost stunning that no one during this period drew up a proposed plan of action. One would have thought the United States had learned in June 1950, when Harry Truman's government had been surprised at the North Korean attack on South Korea. Even though war in Korea had loomed for some time, Americans had made no useful plans for such an eventuality. As a result, when it came, Truman and his advisors stumbled around and made a series of costly blunders. For Kennedy's New Frontiersmen, who prided themselves on their rational control over events, to fail in the same way is amazing.

The administration ignored Hilsman's pleas.

October 5

Another U-2 flight over eastern Cuba revealed nothing.

October 8

Cuban President Osvaldo Dorticós came to New York and spoke to the UN. He expressed concern over Congress' recent joint resolution about Cuba. (Castro's government may have been worried that the resolution augured an invasion.)

Dorticós admitted that Cuba had received Soviet arms. But his country had a right to arm herself, he said, especially in light of the "warlike hysteria" in the United States. He noted that his government had often pleaded with America to negotiate their differences. Cuba, he said, was even ready to indemnify Americans who had had their property expropriated early in the revolution. He reminded the UN that Cuba's Council of Ministers had recently declared that if the United States would give "effective guarantees and satisfactory proof" that it would not invade the island, and if it would cease supporting exile attacks, Cuba would not need these weapons.

Would Castro's government have been really willing to stop arming itself, even remove the Soviet missiles, if the United States gave "effective guarantees" of peaceful intentions? It is very doubtful the Kremlin would have accepted such an eventuality. But it is interesting to speculate what might have happened if Cuba had decided that the missiles had to be taken away and the Kremlin had disagreed.

Adlai Stevenson, ambassador to the UN, delivered America's reply. "The United States," he said, "will not commit aggression against Cuba." But neither would it negotiate with Castro's government, at least so long as Cuba retained any ties with Moscow. "The maintenance of communism in the Americas is not negotiable," Stevenson orated.

America's position, as it would be throughout the sixties, remained painfully, almost fatally rigid.

October 9

COMOR met again. They admitted they had found no substitute for the U-2. They decided they had no choice but to use the spy plane over western Cuba.

There remained another delay while SAC pilots learned the intricacies of the CIA U-2. McNamara had insisted for some time that since one of these planes might be shot down it would be better if the pilot were a regular Air Force officer, not a civilian (by definition, a "spy"). (CIA pilots, of course, were not exactly civilians. They were Air Force officers, paid by the CIA and dressed in civilian clothes. They called their "separation" from the service "sheep-dipping.") The controversy over who flew the U-2s was partly bureaucratic. The CIA did not want to relinquish control over their planes and appealed to the White House. The President, however, agreed with McNamara. It took the Air Force pilots several days to train in the CIA's specialized planes.

The weather over San Cristóbal remained cloudy.

Senator Keating in the Senate made a long, discursive speech, containing all his previous allegations, adding nothing new.

Analysts, working on photographs of the *Kasimov*'s crates, compared them with others seen in Egypt and Indonesia. They discovered an exact match. These crates, they concluded, contained Soviet (Beagle) IL-28 light bombers. Six months earlier, intelligence had predicted that Russia would give Cuba some Beagles.

This plane was capable of carrying atomic loads, but it flew relatively slowly. American fighter interceptors could fly twice as fast and blow it out of the sky. The Beagle's radius was only 600 miles, not far enough to reach the Panama Canal or Atlanta or New Orleans. Khrushchev later said they were obsolete. In a way he was right. Beyond dividing America's attention and thereby being an irritant, the IL-28s would not have been of much use in a full-fledged war between the United States and Russia. The Soviet leader called the planes strictly defensive, saying "they would be useful against an enemy landing force," and that "they were well suited for coastal defense." But since the planes theoretically could reach targets in Florida (about as far north as Tampa), and also America's base at Guantanamo, their arrival in Cuba could be looked on as "dangerous." (It should be pointed out, however, that in 1971 Moscow wanted Washington to include in the SALT talks the fighter-bomber the United States retained in Western Europe, planes very similar to the Beagle. The United States refused on the grounds that their bombers were solely "defensive.")

October 10

Kenneth Keating gave another speech. He included new information. "Yesterday," he said, "I spoke on the subject of Cuba. At that time I did not have fully confirmed the matter to which I shall address myself now." He announced that, "construction has started on at least a half-dozen launching sites for intermediate-range tactical missiles." (If he had said that at the present time the Russians had "half a dozen launching *pads* for medium-range ballistic missiles," he would have been quite close.)

Where did Keating get this information? The late senator never told. He did say on an NBC interview program that he had gotten his information "from official sources or had it from others and confirmed by official sources." In an interview with *U.S. News and World Report,* he would say that "only one prominent person in the high councils placed the same interpretation upon [the various pieces of information] that I did." Elsewhere in the same issue of the magazine, listed under "Washington Whispers," would appear a small item noting that John McCone's reputation had been enhanced by his "early reporting and correct appraisal of the Soviet buildup." If one assumes that McCone was Keating's "Deep Throat," that the Republican CIA director was using the senator to goad liberal Democrats into greater action on Cuba, one still does not know how McCone *knew* about the missile sites. Maybe he (or whoever else the senator's source may have been) had told Keating that intelligence officers *suspected* the Russians were building six IRBM sites, and Keating just rushed ahead as if it were true. The mystery is a fascinating example of the subtle inner workings of bureaucratic Washington.

PART TWO

The Chinese have a character for the word "crisis."
It is made by combining two other characters,
one "danger," the other "opportunity."

6 *Discovery*

Time magazine recently recalled the 1962–1963 era as the best time in history, a moment of peace and optimism. Poverty, ignorance, and wars preceded it; Vietnam, Watergate, and inflation followed. It seemed a Golden Age, an era of simplicity and decency: Camelot.

This theory of course is patent nonsense. Any moment is good for some, bad for others.

The United States was not at "war"—but it was certainly not at "peace." NBC paid $7,500 for a film showing Germans digging a tunnel under the Berlin Wall. The *New York Times* pontificated on NBC's action: "With *peace hanging by a thread* it is not time for adventurous laymen to turn up in the front lines of world tension. *No one knows what small provocation might be grasped as an excuse to press the proverbial button.*"

Among the bestsellers that autumn were *Seven Days in May*, about a military coup in Washington, and *Fail-Safe*, about how a tiny mechanical failure could lead to a nuclear confrontation. In October the movie *The Manchurian Candidate* opened in New York. It told of a man brainwashed by the Chinese Communists for assassination.

Few Americans, to be sure, felt in immediate danger of atomic holocaust. A sense of doom did not dominate the era—far from it.

But a decade of children by now had learned atomic drills, and most school-age Americans knew that when a siren shrieked for a full minute, it was time to turn on a radio. The Berlin Wall crisis of 1961, when headlines had rumbled ominously, had made some people, particularly servicemen, jumpy.

In its race relations the United States still had far to go. If you were a typical member of America's white Protestant majority, and someone knowingly leered, "Guess who's coming to dinner?" it was probably an Irish Catholic, possibly a Jew—certainly not a black man. College liberals discussed the civil rights movement with their more conservative classmates. They sat up late at night (in dorms where almost no blacks resided) and debated the recent trend toward sit-ins. Liberals thought such actions were good and right, though few could honestly imagine doing such things themselves. And they were stumped by that vintage American query: "Yeah, but would you let your sister marry one?"—the question neatly combining racism and a sexist assumption that males had the right to control the actions of their sisters.

In Rapid City, South Dakota, right next to the "Shrine of Democracy," where Mount Rushmore's four stone-faced Americans look dignified, 90 percent of the town's bars and barber shops and 30 percent of its restaurants and motels refused to accommodate blacks. "We don't serve colored people," hat check girls said defiantly. One restaurant owner exclaimed: "The only thing we're scared of is the young ones [blacks] coming in and trying to intermingle."

In late September, as the administration mulled over the Cuban arms buildup, a black man named James Meredith attempted to enter the University of Mississippi. Tension and violence grew so high the White House sent troops.

In Los Angeles that year a college student named Kenneth Young, going to summer school, sported a beard for the occasion. His family grew angry and ashamed. What would people think? they asked. His aunts and uncles called him a beatnik, a Castroite, an anarchist, a Communist. His crime actually was not so much in being too leftist, but in being different, in not fitting in.

The high school in Cohasset, Massachusetts suspended four students because their hair was *too short*.

A school in Springfield, Ohio actually expelled the sixteen-year-old daughter of a part-time pastor for refusing to wear bloomer-type shorts to gym. Judy Rae Bushong's objection was not that the shorts were ridiculously dowdy and Victorian, but that they showed her knees. Judy Rae was very moral. "I would like to convert heathens in Mexico or Germany or something like that," she said.

Nor was she alone. In Lubbock, Texas a high school suspended two girls who did not want to wear sleeveless blouses and Jamaica shorts and participate in "immodest exercises."

Mid-October

A glorious season of the year. School bands happily and sweatily played their ragged songs while adolescents shouted encouragement to their teams and others stood beneath the stands drinking too much Southern Comfort. Leaves tumbled silently toward the ground to lie in thickening mats, until energetic rakers piled them up and lit them. The bacony smell of burning leaves filled the crisp evening air. Tired shoulders and blistered hands were the badges of fall. City kids missed that part of Americana, but had other entertainments.

As usual, few young people got excited about racial problems or even God's strictures. In New Milford, Connecticut a local radio announcer, calling himself Donald Baron, did his Saturday night show live. "Right *here* in the *gymnasium.* Come on *in! All* you guys and gals! Take off your *shoes* and dance in your *socks!* We're gonna play Chubby Checkers—Doin' the Twist!"

The Twist that fall became almost a mania. Social historians have noted that about once every decade or so, a large percentage of the American population feels a primal need to sway or stomp to music. No one knows why, apparently just a rhythmic fad. In the early 1960s a group of well-to-do prominent Americans rediscovered dancing. They twisted, they flyed, they mashed-potatoed, they hully-gullied. Ladies in New York, their hair neatly bouffanted, expensively clothed in Pucci or Lilly, escorts in tow, wriggled into *discotheques:* Le Club required that you be a member to get in; the Peppermint Lounge was now "out," dying from discovery by the masses.

At the center of the social swirl, for the first time in American history, was the White House. With his bad back, John Kennedy could hardly attempt the Twist. Nor did he care much for the "Jet Set" (a phrase invented during this period by the society columnist Igor Cassini). But stories about Kennedy and his photogenic family, and his young, handsome, energetic staff, sold newspapers and magazines. Certainly much of the excitement about the Kennedys was due to a cosmetic change from the Eisenhower and Truman administrations. One would have to go all the way back to Teddy Roosevelt, the previous youthful denizen of the White House, to find this sort of bubbling excitement. Like TR, Kennedy clearly understood journalism and its practitioners.

Years after John Kennedy died, some people would say that his presidency was all cotton candy, just sugar and empty air, that very little actually got done. But a President can affect the nation's style, its attitudes, its feeling about itself. Just as Teddy had made "Reform" respectable, Kennedy elevated wit, intelligence—and Vigor. He was therefore generally "popular" with those who aspired to wit, intelligence, and vigor. He was of course not universally appreciated. Many people—on both left and right— had disdain for him (and for the fluff of fan magazines that enveloped him). Even elements in his own State Department felt uneasy about their President, considering him a little too young and liberal. A foreign service officer recalls: "The embassy community was very conservative in those days, very anti-Communist, and basically anti-Kennedy."

Politically Kennedy was in trouble. His programs in Congress had stalled. Sniping at him from all sides had increased. He had decided to spend October politicking. On Saturday, October 14, he flew to Indianapolis. There, Homer Capehart's demands for an invasion of Cuba had become noticeably shrill. Kennedy told his audience that the Indiana Republican was a warmonger. "These self-appointed generals and admirals who want to send somebody else's son to war ought to be kept at home by the voters and be replaced by somebody like Birch Bayh, who has some understanding of what the twentieth century is all about."

Kennedy then flew on to Buffalo to celebrate Pulaski Day. He spoke on the steps of City Hall to a crowd estimated at 150,000, many of them Polish-Americans. *"Jeszeze Polska nie zginela!"* he shouted. "Poland is not yet lost!"

In Indiana he had praised moderation. In Buffalo, he stoked Cold War, anti-Soviet angers.

In Cuba life went on as usual. The United States maintained 127 military bases in eighteen foreign countries. In October 1962 Cuba was the only nation in the world to house both a Russian and an American military installation. While Soviet troops secretly built their missile sites, Americans at Guantanamo pondered what was going on.

In 1903 the newly created Cuban government ceded Guantanamo Bay to the United States. By 1962 Cuba was receiving two checks for America's use of the facility: $14,000 a month to supply it with fresh water, $3,500 a year rental for the base. (Castro did not cash the latter since he refused to recognize the treaties with the United States.)

The Guantanamo reservation consists of 28,817 acres. Nine thousand of these are actually water. The land of the base (known to American residents as "Gitmo") is about 30 square miles, or the size of a typical town. It provides one of the best naval facilities in the world and was used as an important training base for America's Atlantic Fleet. The installation in 1962 also had two air strips, 1,400 buildings, and a Marine garrison.

If Cuba decided to attack it, Guantanamo would be hard to defend. The Marines there had to guard a 7-foot wire fence stretching 24 miles around, and another 10 miles of seacoast. Surrounding much of Guantanamo are hills. Artillery emplaced here could make it untenable. Cutting off the water supply, which Castro did in 1964, could also cause problems.

By 1962 Guantanamo's importance had actually begun to decline. Missiles and atomic submarines had begun to make it less essential, and the American anchorage in Puerto Rico, only 500 miles away, was becoming a satisfactory substitute. (But the United States retained the base—partly to show its strong opposition to Castro's regime and also to prevent the Russians from gaining access to such a valuable naval installation.)

Almost a thousand Cubans lived on the base, working as

domestics. (Most American families stationed there had at least one "girl" to baby-sit and clean the house.) Another one or two thousand Cubans entered each day to work on the grounds and do other unskilled manual labor. Some commuted by water taxi; most entered from the Cuban town of Guantanamo just outside the base. Cuban workers at the base received an average of sixty cents an hour, high by the island's standards. A percentage of these earnings went to their government.

Life was rather pleasant for Americans there. About 6,000 of them lived on the base, plus almost 1,600 service employees, and another 4,000 to 5,000 aboard ships operating out of its waters. They had barbershops, schools and churches, a dry cleaner's, a radio station, a roller skating rink, a skeet range, a golf course, and a hospital where an average of twenty babies were born each month. They also had the Caribbean sun and palm trees and beautiful blue water for fishing and boating and beaches to lie on.

In mid-October, the base's children were preparing for Halloween. Lee Ann Dwyer, age five, an attractive, round-faced little girl played in the sun. Her father, George Dwyer, a naval lieutenant, had been stationed there since March 1961. Every month or so, the base held a readiness alert, and Lieutenant Dwyer had to leave. These separations from his family gradually became routine.

Early that year directives were given out to each family. Each wife was supposed to keep a suitcase packed at all times. Few women did so. As one said, "I never believed we'd go out, so I said, 'Nuts.' "

In June 1962 Castro declared the area around the base a militarized zone and began to move people away.

In Havana, several hundred miles across the island from where Lee Ann Dwyer played, lived Isidro Rodriguez. Isidro was in many ways an average Cuban male, rather short and compact, with swarthy skin and wavy dark hair. Normally reticent, he was invariably generous, charming, and gracious. Forty-six years old, usually a man of dignity and control, he positively loved to dance and had begun practicing the hully-gully. He also loved to swim and lie in the sun and get tan. A factory worker, he had originally heard of Marx's ideas from his friends and had joined the Communist party in 1936. In 1962 he was working in a little factory, repairing irons, fans, and other small appliances. He was in charge; twenty-four men worked under him. Señor Rodriguez was also in the militia. He felt great devotion to the revolution and would gladly die for it. A militiaman was really a civilian who spent two or three morning hours every few days learning military rudiments: lying down, digging a trench, putting a gun together, marching, a little discipline. If the Americans attacked Havana, it was Isidro's duty to defend his factory to the death.

Blanca Rivero, an attractive forty-year-old, was also in the militia. In case of an invasion she had to guard the jewelry store where she worked.

Teresa Mayans was a lovely, dark-haired young woman. Married at thirteen, she had continued school, taking her infant son in a bassinet with her. She had become part of the anti-Batista underground, a bomb-thrower. Once arrested by Batista's police, she had been lucky to get out alive. In 1962 she liked to take her eight-year-old son to the beach to swim. She would sit in the sun and watch him make sand castles. Close by stood concrete pillboxes, facing out to sea.

Perhaps more than anything else, those small gun emplacements symbolized Cuba in 1962. Castro's government had sprinkled some of these structures, each about 10 feet in diameter, above a few of the island's beaches. Each had two slots, one for an artillery piece and one for a machine gun. On each one's top was a tiny platform with a wooden railing; a man could stand there and look at the horizon, watching for an American invasion. When an alert occurred (by that autumn one took place every few weeks), a designated sentry would rush to his platform and look out. Other soldiers with guns would clamber down inside and wait. There would not be much protection there; a hand grenade could destroy it. To civilians it may have looked martial, and perhaps Teresa Mayans felt safer knowing it was there.

The aircraft seemed more like a giant silver-and-black bird than a plane. Its wings, stretching out much longer than its short body, had a tendency to flap in the wind. Its purpose was to fly *high*. The man who designed it, Clarence L. (Kelly) Johnson, a Lockheed vice president, had promised the Air Force he could put up a plane that would fly at 70,000 feet (13 miles) and that he could accomplish this in only a year. His promise had seemed unbelievable. At the time (1954) the record altitude for a plane, held by the British, was 54,000 feet. But his concept had appeared simple: Take a glider and put a jet engine in it. Get rid of every nonessential part. Instead of three sets of wheels (one under each wing and one under the tail assembly) use two. One would go under the nose, one under the rear. When on the runway taking off, each wing would have a "pogo"—a stick with small wheels to run along the ground holding up the tip. At takeoff, these would drop away. A pilot had to land with only two sets of wheels, like bringing in a bicycle. If all went well, he would taxi his plane toward a grassy section, hoping to arrive there just as it stopped. One wing, slightly reinforced in the tip, would drop down on the turf and balance the plane.

For ten months Johnson worked twelve to fourteen hours a day at Lockheed's secret plant in Burbank, California. The few men who knew about the project simply called it "Kelly's plane." Later it would be known as the U-2.

In August 1955 Johnson finished the first one—and it worked. Lockheed only produced fifty-five of them. Each was hand-made.

The plane had two basic purposes. Air Force pilots of the 4,028th and 4,080th Strategic Reconnaissance Squadrons, under the supervision of SAC, had a few of the aircraft. They collected air samples at high levels, particularly around the Soviet Union, checking for signs of nuclear activity. They also checked atmospheric and meteorological conditions. The CIA had its own models which carried different equipment, including cameras peeking out of seven portholes in the underbelly.

Each pilot received intensive training. Flying a U-2 required concentration and precision. At high altitudes an unprotected man would explode, so a pilot wore a special suit to protect him in case his cockpit lost pressurization. The suits were weatherized and airtight and fit tightly against the skin. Once the helmets were locked into place, the suits allowed no ventilation. Heat built up inside them and a pilot sometimes lost ten to twelve pounds during a flight. Men often staggered off their planes. Because of exhaustion, a flyer was not allowed to go up again for two days.

The U-2 had certain peculiarities. It took off almost straight up and only needed 1,000 feet of runway. Within moments it was out of sight. It flew at 460 miles an hour, but it had a very narrow range of speed. If it went too fast it began to buffet; too slow, and it would stall. Pilots called the range "coffin corner."

Despite all the plane's idiosyncrasies, flying a U-2 offered something special. At 13 miles up, on a clear day one could see the ground below for hundreds of miles in every direction. The sight could be breathtaking. A person felt a sense of peace, of . . . aloneness.

Major Rudolf Anderson, Jr. flew U-2s for SAC. He was a handsome thirty-five-year-old with deep-set eyes and a crew cut. He had married a girl from Georgia and they lived with their two small children in Texas. His present tour of duty was at Laughlin Air Base in Del Rio. Anderson gave the appearance of the classic Air Force officer—quiet, dedicated, conservative. His childhood home had been Greenville, South Carolina, a lovely city in the foothills of the Carolina mountains. He came from a locally prominent family. His father, a nurseryman, was rather well-to-do, and young Rudy grew up a typical middle-class Southern boy. He won his letter playing on a high school championship team. He impressed others as being pleasant and likeable.

He graduated from Greenville High in June 1944, just after the Normandy landing, but, unlike many of his classmates, did not immediately enter the service. Instead he went to Clemson, 20 miles down the road, where he studied textile engineering. South Carolina had a number of textile mills and this academic major seemed a good way for an ambitious young man to make good money. When he graduated he took an accounting job with a local mill. He worked there three years.

When the Korean War started, Anderson still felt little inclination to join. But after the Chinese entered the war, pressure increased on young American males to do their part. The draft loomed over Anderson's head. In November 1951 he signed up for the Air Force. It seemed better to do that than slog it out in Korean mud. The government trained him on jets and sent him to Korea. By the time he arrived the war was over. Yet there was still "military" work for a pilot. Asia had become part of the Cold War. The American government wanted constant reconnaissance flights. Would the North Koreans attack again? it wanted to know. Were Chinese troops massing for an invasion of Formosa? For two years Rudolf Anderson flew Super-Sabre jets on secret reconnaissance missions in the Far East. He won a Distinguished Flying Cross with two oak leaf clusters and an Airman's Medal. He returned from Asia in the spring of 1955, just before Kelly Johnson completed his first U-2. By this time Anderson had discovered himself in the Air Force. He enjoyed the camaraderie and the security. He loved flying. It satisfied his hunger for quietude. He was therefore a natural choice to fly Lockheed's new planes. (In August 1962 he and his wife Frances visited his parents in Greenville. He couldn't tell them what he was doing, he said, but he gave his father a model plane he had carved out of wood. Its wings stretched out much longer than its body.)

Before dawn on October 14 Anderson pulled on his rubberized flight suit and climbed aboard his plane. He first circled south, far below Cuba, then cruised north. He had been told the Russians might fire SAMs at him. As he approached the island, just before dawn, the sky was clear. He could easily see all the way across the island, and even the waters lapping the other side, dark gray this early in the morning. The whole flyover would take only eight or nine minutes.

The San Cristóbal region was mountainous and heavily wooded with royal palms. To a pilot high above, the land must have appeared lush and green, a lot like the area around Greenville. As the U-2 sped across the island, its cameras gave off low, whirring sounds. (These cameras were remarkable. In 1955 the Air Force had released pictures of a golf course taken from 50,000 feet. One could pick out golf balls on the green. The lenses of these cameras were so sophisticated that one could see an ace of spades at 8 miles or read a newspaper headline at 12. An expert could distinguish between foliage and camouflage.) As soon as Anderson landed, ground crews ripped out the plane's film magazines, put them aboard a waiting jet to send them off to Washington.

There the film was taken directly to a decrepit building in the heart of the city. Inside was the National Photographic Interpretation Center, the hub for the photo intelligence of all of America's secret agencies. A team of experts led by a man named Art Lundahl began poring over the film. First it had to be developed, then interpreted—this latter a complex job. The men had before them a line of pictures that could stretch for miles.

Art Lundahl's equipment to read the photos was almost as magical as the cameras. The pictures arrived in pairs. Placed side-by-side they produced a three-dimensional effect like an old-fashioned stereopticon. A photo interpreter using the proper machinery could judge the height of an object *within a fraction of an inch*. Each print also had recorded on it the exact longitude and latitude. If Lundahl's crew saw anything interesting, they knew *precisely* where it was.

During the afternoon of Monday, October 15, while the photo experts worked feverishly, John Kennedy was across town at a White House reception for Prime Minister Ben Bella of Algeria. The President was tired. He had gotten in from New York at 1:40 in the morning.

A few blocks away at ABC's Washington television studios Mac Bundy was saying to news interviewers: "I think there is no present likelihood that the Cubans and the Cuban government and the Soviet government would, in combination, attempt to install a major offensive capability."

John McCone was entering a plane in Washington, taking off for California. The trip involved a personal tragedy; his stepson, Paul J. Pigott, had just been killed in a sports car accident. McCone was going to Los Angeles to pick up the body, to take it to Seattle for the funeral.

Robert McNamara left his Pentagon office earlier than usual. He wanted to change before going to Robert Kennedy's house. The attorney general was holding what Washington called a Hickory Hill Seminar, an informal study group which met every so often at Bobby's place in McLean, Virginia. The speaker for that evening was John Ford, a computer analyst. He was going to explain how the Russians were using computers for their space probes. These "seminars" were always popular. Bobby and Ethel and all the children and animals seemed so *alive*. No one would want to pass up an invitation. Tonight was special to McNamara because it was his turn to be the seminar's revolving official host.

The United States as usual had military vessels up and down the eastern seaboard from Nova Scotia to the Caribbean. The Navy and Marines were carrying out training exercises in half a dozen spots. In the South Atlantic a small fleet conducted anti-submarine warfare (ASW) exercises.

Another routine operation was called PHIBRIGLEX 62 (standing for Amphibious Brigade Landing Exercise). Each year naval and Marine units practiced assaults, storming some "enemy" stronghold. This year their objective was Vieques, a tiny, almost unpopulated island off the southeast coast of Puerto Rico, often used by Marine units for maneuvers. Their orders were to take the island and overthrow its tyrant, "Ortsac" (Castro spelled backwards). This exercise—involving four aircraft carriers, fifteen destroyers, fourteen amphibious ships, three submarines, and a Marine brigade—was being carried out not far from Cuba. No wonder Castro's government was nervous.

At a secret base in the Florida keys, CIA agents (unaware of Anderson's U-2 flight) briefed a small commando group of Cuban emigrés. The Cubans were to leave in a few days on a special mission which the CIA's JM WAVE section had planned for months. The object would be to knock out the Matahambre copper mine operation. The ore from the mines was taken by elevated cable car to the sea. Huge towers supported the cable car system. The commandos were to blow up the towers with dynamite. By coincidence, the Matahambre mines were in Pinar del Rio.

Somewhere in the Caribbean, through a mysterious process of temperature changes, hot winds picked up swirling speed, becoming Hurricane Ella. She was massive, 650 miles across. Her winds shrieked at 100 miles an hour. The waters beneath her turned frothy and waves rose to 45 feet. For the next several days she would make her presence known all the way across the Atlantic.

A photo interpreter in Washington, looking closely at Anderson's film, spotted something in the woods near San Cristóbal. "Hey," he is recorded saying to a companion, "take a look at this."

Others gathered around. They examined the picture carefully. Gradually they picked out missile transporters and erectors, propellant vehicles, and off to the side a haphazard bunch of tents. Intelligence analysts realized what it meant: long-range missiles. (The site was just where Colonel John R. Wright had suggested back in late September.)

The photo interpreters knew their discovery was important. They tried to contact the CIA director, but at this moment, McCone (whose somber prophecies had just been proved accurate) was somewhere in the sky nearing Los Angeles. So they told his second-in-command, General Marshall S. Carter, and Ray Cline, the head of the agency's intelligence desk and the man responsible for gathering, sifting, and categorizing information. These two men began telephoning some of the government's highest officials.

Carter, the military man, first called the director of the Defense Department's intelligence branch, General Joseph F. Carroll, who promised he would inform his superiors. The two men agreed to meet later that evening at General Maxwell Taylor's quarters at Fort McNair in southwest Washington. Taylor, recently appointed chairman of the Joint Chiefs, was hosting a black-tie dinner, including music by the Army chorus.

Roswell Gilpatric was dressing for General Taylor's dinner when his special Pentagon telephone rang. It was General Carroll. The latest photos from Cuba, Carroll said cryptically, revealed something new. Intelligence men would soon arrive at Gilpatric's apartment in the Towers and show him the pictures.

Within minutes, just as Gilpatric finished arranging his tie, two photoanalysts arrived. The three went into the bedroom. The photographs, a little gray and cloudy, did not seem so clear to Gilpatric as to the experts. All he could make out was hundreds of dots. But as the photoanalysts pinpointed them, he could discern trucks and trailers over here and the slashes through the trees of new-cut roads over there and a sprinkle of tents. The two analysts showed him the launchers and erectors; these, they said, could only be for long-range missiles.

Gilpatric later recalled that his first reaction was dread: A confrontation was about to begin. The President, he thought, would not tolerate this new development.

It was about eight o'clock when he left for Maxwell Taylor's house. By the time he arrived, General Carroll was already there and had briefed the chairman of the JCS. The top officials at the dinner spent the rest of the evening in whispered conversations and hushed telephone calls. The men agreed to meet the next morning at 7:30 at the Defense Department. (Exactly when Secretary of Defense McNamara was originally told of the situation he himself cannot now recall, but he was shown the photographs around midnight, after he left Robert Kennedy's.)

Meanwhile, Ray Cline—a stocky Ph.D. with a quick, analytical mind—had called Roger Hilsman. Hilsman, after telling his children to avoid using the regular house phone, began to call others in the department.

He contacted, for instance, Edwin M. Martin, in charge of State's Latin American section, who at that very moment was speaking to the Journalism Society, Sigma Delta Chi, on the subject of Cuba. "This military buildup is basically defensive in character," he was telling the newsmen. Since Martin was still talking when Hilsman called, an aide came to the Press Club phone. "Is it urgent enough to interrupt?" he asked.

"For God's sakes, no!" Hilsman quickly gasped. "But it is important enough to have him call me when he's finished—so long as it doesn't attract attention."

After his speech, the aide whispered Hilsman's message to Martin. The Latin American expert apologized to those around him and said he had to call his wife and tell her when he'd be home. He hurried to a telephone booth and called the intelligence man.

Hilsman also phoned others like George Ball and Robert Hurwitch of State. They all agreed to meet in Ball's office the next morning at 8:30.

Secretary of State Dean Rusk was at a black-tie affair on the eighth floor of the new State Department annex. The occasion was a stag dinner for the Foreign Minister of West Germany, Gerhard Schroeder. Rather than call Rusk directly and disturb the dinner, Hilsman first contacted Rusk's bodyguard and told him to give the secretary unobtrusively a message to call back. The bodyguard persuaded a waiter to pass a note to the secretary while giving him a clean plate. Rusk glanced behind his napkin at the note, then put it in his pocket. A few minutes later he excused himself and stepped into the pantry where he phoned Hilsman. The two men carried on the kind of double-talk conversation simultaneously occurring all over town.

"You remember the thing that I've worried about the last few days?" Hilsman asked.

"Yes," Rusk replied.

"Well, very preliminary analysis indicates that something is there."

"Are you sure this is it?"

"From what I can get over the phone," Hilsman said, "there doesn't seem to be much doubt."

"Well, I'll meet you in my office the first thing tomorrow morning."

Rusk hung up and returned to the table. Later in the evening he took aside Paul Nitze, assistant secretary of defense for international security affairs, and on the terrace overlooking the Lincoln Memorial whispered the news to him. (Gerhard Schroeder told some German friends the next day that he wondered why Rusk had been on the phone in the pantry so long.)

Ray Cline called Mac Bundy that evening. Bundy was at home giving a dinner for Chip Bohlen, just appointed ambassador to France and on his way to Paris. Presidential assistant Bundy now had a decision to make: Should he call John Kennedy?

The President was having dinner with his father who was visiting him that week. Bundy decided to wait. As he later told the President: "What help would it be to you to get this piece of news and then tell you that nothing could be done about it until morning? . . . You were tired [from] a strenuous campaign weekend. . . . So I decided that a quiet evening and a night of sleep were the best preparations you could have."

Intelligence experts at CIA headquarters in Langley worked all night preparing a report to present to the White House the next morning.

The Cuban missile crisis had begun.

7 How Tojo Felt

Tuesday morning, October 16, 1962

A crisp sun rose slowly, soft and warm, tanning October's leaves. McGeorge Bundy left his residence a little after seven o'clock. His car entered the early morning traffic streaming toward the center of the city. Around him, wrapped in their own thoughts, were thousands of other government workers. They were the city, coming awake—secretaries and congressmen, lobbyists and elevator operators.

Mac Bundy looked like a Russian chess master: thinning lackluster brown hair jutting almost straight up from his scalp; an extremely high forehead that seemed to promise analytical abilities far beyond the norm; cool, intelligent eyes peering from behind no-nonsense glasses; a clever mouth. He dressed in dark suits and narrow ties. He had the appearance of a man you would choose to carry military secrets, or to push nuclear buttons—trustworthy, cool, a touch humorless. He had a Yale degree, Phi Beta Kappa, and had been a professor at Harvard, then dean of its faculty of arts and sciences. He possessed an absolutely impressive mind. They told a story about him, about when he had once forgotten an assignment in school, and how he had held some blank papers in front of him and "read" a report so well worded and organized that

99

his teacher, not knowing it was extemporaneous, considered it among the best he had ever heard.

Bundy was John Kennedy's aide specializing in national security affairs, holding the same position in the New Frontier that Henry Kissinger would later have in Nixon's first term. One of Bundy's main tasks, and the source of much of his power, was his control over the Situation Room, down a short flight of stairs from his office. Of the White House's 132 rooms, the Situation Room was one of its most important and secret. Armed guards stood before it. As one entered its door, one's first impression was of machinery—and of the constant clatter of various teletypes: of AP, Reuters, and UPI. Classified equipment filled the room, bringing in a steady flow of information from around the world, from CIA and the Department of Defense. Wall maps showed the position of American forces. During crises, other maps, like those detailing the sea approaches to Cuba, appeared on the walls. Here in this room were closed television circuits, a highly intricate telephone that allowed the President to speak directly to Prime Minister Harold Macmillan, and a long table for those who wanted to hold conferences. Bundy would usually come here early in the day and go through all the dispatches from the night before.

This morning, as he entered his basement office in the West Wing, three men awaited him, two photoanalysts and an intelligence man. They had with them the special report the CIA had developed during the night and the San Cristóbal pictures. Bundy listened carefully, asking a few questions.

He made a decision. Whatever was happening in Cuba had to be kept absolutely secret. Kennedy's government would want time to decide what course to take, would want to preserve its independence of such gadflies as politicians and newspapermen, to say nothing of the Kremlin. He called the State Department and spoke to Roger Hilsman. How many people had Hilsman told about Cuba? Seven, Hilsman replied, and he named them. Okay, Bundy said, but don't tell anyone else without getting further instructions from the White House. He hung up and left his office to go upstairs where the President lived.

John Kennedy was sitting on the edge of his bed in his bathrobe and slippers. Up to this moment he had heard nothing about the missiles. As was his custom, he was sipping coffee and skimming through half a dozen morning newspapers before going to his office. When Bundy entered his room, Kennedy immediately started giving orders to his aide, simultaneously commenting on some of the things the papers were printing.

Bundy interrupted. "Mr. President," he reportedly said, "there is now hard photographic evidence, which you will see a little later, that the Russians have offensive missiles in Cuba."

Like a panther, suddenly aware of the presence of a new enemy, Kennedy became instantly alert and intent. He began to snap out commands. He wanted a meeting immediately—say 11:45. He dictated the names of those he wanted there. They included Vice President Lyndon Johnson (Kennedy had been well aware of Johnson's sensitivity towards some of the New Frontiersmen and their sneers, and tried to include him in every important decision); Rusk and McNamara, of course, because of their high-ranking positions; Taylor from the JCS; General Carter representing the CIA; Ros Gilpatric from Defense and George Ball, his counterpart at State, both highly talented and respected for their judgment; Ed Martin, the Latin American expert; Ambassador Bohlen, the government's main Kremlinologist; Bobby Kennedy and Ted Sorensen, Kennedy's closest professional advisors; Douglas Dillon, secretary of the treasury, a moderate Republican, originally added to the Cabinet to satisfy the nation's bankers; Kenneth O'Donnell, one of Kennedy's earliest political companions, tough, canny, a Massachusetts gutfighter, at the center of Kennedy's so-called Irish Mafia; and finally, Bundy himself.

Kennedy, since the days of his presidential campaign and before, had often chosen ad hoc groups to advise him about some issue. If he wanted a position paper on Africa or the complex subject of conservation he would ask several (often about a dozen) people to form a task force and hammer out a solution. He normally preferred not to use established committees—like the National Security Council. They seemed to him rigid and bureaucratic. Their unwieldiness made it difficult for them, he thought, to come to a decision, to take action. Kennedy, like Truman before him, prided himself on his decisiveness, not on any subtle cerebrations, nor on his idealism—he could leave those to theorists like his speech writers, Arthur Schlesinger, Jr. and Richard Goodwin (both experts on Latin America), or to idealists like Hubert Humphrey. Kennedy was in most ways rather conservative, but he liked to cut across institutional lines. Perhaps it was his obvious impatience with form, his tendency toward anti-institutionalism that made him *seem* (especially after his death) like the progenitor of the late-sixties radicalism. Whether his methods were effective in accomplishing his goals is debatable.

Why did Kennedy choose these particular fourteen people? Why did they come *first* to his mind? Several of them were obvious: Johnson, Rusk, McNamara, Carter, Taylor, Bundy, Gilpatric, Ball, Martin, and Bohlen. Each of these had an *official* relationship with the problem; their expertise or their office clearly overlapped it. His choice of the other four—Bobby, Ted Sorensen, Kenny O'Donnell, Douglas Dillon—is more interesting. None of the four was much of an idealist, nor a striker of poses, nor a talker. Sorensen, O'Donnell, and Bobby had each been with him a long time and he trusted their loyalty *to himself*.

His choice of Douglas Dillon is the most unobvious, and therefore, perhaps the most telling. The only person (outside the fourteen) Kennedy is recorded as calling that morning was a Republican, Wall Street lawyer John J. McCloy. Kennedy respected McCloy—he liked his pragmatism. (McCloy once said about the UN: "World opinion? I don't believe in world opinion. The only thing that matters is power.") It is revealing that in this moment of possible crisis, Kennedy turned to his brother Bobby, two trusted political advisors (Sorensen and O'Donnell), several official experts (like Rusk and Bohlen), and two New York Republicans with Cold War experience and connections to international corporations. Karl Marx would have been entranced with the inclusion of Dillon and McCloy, but probably all it meant was that the President respected the kind of mind developed in the concrete canyons of southern Manhattan. McCloy and Dillon were men who *did things*, who could parse a problem, who, Kennedy must have thought, knew how to "deal with the Russians." (He may also have phoned McCloy and included Dillon partly because they were Republicans and their involvement might make whatever actions Kennedy took less open to partisan attacks. Roosevelt and Truman had often done such things.)

As soon as Bundy left, the President called Bobby and asked him to come right over. The two brothers discussed the situation, and afterward Robert Kennedy went directly to a session of the Special Group (Augmented), the committee to oversee Operation MONGOOSE. This meeting had been scheduled several days earlier, but most of its members failed to appear since they were working on the new problem. (It is interesting that the membership of SGA—Bundy, Maxwell Taylor, Robert Kennedy, Ros Gilpatric, Rusk, McNamara, McCone of CIA and Alexis Johnson of State—overlapped the fourteen names the President had just chosen.) Bobby, clearly excited about his brother's revelations, told SGA's staff that the President was dissatisfied with their project. MONGOOSE, he said, had been going on a long time without much success. (Apparently the President, in light of the news he had just received, had asked Bobby what SGA had accomplished recently. No doubt the attorney general had been embarrassed by his committee's obvious lack of success and now took out his frustrations on its staff.) He told the committee that henceforth he would be giving "more personal attention" to the project of getting rid of Castro, and that from now on he would hold daily meetings with them. As it turned out he would not, but his momentary mood is evident.

Meanwhile, at the White House Kenny O'Donnell was standing by his desk, glancing through some newspapers, when the President poked his head in and said, "You still think that fuss about Cuba is unimportant?"

"Absolutely," O'Donnell replied. "The voters won't give a damn about Cuba. You're wasting your time talking about it."

"You really think it doesn't amount to much?" Kennedy asked again, relishing his secret advantage. (Having the "inside dope" gives one a delicious sense of power.)

"Not as a campaign issue," O'Donnell, the practical politician, responded.

"I want to show you something," Kennedy said, taking his appointments secretary into his office and showing him the photos on his desk. "You're an old Air Force bombardier," he said. "You ought to know what this is." He held a magnifying glass over a spot on one of the pictures. "It's the beginning of a launching site for a medium-range ballistic missile."

"I don't believe it," O'Donnell remembers gasping.

"You better believe it. . . . We've just elected Capehart in Indiana, and Ken Keating will probably be the next President of the United States."

It is perhaps significant, assuming O'Donnell's recollections about this conversation are accurate, that Kennedy did not mention the Russians or the threat of war. He seemed mainly worried about his Republican enemies, not his foreign foes. (There is a rumor that when Bundy that morning had first told the President, John Kennedy had wondered if he could put off any action until after the coming elections.) During the next two weeks, Kennedy never publicly mentioned the political ramifications of the Cuban missiles. He remained statesmanlike and above such mundane matters but, as a consummate politician, they gnawed at him. He later said to Sorensen that he had been concerned that if he had done nothing, the Democrats would have been seen as "soft on communism, soft on Castro," and if he had done too much, they would have been called the War Party. But "the worst thing of all would be to do nothing."

He now told O'Donnell: "Not a word to anybody about what it's all about. Stick to all the other appointments for today. We want to look as though nothing unusual is going on around here."

The President was anxious to take some concrete action. He had no patience for any proposal that might take time—diplomatic bargaining, for example, or working through the UN. He was worried that while the diplomats talked, the missile sites would be completed. To "do nothing" would damage his own reputation within the government and around the world. He told O'Donnell that week: "If I don't do anything about removing those missiles from Cuba, I ought to be impeached." Dean Rusk later reflected that Kennedy had seemed to feel that unless he took some decisive action there would have been demands for his resignation. Whether or not Kennedy had truly believed this, his own character and temperament would have made it difficult for him to sit still.

But more than personal inclination or fears about his reputation drove him. The Soviets had entered America's private preserve, the Western Hemisphere, not just with a few "technicians" or some military equipment, but with something which could actually threaten the United States. And they had done this after Kennedy had told them not to. This Soviet affront seemed downright insulting.

Were the missiles *militarily* dangerous? Yes, as all weapons are, but they would hardly alter the balance of power—and Kennedy knew it. He recognized that the United States still retained overwhelming superiority.

Was there, therefore, any real threat? Yes, Kennedy thought: not to America's immediate strategic position, but to its *prestige*. The missiles might have, as he later said, "politically changed the balance of power." They would have "appeared to [be important], and appearances contribute to reality." Their presence would have become a *symbol* which would have damaged America's prestige. Kennedy's *courage* itself would have been questioned. (He was very proud of his reputation for courage. The fact that he constantly used a PT-109 emblem indicates his pride in his own bravery.) He believed that America's position in the world required an aura of toughness. Without it, the Soviet Union would become more audacious and try something, probably in Berlin.

In retrospect one is struck by Kennedy's surprise about the missiles. COMOR, the intelligence committee, obviously had not informed him of its strong suspicions. Two agencies (DIA and CIA) had concluded two weeks earlier that missiles were likely being placed in Pinar del Rio. Maybe the intelligence men had felt the President did not want to know such things. He and his fellow Democrats had been campaigning on their ability to improve relations with the Russians, to cultivate détente. Did the intelligence agencies fear telling him without proof since he had taken such a strong public stand on Cuba in early September? (McNamara himself, when first looking at the photos and seeing only the sites but no missiles, had decided the evidence was *still* not hard enough to alert the President.) There was obviously terrific internal pressure not to confront Kennedy with one more piece of bad news about Cuba.

The President's first official appointment that morning was with astronaut Walter Schirra and his family. When they arrived, the President handed twelve-year-old Walter III one of those PT-109 tie-clasps and gave little Suzanne Schirra a lovely chain bracelet. He led them all out to the lawn to see Macaroni, his daughter Caroline's pony. He chatted with the Schirras for eighteen minutes. One wonders, thinking about that scene, if the President, standing next to those two children, pondered the implications of nuclear war. Often before, when the subject of a nuclear confrontation had come up, Kennedy had said to O'Donnell: "I keep thinking of the children, not my kids or yours, but the children all over the world." Maybe, peering down on little Suzanne Schirra, he once again thought about nuclear war and children.

Later in the morning Pierre Salinger, the press secretary, came in to discuss news releases. Afterward Salinger recalled how grim and angry Kennedy seemed. "The President sat at his desk, drumming his teeth impatiently with his fingertip," a sure sign he was in a bad mood. As Salinger started to check through the list of what important events were coming up, Kennedy interrupted him.

"I haven't time to hear the rest of it. But I have one you can put on top of that list. I'm going to see Gromyko here Thursday."

What is the purpose of the visit? Salinger asked.

"I don't know what he wants," Kennedy replied. "He's coming on his initiative, not mine." The President stood up and said, "There's another thing. I expect a lot of traffic through here this week—Rusk, McNamara, Stevenson, the chiefs of staff. If the press tries to read something significant into it, you're to deny anything special is going on."

Across town that morning other meetings took place. At 7:30 Maxwell Taylor, McNamara, and Gilpatric, after studying the San Cristóbal photos, conferred with the Joint Chiefs. Gilpatric also met with George Ball and Douglas Dillon later that morning. At the State Department, Alexis Johnson, Hurwitch, Hilsman and Ed Martin talked with Dean Rusk. They all kept asking themselves the same question: What did the missiles mean? All anyone knew so far was that a U-2 camera had picked up some medium-range missile installations. Beyond that everything was guesswork.

At 10:40 Dean Rusk left his office and drove to the airport to meet the Crown Prince of Libya, Hassan al-Rida al-Sanusi. As the President had told Salinger, appearances had to be maintained.

At 11:45 the men Kennedy had designated began to rendezvous at the White House.

The Cabinet Room is not particularly large. Along one side are two French doors. Directly across from them are shelves filled with books and models of old three-masters. Dominating the room is the table, shaped a little like a rowboat. (It was designed in the forties by the slightly deaf Jesse Jones who wanted to be able to observe everybody's lips.) The chairs are of fine black leather, each with a metal plate on its back, listing the name of the official owning it. Kennedy sat in the middle on one side, facing the bookshelves. From his chair he looked directly at a small, handsome bust of Abe Lincoln.

The President was in his office quizzing Chip Bohlen about possible Russian motivations and arrived a few minutes late to the meeting. He opened it by calling on General Carter and his CIA experts to provide them all with the latest information. Once again the agency brought out its photographs of San Cristóbal. Using pointers the intelligence men indicated where the trucks were and the tents and so on. Almost everyone in the room had already seen the pictures by this time, but once again they stared intently at the gray and white spots, trying to visualize what the CIA men were describing. It was hard to imagine that those little specks meant anything. "I for one," Robert Kennedy later said, "had to take their word for it." Carter told the group that his analysts had determined that the site was for MRBMs, which had a 1,100-nautical-mile range, blanketing the entire eastern seaboard past New York.

Kennedy called for questions. How soon would the installations be ready? someone asked. Were the missiles ready to fire now? McNamara pointed out that since no guards were visible in the vicinity, the missiles were probably not operational. General Carter estimated that they would, however, be ready in two weeks, possibly even one.

Kennedy thanked Carter and complimented the photo-intelligence team for its efforts. He gave out his first directive. Since additional information was obviously needed, he ordered more U-2 flights. (Six U-2s that day flew over the island taking pictures. Art Lundahl's crew was about to have a lot more work.)

Dean Rusk opened the discussion. The secretary of state was a remarkable man with finely tuned abilities. Born in Georgia and educated at Davidson College in North Carolina (Phi Beta Kappa), Rusk had been a Rhodes scholar and a college professor. He had entered the service during World War II, then remained in Washington, specializing in foreign affairs. From 1952 till 1960 he had been president of the Rockefeller Foundation. He had an excellent if unoriginal mind, but he lacked the Kennedy style. He had humor but little wit. He was perhaps too shy and sensitive for gaiety, for easy jokes, the clever remark, the biting tongue that marked so many members of the New Frontier. Nor was he as physically active as his colleagues. He was becoming a trifle stout, his head gradually rounding like a basketball. He understood how important the appearance of vigor was to the administration— young men attached to the American Embassy in Uruguay were advised early in 1961 to drop golf and take up tennis if they wanted to get ahead—but he himself ignored such pressures. He would get by, as he always had, through hard work and self-control, not flair. He took no strong stands. He never had. Between 1950 and 1951 he had headed State's Far Eastern desk, yet was overlooked by Senator Joe McCarthy. Only a very careful man could have remained so unscathed. Temperamentally Rusk detested controversy. When he took over State, he claimed that he believed his new position required him to remain apart from partisan issues. It was of course what he would have done in any case. He was an absolutely decent man with fine instincts and the inclinations of an Oriental diplomat. Observers often used the word "inscrutable" to describe him. Perhaps this was partly due to the heavy bags under his eyes which hid emotions flickering there. His greatest strength lay in his ability to listen to several people argue about a problem, then calmly and lucidly sum up all points, giving due weight to every side.

Now, when Kennedy called on him to open a general discussion of the Cuban missile crisis, he was prepared, having spent the morning with his aides debating the topic. He clicked off various possible courses of action.

The United States could take a series of *political* actions, putting pressure on the Soviets and the Cubans, leading up if necessary to a partial mobilization of the American Army, a reinforcement of Guantanamo, and a blockade of the island. (Douglas Dillon, for one, said he didn't like this course of action, as it gave the Russians too much time.)

Rusk also raised the possibility of a surprise air strike. General Taylor immediately supported this approach, but noted that a single air strike would be insufficient, that a number of attacks should be undertaken. (Robert Kennedy later recalled passing a note to his brother: "I now know how Tojo felt when he was planning Pearl Harbor.")

McNamara now spoke. He knew what an air attack would involve. He had begun the day with a number of Air Force officers. They had reminded him of their contingency plan for an attack on Cuba, concocted several months earlier by General Paul DeWitt Adams. Planes would fly in low to avoid radar. They would knock out any radar installations, then Cuban airfields. As General Adams himself later remembered: "We had air units assigned to every target that amounted to anything. . . . We could neutralize the enemy air, then move in with airborne troops. . . . When the last MIG went down, the commander of the 82nd Airborne Division would be following it." (Adams had outlined his scheme to General Curtis LeMay back in June. "LeMay became so interested," Adams recalled, "I was a little fearful, jokingly, that he might go out and crank a bomber.")

McNamara described some of the more subtle ramifications of an air assault on Cuba, how a simple attack on a missile site would be insufficient. Radar should be first knocked out and anti-aircraft installations and so on, just as Taylor had suggested. The attack would have to be extensive.

One senses that McNamara was not so much making a *proposal*, as diagramming the implications. As a matter of fact, given McNamara's later open opposition to such an attack, one suspects the secretary of defense was intentionally outlining a drastic scenario, to jolt his listeners *away* from such actions. If he was subtly attempting to prevent such an attack, his tactic seems to have worked. While most of the men in the room that day at first approved of an air strike, Bobby Kennedy's instant repugnance—seen in his "Tojo" remark—eventually grew to revulsion. And it would be the attorney general, backed by McNamara, Rusk, George Ball, and Ted Sorensen, who would successfully argue against the air attack. But at this first meeting, the coalition against such an assault had not yet formed. Most of these men, the President included, clearly leaned toward a surprise air attack, at least on the missile sites. Certainly there was no *open* opposition to such a plan.

The group's major agreement was that Guantanamo Bay should be reinforced, and that dependents there should be evacuated.

Closing the meeting, the President asked them all to spend the afternoon working on the problem. He wanted another session right here at 6:30. He reminded them about the importance of secrecy—a subject certainly on his mind. This was at least the fifth time that day he had brought it up. He did not want this matter to leak out. He wanted no one to talk to reporters, something high officials had a habit of doing.

With that, the meeting broke up and the men filed out. Several had not said a word, or at least no one recorded any of their remarks. Kenny O'Donnell, for instance, remained silent, as was his way. (Throughout the crisis he only went to meetings the President himself attended. "My assignment from the President," he recalls, "was to watch and listen to the proceedings so he could talk with me later about what he had said and compare his impressions and conclusions with mine.") Nor did Lyndon Johnson say anything. As a matter of fact, the Vice President added almost nothing to any of the crisis discussions. In light of what the nation would later learn about this man's volcanic energy and pride, his muteness at this time echoes loudly. He must have felt he had nothing to add, no thoughts, no expertise, no knowledge. No one even recorded when Johnson was first shown the San Cristóbal photos. No clearer evidence exists of the low point he had sunk to.

Others were also quiet that morning. George Ball, for example, a man of wisdom and ideas, and Roswell Gilpatric, and Ed Martin. All three stayed silent, allowing their superiors to speak for their departments.

The discussion in the Cabinet Room had not been a good one. Apparently the presence of the President, particularly in his present mood, restricted any give-and-take. He obviously was angry; it seemed unlikely he would brook any discussion of compromise. The others in the room were undoubtedly aware of this, and acted accordingly. The silence of men like George Ball probably also resulted from bureaucratic inhibitions. Those below the top only speak when called upon.

After the meeting was over, Robert Kennedy walked back to the mansion with the President. The two brothers talked about the session just over, and how stilted it had seemed. They agreed that the President's presence may have been the cause. John Kennedy agreed that after today he would stay away from future meetings for a while. Then he hurried off to a luncheon for the crown prince of Libya.

One of the luncheon's guests, having just flown in from New York that morning, was Adlai Stevenson. In 1956 Kennedy had campaigned for Stevenson in twenty-six states, but he did not much like the governor nor respect him. Many people have suggested reasons—the differences in the two men's backgrounds, Stevenson from old money and Kennedy from new; their age difference—not merely chronological but the fact that the President seemed so much tougher, more calculating, perhaps hardened by the years after 1939. Maybe the coolness between them resulted from the period between 1956 and 1960 when they were rivals for the leadership of the Democratic party, two bulls fighting for control of the herd, the younger one winning in the end, the older sulking on the sidelines, becoming fat and vaguely pathetic. If Dean Rusk, because of his disinclination toward organized sport, was almost an outcast in the New Frontier's social swirl, poor Adlai Stevenson, his hips ballooning, beginning to waddle, seemed totally out of place. No touch football or 50-mile hikes or swimming parties or tennis for him.

But the enmity between the two men stemmed from more than their physical or emotional differences. Stevenson—a man of character and high principle, of remarkable sensitivity and honesty, his eyes failing to hide a certain shy vulnerabilty, a man capable at times of great eloquence—had grown a touch pompous. His tone had become moralizing, almost prissy, as if he were delivering schoolish homilies. The New Frontiersmen, who felt they understood the world better than he, had turned him off. Possibly a reinforcing cycle may have been at work here. Kennedy had begun to regard Stevenson with slight scorn but felt he owed him something (or at least needed the backing of Stevenson's liberal supporters), so he had placed him in the UN. New Frontiersmen held no more respect for the United Nations than the New York lawyer, John J. McCloy. A graduate student, writing a dissertation on the crisis, later interviewed Dean Acheson, Paul Nitze, Dean Rusk and Maxwell Taylor, and concluded that they "considered that just to bring the issue [of Cuba] before the United Nations was tantamount to *doing nothing.*" Since New Frontiersmen revered Action, they would hardly admire those committed to an organization which "did nothing." In other words, Stevenson may have been at the United Nations because the Kennedy men did not much admire his abilities; and their respect for him then declined further because he had become ambassador to the UN.

Whatever Kennedy's personal attitude towards Stevenson, he now felt it necessary to inform the ambassador about the missiles. As soon as the luncheon for the Libyan prince ended, the President excused himself and guided Stevenson into his study on the second floor. He laid out the photographs.

"We'll have to do something quickly," Kennedy said. Then, reflecting the apparent consensus of the Cabinet Room, less than two hours earlier, he added, "I suppose the alternatives are to go in by air and wipe them out, or to take other steps to render the weapons inoperable."

Stevenson was alarmed that Kennedy's first reaction was military. "Let's not go to an air strike until we have explored the possibilities of a peaceful solution," he said. He reminded the President that eventually the situation would come to the UN and it would be "vitally important we go there with a reasonable cause."

Kennedy asked the ambassador to join the other State Department officials meeting that afternoon. Stevenson left and drove over to State where he talked to Dean Rusk. He was concerned about the President's bellicose mood. The next morning he sent Kennedy a rambling note explaining his misgivings. Bombing

Cuba, he said, would invite Soviet counterattacks on American bases overseas. A surprise assault, moreover, would alienate both Western European and Latin American nations. Before doing anything, Stevenson advised, Kennedy should make it clear, "that the existence of nuclear missile bases anywhere is *negotiable*," and Stevenson underlined this word twice. He emphasized the importance of "talking" and of a "first announcement." He pontificated that "the judgments of history seldom coincide with the tempers of the moment."

Eventually others in the government would reject an air strike, but the ambassador was the first important official to place himself firmly in favor of negotiations *before* any military actions. Those who first propose peace often acquire a reputation as Nervous Nellies and exude an aura of weakness. ("Adlai's not soft on communism," one New Frontiersman later said, "he's just soft.") Stevenson knew what the others thought of him. He would reply to their charges: "It seems in our age anyone who is for war is a hero, and anyone who is for peace is a bum." (Those interested in the pressures of group psychology should note that Stevenson had *not* attended that first meeting in the Cabinet Room when the President's anger at the Russians blanketed the discussion. Had he been there, he might have been pressed by "group will" into a different initial stance.)

During the afternoon, while Kennedy met the Libyans, McNamara was having a luncheon meeting at the Defense Department with Ros Gilpatric and the Joint Chiefs. They began preparing plans to ready America's military for any contingency, including a possible invasion of Cuba.

At the State Department various officials spent the afternoon in conference or phoning each other. Roger Hilsman, for instance, took four calls from Ed Martin and met with him three times. He talked to Robert Hurwitch twice on the phone and also met with him for an hour. Rusk spent all afternoon with Chip Bohlen and Llewellyn Thompson pondering Soviet motives. What did the Russians want? What would they do next? How would they react if the United States bombed the sites?

(No doubt the State Department officials discussed a curious event that had occurred that very day in Moscow. Khrushchev, returning from vacation, had asked to see American Ambassador

Foy Kohler. When Kohler arrived, Khrushchev seemed quite amiable. The Soviet leader apologized if Castro's recent announcement about setting aside a fishing port for the Russians had embarrassed President Kennedy. The situation, the premier said, would not have arisen if he had not been out of town. He really did not want to cause Kennedy any political problems with the election coming up. The premier also reminded Kohler that Russia's purposes in Cuba were absolutely defensive.)

At five o'clock most of State's highest officials got together to exchange whatever new information or ideas they had gathered during the afternoon. Just before six Ball, Rusk, and Martin left for the White House to attend that evening's meeting.

Meanwhile Kennedy had kept himself busy. During the hour between the luncheon and another, more private, five o'clock meeting with the Libyans, he drove over to the State Department auditorium to address a conference of newspaper editors and radio-TV people on the subject of foreign policy. He gave a short speech, about fifteen minutes long, obviously written beforehand, which in retrospect seems filled with meaning. "I don't think it is unfair to say," he said, "that the United States—and the world—is now passing through one of its most critical periods. And it may be that it will continue to pass through a period of comparable criticality for the next few months—maybe years." He closed with a little poem:

> Bullfight critics row on row
> Crowd the enormous plaza de toros,
> But only one is there who knows,
> And he is the one who fights the bull.

The Cabinet Room filled up. Dusk was settling outside. Most of the city's workers were home by now, many watching the news on the television. In the Cabinet Room the soft ceiling lights reflected across the polished walnut table.

The group was a trifle larger this evening. Paul Nitze, an extremely bright assistant secretary of defense, had joined them; so had Llewellyn Thompson, who had just returned from Moscow where he had served as ambassador.

(This group was like a live thing. During the next two weeks it would split up into smaller parts for separate discussions—State, Defense—then collect again. It would grow larger, and smaller. Experts would come in for a few moments, for a meeting or two, providing whatever specialized information they had, then leave. Later on, when the story broke, reporters, looking for a handle, something to lead with, dubbed them "ExCom": the Executive Committee of the National Security Council. They were no such thing. They were merely a bunch of men Kennedy had wanted to see when he had first heard about the missiles. As he wanted others, they too would join. As a group, they had nothing official to do with the National Security Council. They were the outgrowth of John Kennedy's immediate perceptions about his needs. But a tradition has now hardened around their title, so ExCom they will always be.)

One senses that this evening's session was slightly different from the morning meeting. Perhaps Kennedy had cooled down or maybe they all had. No longer did they talk only of bombing attacks. McNamara told the group that in his opinion the missiles changed nothing very much. The United States was still infinitely more powerful. And if the Russians wanted to make a surprise missile attack, their ICBMs from the Soviet Union could do the job. "A missile is a missile," he said. "It makes no great difference whether you are killed by a missile from the Soviet Union or from Cuba." Mac Bundy agreed with McNamara but not very vehemently. Paul Nitze, however, strongly opposed McNamara's position. Nitze emphasized how these missiles were capable of taking out most of America's SAC bases, many situated in the threatened Southeast.

George Ball backed up McNamara. Apparently Ball in this instance was speaking for the State Department's leadership—Rusk, Alexis Johnson, Ed Martin, and Roger Hilsman—who had just been meeting together. Ambassador Thompson (who had also talked to Rusk that afternoon), when asked his opinion said he thought an air strike would be a mistake. It might cause Khrushchev to counterattack.

This anti-airstrike coalition, however, could still offer no concrete alternative, and there lay its greatest weakness. Those men favoring forceful action were so powerful and determined, it behooved those who opposed an air strike to come up with some *acceptable* alternative (not Stevenson's "negotiations"). John Kennedy, more Cold Warrior perhaps than many in the room, worrying about America's reputation (and maybe his own) for toughness, still demanded *something*. He, along with Dillon, John McCloy and Paul Nitze, wanted—possibly felt *driven*—to take some Action. (It is perhaps worth noting that Nitze, like Dillon and McCloy, was involved in New York investment banking and had even worked at Dillon, Read & Company for a decade. In fairness it should be pointed out that George Ball, also a lawyer-investment banker, totally opposed bombing.)

The meeting broke up a little before eight, nothing decided. Dean Rusk left for a formal dinner for the Libyans in the State Department's eighth-floor dining room. He stayed there an hour and returned to his office where he met again with his assistants until eleven.

Kennedy drove to Georgetown where his friend, the columnist Joseph Alsop, was giving a goodbye party for Chip Bohlen, leaving the next morning for New York, from there to sail to France. The President liked Bohlen and trusted his judgment about the Soviet Union, a subject the ambassador had specialized in since his days as a young foreign service officer. Llewellyn Thompson was also an expert, but Kennedy did not know him as well, nor feel quite as comfortable with him. Both Rusk and Bohlen had believed that it would be much less conspicuous if the ambassador left on schedule the next day, but Kennedy was unconvinced. As he said goodnight to Bohlen's wife Avis, he told her, "I wouldn't be too sure about his leaving."

Adam Yarmolinsky, a middle-rank official in the Defense Department, went to a small theater in Washington's Northwest section to see the special preview of a new movie, about to open all across the country. It was a melodramatic, Cold War documentary about the history of the Soviet Union. Its title was: *We'll Bury You.*

Nikita Khrushchev and Richard M. Nixon, September 27, 1959. (*USAF*)

John F. Kennedy and General Curtis E. LeMay, May 4, 1962. (*USAF*)

Cuban *bohío*, today.

Cuba: a small-town street today.

U.S. Jupiter (MRBM). (*USAF*)

U-2. (*USAF*)

Poltava, September 15, 1962. (*USAF*)

The port of Mariel. (*U.S. Navy*)

Soviet Military Buildup in Cuba

SAN CRISTOBAL MRBM SITES

GUANAJAY IRBM SITES

(2)

(2)

SAGUA LA GRANDE MRBM SITES

REMEDIOS IRBM SITE

! SA-2 SAM SITES (24)

◣ SSM CRUISE SITES (5)

⚓ G.M. PATROL CRAFT BASES (2)

⊘ MIG-21 AIRFIELDS (3)

□ GROUND FORCE INST (4)

★ IL-28 AIRFIELDS (2)

▌ MRBM SITES (6)

▌ IRBM SITES (3)

Soviet military
buildup in Cuba.
(*USAF*)

John F. Kennedy and Andrei Gromyko, October 18, 1962. (*National Archives*)

John F. Kennedy and the Schirras, October 16, 1962. (*National Archives*)

San Cristóbal MRBM site, October 14, 1962. (*USAF*)

SAM site: Bahía Honda, October 23, 1962. (*USAF*)

8 Nations Make Love Like Porcupines

Wednesday morning, October 17, 1962

John Kennedy received two visitors, Mac Bundy and John McCone. They gave the President the latest information, though it was not much more than they had had the day before. Work, they said, was progressing on the San Cristóbal installations.

(Later this day, U-2s would photograph the first scratches of the Guanajay IRBMs. Interestingly, no one recalls first hearing of Guanajay. Maybe the initial shock of the San Cristóbal discovery had deadened Washington to this new information: The *fact* of Cuban missiles seems to have made much more impression than their *type*. The administration was more troubled about how soon the missiles would be ready than how far they could fire. The New Frontiersmen were worried about symbols, not strategic military might. The United States was embarked on a public relations contest. Whichever country in this particular crisis first said, "I'm ready," was presumed to be the victor. The missile crisis was part of the mystic world of Image, of packaging—of space races and falling dominoes. The White House was anxious to beat the Russians to an *announcement*. Therefore the Guanajay sites which would not be ready for many weeks were much less distressing than San Cristóbal's.)

As soon as Bundy and McCone left, Kennedy went to the

Cabinet Room where he met Gerhard Schroeder for some high-level discussions of Germany's problems. The President did not mention the Cuban missiles to the German although he believed the rockets directly involved Berlin.

Afterward Kennedy and Dave Powers had time only for a short swim before they both went to a luncheon at the Libyan Embassy. On the way, the President stopped at St. Matthew's Cathedral.

"We're going in here to say a prayer," he told Powers.

The church seemed almost empty, and Dave Powers was surprised at the stop.

"Have you forgotten that I proclaimed today as a National Day of Prayer?" Kennedy said. "Right now we need all the prayers we can get."

About three o'clock Kennedy flew to Connecticut to help his friend, Abe Ribicoff, in a Senate race. His plane landed at Bridgeport at 4:25. It was a fine fall day and more than ten thousand cheering people awaited him. It was the kind of scene that invigorates a politician. Kennedy turned to Powers, still tagging along, and exulted, "My God, doesn't anybody have to work on Wednesday afternoons around here?" He was officially greeted by Ribicoff, Governor John Dempsey, a Democratic national committeeman, and the Bridgeport mayor. He spoke a few words to the crowd and they applauded almost every sentence. He then clambered into a waiting limousine for a motorcade the thirty miles or so to Waterbury. There the crowd was even bigger, fifty thousand of them. Waterbury is a rundown, depressing town with a large Catholic population. A presidential visit was something very special, particularly on a pleasant October evening just after work. Whole families had rushed through dinner to be on time at the town square, a small grassy rectangle surrounded by aging buildings. The last time Kennedy had been in Waterbury had been in November 1960, just before his election. That occasion had also been a clear, crisp evening, and Waterburians had turned out in vast numbers.

Kennedy in his speech now referred back to 1960. "Waterbury either is the easiest city in the United States to draw a crowd in, or it has the best Democrats. I'm coming back here to finish my campaign in 1964, just as I did in 1960." Happy shouting and whistles echoed loudly across the square. Locals would talk about that night for years. "I saw Jack," they would say, "President Kennedy, you know. He drove his car right by here. Back in 1962 I think it was. Gave a hell of a speech."

Throughout this day—on planes and cars, behind podiums—everywhere Kennedy went, he was surrounded by reminders of the outside world. Secret Service bodyguards stayed with him constantly, eyeing the crowds for maniacs. A telephone remained within reach. John Kennedy could, if necessary, speak to Dean Rusk or Maxwell Taylor in seconds. And an unobtrusive man toting a black box always stood near him. The man carried that day's codes to order a nuclear attack.

From Waterbury Kennedy motorcaded to New Haven. Two candidates for the House of Representatives rode in his car with him. They chatted about Connecticut politics.

In New Haven, home of Yale University which had recently bestowed on Kennedy an honorary degree, a few students booed him as he came into town. In his short address he mentioned this lightly. "I've enjoyed that warm reception I have gotten from my fellow Elis as I drove into the city. But they will learn, as this country has learned, that the Democratic party is best for them, as it is best for the country."

For Kennedy it had been a marvelous afternoon. The large crowds, the friendly ovations—five hours away from the tension-filled capital. That evening, as the presidential plane flew back to Washington, a reporter friend of Kennedy's, Charles Bartlett, talked to him. They spoke about the campaign a while. Kennedy seemed gay and full of life. Then the newsman happened to mention the ambassador to Mexico. The President's mood changed. Bartlett, not knowing what it meant, was startled by the transformation. He recalls: "And just the mention of Mexico—it was an amazing thing. The sheer buoyancy of having been out in the fresh air and campaigning with cheering crowds and all that, the buoyancy just left him and he almost—his shoulders sort of bowed, his face took on lines and he said, 'Boy, Charlie, do I have problems down in that region.' "

Wednesday and Thursday, October 17–18, 1962

From now until the end of the crisis the intelligence board met every morning in an old brick structure called the East Building. The flow of information into them increased steadily. Their job was to prepare a daily status report. Each morning they surveyed the entire world. The Cuban missiles, they worried, might be merely part of a much bigger, more ornate plan. So they scrutinized troop movements in East Berlin and Bulgaria, shipping lanes in the Baltic and Mediterranean, border tensions in Korea. A semi-guerrilla war was going on in Vietnam. Was there any connection? Then to complicate matters during this week, the Chinese invaded India. Could this, they asked themselves, be the beginning of a vast conflagration? Each day they checked their reports and made their predictions.

At the State Department experts pondered the international implications of the missiles. What would the Latin American countries do? Lately the United States, for example, had been having problems with Brazil. How would Brazil react to an American bombing of Cuba? How about Venezuela? Or Chile? What would happen if the United States brought the issue to the OAS, the Organization of American States? How about Africa? How about Europe? And so on. The personalities of hundreds of world leaders had to be analyzed. (At one meeting, after Rusk summarized possible foreign reactions, Sorensen asked: "Are you saying in effect that if we take a strong action the Allies and Latin Americans will turn against us and if we take a weak action they will turn away from us?" "That's about it," Rusk answered. Those around the room chewed on that thought a moment, then Max Taylor spoke up: "And a Merry Christmas to you, too!")

In the Pentagon the generals and their civilian leaders debated the situation. Many of them slept on cots in offices. "I didn't leave the Pentagon for over a week," one general recalls. A number of the military leaders, being quite conservative in their tempera-ments and training, detested communism and personally would have loved to invade Cuba and destroy Castro's leftist, irritating regime. But, despite later rumors to the contrary, the generals were not a mob held in check by humanistic civilians. Their inclination was to attack the Cuban missiles, but not because they were bloodthirsty. They just did not appreciate weapons being pointed at them, and they believed that in the case of Cuba the United States could do something. Moreover, they were not that concerned about the specter of nuclear war with the Soviet Union. The Russians were strategically far behind the United States. As long as America did not *directly* threaten the Soviet Union, they thought, the Kremlin would not go to war. The Russians would not venture national suicide unless their vital interests were at stake. The generals could not believe that Moscow considered Cuba "vital." The generals tended to see the Cuban missiles as a military problem—not a diplomatic or political or a psychological one. And if the Soviets wanted to make a fight of it, there were few places in the world where the United States had such an overwhelming supremacy as the area around Cuba. The Russians were far away and America close. The Soviet Union could not militarily compete with the United States in the Caribbean.

The Joint Chiefs planned several alternatives, but they personally favored a generalized air assault on all airfields and radar installations, in addition to the missile sites. The JCS figured that a long bitter period would follow the attack, during which Cuba might try to retaliate in any way it could. The United States would be wise, they thought, to destroy all Cuban capabilities to bomb American cities or attack Guantanamo Bay or launch torpedo assaults on the Florida keys.

Not knowing what the White House might decide, Pentagon planners also mapped out an invasion. None of the Joint Chiefs wanted one. They knew from their own experience in World War II how risky getting into a land war could be, and they had learned at Korea that once you were in, you often had to commit more divisions than you had originally expected. What might seem a police action could turn out to be a long conflict, followed in Cuba by years of guerrilla warfare in the mountains. An invasion, moreover, would be impossible to spring without warning. The United States could not mask all preliminary troop movements. And the logistics of an invasion—the landing ships, the equipment, the time schedules—were awesome. So many men and so much matériel would be required that the United States would weaken itself elsewhere. If the Russians simultaneously started something in Berlin, the military would be hard-pressed to meet it.

Officials all over town dreamed up alternatives. One State Department man suggested bombing Cuban oil refineries. While, he believed, American newspapers headlined *this* bombing, the United States could slip in and knock out the missiles. Another man proposed a commando raid. Troops would fly in by helicopter under air cover, land and knock out the missiles, then leave. The Pentagon considered this option quite carefully but rejected it as too uncertain. Walt Rostow—Rhodes scholar, college professor, now Mac Bundy's assistant, an intellectual positively entranced with James Bondian paraphernalia—suggested flying over the installations and shooting the rockets with pellets, fouling their engines.

McNamara himself reportedly had a rather strange notion. He supposedly quizzed Curtis LeMay, the barrel-chested, cigar-smoking, tough-talking chief of the Air Force, about whether his planes could bomb the missiles with *total* precision. Another general, no fan of McNamara's and perhaps a poor witness, later recreated the conversation.

"Now, Curt," McNamara said, "we are pretty sure those are Russian technicians down there. I want to go in with an air strike. I don't want to kill any of those technicians but I would like to wound a couple. Can we do that?"

LeMay looked at him for a long moment, then replied. "You must have lost your mind."

From Wednesday morning until Thursday night ExCom met repeatedly, almost continuously. President Kennedy sat with them twice but generally stayed away, keeping in contact by phone or talking privately to one or another of the members.

The sessions were sometimes haphazard. Often no firm meeting times had been arranged. Individuals would slip in during a discussion, sit down, and would have to be brought up to date. Others would leave for another meeting or to receive a telephone call, then return. Sandwiches and coffee were brought in. Except for Robert Kennedy's willingness to be what Adlai Stevenson called "a bull in a china shop," no one led the discussion. Traditionally,

Rusk, as secretary of state, would have done so, but he was often absent in conclaves with foreign officials like Gerhard Schroeder or the Libyan prince. Crisis management had never been his forte: He was not tough enough (or perhaps not rude enough) to ride herd on a bunch of men as individualistic as those in ExCom. McNamara, certainly steely enough, refused to supplant Rusk. This left Bobby. The attorney general was good at Socratic questioning—pressing each speaker, demanding clarity of thought—but he lacked a well-organized mind, and under his influence discussions sometimes became disjointed. No one even made up agendas for the meetings. The sessions therefore were often, as Acheson later called them, "repetitive, leaderless, and a waste of time."

They were also exhausting. Anyone who has sat in meetings for any length of time realizes how draining they can be. One assistant secretary apparently fell asleep at the wheel on the way home one night and crashed into a tree. Tempers began to fray.

Poor Ted Sorensen had had an ulcer operation a few weeks earlier. Just three days before the crisis began he had told someone: "I am on a restricted diet for three months—feeling rather virtuous about giving up coffee, cigarettes, whiskey and exotic foreign foods. . . . All I need now is a life without worry, pressure or tension, and full of tender, loving care." What he received during these weeks was the opposite. As he later wrote: "It was an agonizing prospect. In no other period during my services in the White House did I wake up in the middle of the night, reviewing the deliberations of that evening and trying to puzzle out a course of action."

Often ExCom would gather together in George Ball's conference room in the State Department, across the hall from his office. A sign outside its door read, "In a Nuclear Age, Nations Must Make War Like Porcupines Make Love—Carefully."

By early Wednesday, the men had isolated and rejected several alternatives. They had agreed that they had to do something. McNamara and Bundy and even General Shoup did occasionally suggest the possibility of doing nothing, of accepting the missiles, but none of them broached this idea very forcefully in front of John Kennedy. Nor, other than Stevenson, did anyone press strongly for a compromise, a diplomatic solution. Nor, during this period, was there serious discussion of an invasion. John McCone offhandedly proposed "taking Cuba away from Castro," but he did not push it vigorously.

In other words the fond recollections of some of the participants that they had taken part in freewheeling debates, and had carefully probed *all* possibilities, is untrue. ExCom's initial discussions revolved almost solely around two options—bombing and blockading.

Early in the week Secretary of State Rusk phoned Dean Acheson and asked him to come over. The friendship between these two men went back to their days under Harry Truman when Acheson had been secretary of state and Rusk one of his assistants. Their personalities never meshed well—they were quite unalike—but Rusk respected his predecessor—and Acheson, the brilliant Eastern aristocrat, felt patronizing affection for the rather plodding, poor-boy-made-good from Georgia.

On Wednesday Acheson arrived at the State Department. Rusk showed him the photographs and asked his opinion. The older man, with his excellent lawyer's analytical mind, broke the problem into parts. As he saw it, he later said, "the question was, which was more dangerous," to knock them out now, killing some Russians, or try another, more moderate tack and maybe become "paralyzed by talk while the Russian purpose was accomplished." If the latter happened, the "political effect would be terrific." Acheson believed that the President had an obligation to protect the security of the American people, that John Kennedy had a responsibility, a moral duty, to remove the missiles *now*.

With the addition of Acheson and McCone to the meetings, the pressure for an air attack seemed irresistible. Then two events occurred: McNamara proposed a genuine alternative to bombing, and Robert Kennedy began to support him.

Although the notion of a blockade had arisen the day before, no one had thought much about it. The idea of placing ships around Cuba had a number of flaws. A blockade would take time: ExCom called it, "the slow track." The Russians could tap dance around almost indefinitely, shouting and blustering about Washington's bellicosity, while the American fleet forlornly circled Cuba. There might be no positive effect for a long time. The famous Berlin blockade had lasted a full year; a blockade of Cuba might be equally long—or longer. In the intermediate time several things were likely to happen. The missiles in Cuba would become operational. Demonstrations against the United States would take place all around the world. And within the United States pressure would build. As Robert Lovett, one of the President's unofficial advisors, snidely said, "We would be under pressure from the bleeding hearts, the unilateral disarmament groups, and the peace-at-any-price units," to stop the blockade. The waiting could even be politically damaging. (During an ExCom meeting someone passed a note to Sorensen: "Ted—Have you considered the very real possibility that if we allow Cuba to complete installation and operational readiness of missile bases, the next House of Representatives is likely to have a Republican majority?") Castro, never known for his self-control, might even do something rash, like attack the blockading ships or start killing some of his 1,100 Bay of Pigs prisoners.

The blockade also gave the initiative back to the Russians. Suppose the Kremlin ordered its ships to sail right into the fleet, and the Americans opened fire, killing hundreds of Soviet crewmen. And then suppose the Russians revealed to a neutral investigating team that their ships, now blackened by smoke and gory with corpses, had only been carrying medical supplies and baby food. The Navy insisted it could probably stop an oncoming ship by shooting at its rudder, but accidents do happen. ExCom also asked the Navy if it could halt a submerged submarine. Yes, it said hesitantly: It did have such plans on the books, but it could not guarantee their success. And how about planes? ExCom wondered. Could not the Soviets bring in supplies—possibly even unassembled missiles—by air? Would the United States have to start shooting down planes?

Then there was the problem of West Berlin. The longer a blockade around Cuba continued, the more likely the Kremlin would try the same tactic against the German city.

What about other countries? Many nations, including England and a number of Latin American countries, still traded with Cuba. Would the United States dare halt British ships? John McCone, who was something of an expert on the subject of shipping, called their attention to some legal ramifications. Any blockade interfering with a third party's shipping was normally considered "belligerent," and therefore legally an act of war. (Lyndon Johnson only a few days before the crisis began had made that very point in a speech attacking Homer Capehart.) Possibly, if Washington obtained a two-thirds vote from the OAS, it might have some legal claim. But to count on persuading that many Latin American nations, often quite prickly and independent, to support an American blockade seemed overoptimistic. And without OAS backing, the Russians could claim, with some justification, that the United States was violating the UN charter. McCone also noted that without "legal" backing the United States might run into endless litigation over such abstract questions as maritime insurance.

(The blockade, in truth, would be of dubious legality. For years afterward lawyers have debated it in their law journals. Some have raised the following question: Since the Soviet Union had committed no belligerent act, on what legal grounds could the United States stop Russian ships? A vote by the OAS, as even Robert Kennedy said at the time, was a political act, not a legal sanction.)

A final objection to the blockade was simple. In a real sense *it absolutely could not work*. The missiles were already in Cuba, or at least enough of them to give the Russians the bargaining chip they seemed to be after. A blockade might put pressure on the Cubans themselves by denying them certain goods, including perhaps the oil products necessary for their machinery, and one could hope that *they* might ask the Russians to get out. But this prospect seemed unlikely. Soviet support had become too necessary to Castro's government; he would likely be unwilling to insult them. All a blockade could probably accomplish was to prove to the Russians that the Americans were aware of what the Kremlin was doing and angry about it—or, as Walt Rostow wrote in a secret memorandum, it could "impart a sense of our determination." A blockade in other words would be little more than a symbolic gesture.

One could even argue that a blockade might be more dangerous than bombing. Since it could not halt construction on the installations, the missiles would soon be made ready. The only way to root them out then would be to invade—which all members of ExCom agreed was the riskiest approach. The main attraction of the blockade, although few of its proponents would admit it, was not what it was or what it could do. A blockade was really not much at all—nor could it achieve much. Its chief appeal lay in what it was not: an air assault. Unlike bombing, a blockade was not *immediately* violent. It was also more ponderous. Since it in fact involved more time, it put off an ugly decision.

George Ball, along with McNamara and Gilpatric, helped lead the coalition against an air strike. Ball had once been a director of the U.S. Strategic Bombing Survey which had studied the effects on Nazi Germany of Allied bombing. His experience had taught him that pinpoint bombing accuracy did not exist, that something politely called "spillage" was common. Air Force leaders were aware of this fact and did not like it, but they had come to accept it. Civilians, like Alexis Johnson, however, when first confronted with it, grew uneasy. Alexis Johnson was a high State Department official and sat in on some ExCom sessions. On being told, early in the week of the installations, his first reaction had been to favor what he called a "quick, and hopefully clean, air strike." But he changed his mind as the Joint Chiefs pressed for more and more sorties.

In a sense the military men hurt their own position. Part of their problem this week stemmed from the fact that they did not get along well with members of the Kennedy administration. One high-ranking general referred to them disdainfully as "the group across the river" and spoke slightingly of the "real McNamara." Another general, Lauris Norstad, in Europe commanding NATO at the time, privately told a journalist that he was "worried about the judgment and sangfroid of the team in control in Washington"—a rather diplomatic way of saying that he trusted neither the New Frontiersmen's wisdom nor their courage. The vice chief of staff of the Army said about Robert Kennedy: "He was a very difficult fella to get along with, Bobby. The President was very easy to get along with, but Bobby had a chip on his shoulder vis-á-vis the military. And we all felt this."

The summer before the crisis, Paul Fay, a close friend of the President's, had given him the novel *Seven Days in May*, about an attempted military takeover of the United States. After Kennedy read it, Fay asked him whether he thought it plausible. "It's possible," Kennedy replied. "It could happen in this country, but the conditions would have to be just right." If a second Bay of Pigs occurred, he said, then a third, "it could happen."

Perhaps some of the enmity between the two groups was a normal outgrowth of civilian-military disagreements. Or maybe it stemmed from the relative youth of the administration. Generals do not like to kowtow to men the same age as majors or lieutenant-colonels. Many New Frontiersmen had been junior officers during World War II, and possibly some of their attitudes toward the generals (and vice versa) sprang from this.

Some members of the administration had long suspected the military of being much too warlike. Then, in the early days of the crisis, the Joint Chiefs pressed for wholesale bombing. Each time the Air Force added a new target, some of their civilian listeners cringed. The Joint Chiefs may have been *correct* in their assumption that the United States had to guard against a Cuban counterattack, but their dogmatic insistence on it was, among other things, bad salesmanship.

Nor did Curtis LeMay improve their image with the statement he made to the President on Thursday. The Joint Chiefs had come to one of ExCom's morning meetings and were fervently arguing for an air strike. LeMay was particularly forceful. Kennedy, who was attending this session, was dubious.

"How will the Russians respond?" he asked LeMay.

They won't do anything, the general replied.

"Is that what you really think?" the President asked drily. "Are you trying to tell me that they'll let us bomb their missiles, and kill a lot of Russians, and then do nothing? If they don't do anything in Cuba, they'll certainly do something in Berlin." He added, however, that he did recognize the importance of taking action before the missiles became operational.

General Shoup said softly, "You are in a pretty bad fix, Mr. President."

"You are in it with me," Kennedy snapped.

The meeting ended. As the Joint Chiefs left, their rows of ribbons glimmering beneath the soft ceiling lights, Kennedy said to

O'Donnell, "Can you imagine LeMay saying a thing like that? Those brass hats have one great advantage in their favor. If we listen to them, and do what they want us to do, none of us will be alive later to tell them that they were wrong."

A few weeks later Kennedy would tell his friend Ben Bradlee, "The first advice I'm going to give my successor is to watch the generals and to avoid feeling that just because they were military men their opinions on military matters were worth a damn."

Kennedy seems here a trifle self-satisfied. He himself had supported bombing only two days earlier, before his mind was changed by Llewellyn Thompson, the just-returned ambassador to the Soviet Union. Thompson was the only member of ExCom who really *knew* Khrushchev (in fact, much better than Bohlen). The opinion of this pleasant, highly controlled, somewhat sad-looking man took on paramount importance.

Thompson told Kennedy and the rest of ExCom that week that if the United States bombed the missile sites, Khrushchev might go into a rage and order an immediate counterattack. Moreover, if Soviet troops were killed by an air attack, the prestige of the Russian Army would be involved, and Khrushchev might be forced by internal political pressures to take vigorous action. Kennedy listened to Thompson and was convinced. From that time on, he tended to disagree with those like LeMay who continued to support a bombing.

Yet any rational analysis would have to conclude that either method—bombing or blockading—was potentially dangerous. Both were military acts. In fact, since one could argue that blockading held greater dangers, it was somewhat fatuous for Kennedy to suggest that the "brass hats" were dunderheaded warmongers.

One wonders whether the President rejected bombing because of who supported it and who spoke against it, not because of the cogency of the arguments on either side. By Friday those pressing for an air attack were men like Dean Acheson, whom Kennedy respected but in a distant, cool way, and Curt LeMay, whom Kennedy loathed. Those in favor of the blockade included the men whom the President liked and admired, men like the secretary of defense.

Robert McNamara—Berkeley, Harvard (Phi Beta Kappa), Ford Motor Company executive, looking like a tanned, athletic accountant with slicked-down hair and rimless glasses—did not like to be boxed in. He constantly searched for alternatives, always demanding them from the Pentagon brass. When he could, he preferred putting off decisions until their consequences became clear. An assistant of his once said, "He always wants to know what the penalty is for failure."

Such a careful man would find the missile crisis uncomfortable. The generals who demanded bombing could not guarantee the results. Bombing left the next step up to the Kremlin; Washington would lose control over the issue. A blockade would be more flexible. One could twist it this way or that, let some ships through, perhaps a single Russian vessel in order to show restraint, and stop other ships to show determination. At least the scheme looked good on paper. It could be termed "controlled response." At ExCom's meetings, beginning on Wednesday, McNamara argued that a blockade would "maintain our options."

Perhaps, deep down, McNamara dreaded the coming conflict so much that he looked for any plausible, high-sounding way to postpone it. His obvious distaste for bombing on Tuesday led him on Wednesday to seize the blockade proposal. He probably unconsciously concluded that a blockade would be the only alternative acceptable to President Kennedy and the rest of ExCom.

Where had he gotten the idea? He later told others that he and Gilpatric came up with it at lunch on Wednesday. Perhaps, but the notion had been swirling around Washington for two months. In mid-August Robert Kennedy had been worried that the increasing military shipments to Cuba might eventually include offensive weapons. He had asked an assistant attorney general named Norbert A. Schlei to study what the United States could do, under international law, if Russia attempted to install long-range missiles in Cuba. Schlei wrote a long memorandum proposing, among other things, a "visit-and-search blockade," a gimmick under Anglo-Saxon law to stop some cargoes and not others. Robert Kennedy discussed the memo with him, particularly the blockade concept, and sent copies of it to various officials. The President received one; so did Rusk. And so, possibly, did McNamara.

Other men had also been proposing blockades, though less sophisticated in their nature than Schlei's. In September Senators Strom Thurmond, John Tower, Barry Goldwater, Hugh Scott, and Jacob Javits called on the President to institute a blockade. Richard Nixon, campaigning in California, even suggested a "quarantine."

The idea was in the air. McNamara had probably reached out frantically, grabbed on to it, and then argued forcefully for it, presenting it in language natural to himself.

George Ball, Roswell Gilpatric, Robert Lovett, Llewellyn Thompson, Ed Martin, and eventually even Dean Rusk joined forces with him. The White House men—Sorensen, Mac Bundy, O'Donnell—leaned in their direction. Opposing them were the Joint Chiefs (including Maxwell Taylor), Dean Acheson, and, off and on, John McCone. Lyndon Johnson, in a peculiar position, remained uncommitted. Two men of importance were left: Douglas Dillon and Robert Kennedy. Since President Kennedy had recently been often turning to these two, the way they swung would be extremely important.

On Wednesday, the attorney general repudiated bombing. The position he took (which Acheson would call "emotional or intuitive") was the least sophisticated and most human adopted by members of ExCom.

Robert Kennedy was one of the most interesting men ever to hold high position in America. He was simultaneously a rational conservative and a brooding romantic. He lacked his older brother's wit and ironic humor. He was too sensitive and, yes, insecure to take Important Things lightly. Nor was he particularly intellectual. He hated Evil and found any compromise with it, to use his term, "unacceptable." He was not afraid to say, unlike some of his more cosmopolitan colleagues, that some things were "not right," even "immoral." He personally did not swear. He once said the two qualities he most respected were "courage and sensitivity." He had a poet's instinct to *feel* things. Someone once said, "I think Bobby knows precisely what it feels like to be an old woman." He could be narrow and was abysmally ignorant of many things, but he recognized these weaknesses and tried to overcome them. His Hickory Hill seminars were an example of his efforts. All the Kennedys were late bloomers; Bobby was growing. He was changing from the tough, rigid, Irish-Catholic McCarthyite that he had been to the deeper, more thoughtful (but never brainy) man he was about to become.

During Tuesday's meetings he had not talked much, but the note to his brother about how he now understood how Tojo felt indicates his initial reaction to bombing. He had recoiled from the image—not so much of the *people* being bombed, however, as of himself sitting here in the White House calmly planning the slaughter. It is hard to accept oneself as a killer.

On Wednesday ExCom was discussing various practical matters about an air attack—how soon it could be ready and so on—when the bombing advocates stated that everything could be set so that the planes could begin the attack early Sunday morning.

Early Sunday morning? To Robert Kennedy—thin, intense, puritanical, who had been a highly impressionable sixteen-year-old on December 7, 1941—such a tableau was an abomination. It would be, he said, his high voice filled with passion, "a Pearl Harbor in reverse, and it would blacken the name of the United States in the pages of history." He is reported to have said, "My brother is not going to be the Tojo of the 1960s."

Here was an interesting study of the impact of imagery. The morning before he made these statements, just after his brother had shown him the first photographs, he had pressed SGA to "increase their guerrilla raids." He did not, therefore, seem to mind CIA killings, so why did he find the idea of bombings so repugnant? Was his reaction a typical Kennedy reflex, a feeling that to bomb Cuba *openly* would make the administration *look bad?* Perhaps . . . but there are other possible explanations. He may have genuinely believed that bombing was more likely to cause a nuclear war. It is even possible, though uncharacteristic of the man, that he found bombing light-skinned Russians more objectionable than shooting swarthy Cubans. Maybe he found anti-Castro guerrilla raids acceptable because the Cuban leader had become a personal affront to his brother's administration. And possibly the explanation is even more subtle. He may have condoned CIA killings because he had not personalized them. Nothing in his experience enabled him to *feel* the pain CIA raids were creating. But the words "Sunday morning bombing" would have clicked in his unconscious. All of a sudden attacking Cuba would have seemed wrong. In his Catholic way, like a character from a Dublin novel, he may have been standing up for Higher Ethics. While he probably would have opposed the bombing eventually, if the air strike proponents had first suggested, say, "Tuesday evening attack," he might not have reacted so emotionally.

His outburst also had an important effect. When Robert Kennedy made his analogy with Pearl Harbor, Douglas Dillon stared at him, thought for a very long moment, then mentally swung away from the air-strike advocates. As Dillon later admitted, it was at this moment, listening to the attorney general, that he changed his mind. "It had," he said, "never occurred to me before that a surprise attack was a bad thing until Bobby made this point."

With Bobby and Dillon now with the blockade coalition, the bombing advocates were placed on the defensive. Yet ExCom still could not reach a consensus. With all options so uncertain, individuals found it difficult to make up their minds. Though a few, like Acheson on one side or George Ball on the other, remained firm in their stands, many fluttered from one position to another, hesitating to settle anywhere. Stewart Alsop later called the two wings "Hawks" and "Doves." The words had a nice ring to them and would be used to characterize positions on the Vietnam War, but in this case they were misnomers. The blockade was hardly "dovish" in its implications and potential results; Dean Acheson could not really be considered a "hawk," for in fact he believed that bombing was the least dangerous tactic.

On Thursday afternoon Kennedy talked privately to Acheson. The older man would have made a superlative prime minister. He could think analytically and speak gracefully and cogently. With Kennedy now he reviewed the various options, giving the strengths and weaknesses of each. The President, who had already talked the matter over with Bobby, brought up the Pearl Harbor argument. The parallel clearly weighed heavily on the President's mind, as it had with Douglas Dillon. He wanted to see how Acheson would treat it. The ex-secretary brushed it aside scornfully. Had not the President given the Russians fair warning in his September speeches? Acheson admitted, however, that the decision would not be easy. He said he was glad he didn't have to make it.

Kennedy stood up and walked over to the French doors facing the rose garden. He stood there, his back toward the older man, a very long time. Then he turned around and said quietly, "I guess I better earn my salary this week."

"I'm afraid you have to," Acheson said.

Another interesting scene took place after Acheson left. Andrei Gromyko had been in the United States for over a week, but no American official knew exactly why. The Russian had talked to Dorticós, the president of Cuba, and attended the UN. Then he had asked for an audience at the White House. The request had come in about the same time as the San Cristóbal photographs. Had the Russians spotted the U-2 plane? Did they wish to talk to Kennedy to feel out his reactions? Would they use this talk to inform Washington that Khrushchev was at this moment going public about the missiles, revealing his coup before the United States could spring its reaction? Like someone planning a surprise party, the President wanted to be the one to make the dramatic denouement. If Gromyko told him that the Kremlin was about to announce the presence of the missiles, the administration's activities for the past few days would have been in vain. Kennedy no doubt waited for Gromyko's arrival with some trepidation.

Dean Rusk and Llewellyn Thompson came over at 4:30 and the three men reviewed the situation. At 5 o'clock Gromyko entered, accompanied by Dobrynin, two other officials, and two interpreters. Kennedy stood up and shook Gromyko's hand. The men sat down, Kennedy in his rocker facing the fireplace, Gromyko sitting to his right on one of the beige sofas. Cameramen came in, took pictures for posterity, then left. The Russian leaned back against a striped cushion and began speaking—about Berlin. Kennedy must have breathed a deep sigh of relief. It was not about Cuba after all. Gromyko told the President that Khrushchev would do nothing provocative until after the November 6 election.

(Once again the election had come up. Khrushchev was obviously very concerned to reassure Washington. Why? Was it, as Kennedy thought, just a case of Russian mendacity, Khrushchev's desire to lure the United States into somnolence? Or did the premier assume the President was already aware of the missiles? U-2 flights had by now repeatedly flown over the *uncamouflaged* Soviet installations. Did the Soviet leader assume that although Kennedy had accepted the missiles he might be concerned about their potential effects on the elections? There seems no way of knowing.)

Gromyko declared that after the election, if the two powers could not come to an agreement about making Berlin a "free city," the Soviet Union would be *compelled*—and he repeated the word, saying specifically that he wanted to emphasize it—to sign a separate treaty with East Germany.

The foreign minister finally turned to the subject of Cuba. (Did Kennedy tense up again, wondering if now the other shoe would drop?) Gromyko complained about America's support of emigré attacks on Cuba, and about its general hostility toward Castro's regime. He said the weapons the Soviet Union had sent to the island were strictly defensive, protecting the Cubans from another invasion. Gromyko took out some notes and began to read. He wanted to make sure his message was unmistakable. "I have been instructed to make it clear," he said, that the purpose of the weapons "is by no means offensive."

The President listened impassively. Gromyko, Kennedy thought, was lying right to his face. "I was dying to confront him with our evidence," he later said.

When the foreign minister finished reading, Kennedy sent for his September statement warning the Soviet Union about putting offensive weapons in Cuba. He reread it aloud slowly. Gromyko, he afterwards mused, "must have wondered why I was reading it. But he did not respond."

About 7:15, the two-and-a-quarter hour session came to an end. Gromyko left and was immediately surrounded by a large group of waiting reporters. What was said, Mr. Foreign Minister? they shouted as he passed. Gromyko smiled at them, obviously in a good mood, and said that the talks had been "useful, very useful."

Back in his office Kennedy spoke with Rusk and Thompson.

How did they think it had gone? Should he have openly confronted Gromyko with the evidence? No, they replied, he had done just right. At that moment Robert Lovett and Mac Bundy slipped in through Evelyn Lincoln's office. Kennedy grinned at them: "Gromyko . . . in this very room not over ten minutes ago, told more bare-faced lies than I have ever heard in so short a time. All during his denial . . . I had the low-level pictures in the center drawer of my desk and it was an enormous temptation to show them to him."

Robert Kennedy came in through the rose garden door. The six men went over the whole situation one more time: blockade or bombing? Russian reactions? The UN? Latin America?

Black servants popped in advising the President that it was getting past dinnertime. Rusk and Ambassador Thompson left to go back to State where they joined Gromyko for an informal meal. The President asked Lovett to stay and eat. Lovett, pleading exhaustion, begged off and left. John Kennedy went in to dinner.

Earlier in the week a middle-rank official at State had told his superior: "I know there is something going on you don't want to talk about. But if security is all that tight, maybe you'd better tell all those big wheels from across the river [note again the scornful attitude of civilians toward the Pentagon] to get their cars off the street." Outside, black limousines with well-known license plates were lined up. Henceforth ExCom's members parked in State's basement garage.

Thursday evening ExCom, meeting at the State Department, took a straw vote. The results were six for an air strike, eleven for a blockade. The group agreed to tell the President. Ten of them went to the White House. Discretion suggested that they drive over in one car so as not to attract undue attention. Ed Martin, no doubt tired of closed-in, smoky rooms, opted to walk the several blocks. The other nine jammed into Robert Kennedy's limousine—McCone, Taylor and Bobby in the front with the driver, the remaining six sitting on each other's laps in the back. As the ten men jammed against each other, someone said, "What if we get into a collision?" Another added, "It would be some story if this car is in an accident."

At the White House, however, confronted by John Kennedy's gimlet-eyed questions, ExCom's resolution began to collapse. Bundy even reversed himself and argued for no action at all. The "right decision" seemed so slippery. They decided to meet again the following morning and try once more.

Late Thursday night Rolando Martinez, a Cuban emigré, CIA operative, and later Watergate burglar, turned his small boat toward Cuba. On board he carried eight commandos. Still totally unaware of the crisis that encircled them, they were proceeding with CIA's plan to blow up the cable-car system in Pinar del Rio.

Martinez dropped the commandos on the beach and waited not far from shore.

The eight went in quietly, but before they could set their charges, they were spotted by a Cuban patrol. Flares shot into the sky. Both sides opened fire.

Martinez, hearing the guns, brought his vessel back toward the beach. Six commandos ran out of the night and tumbled into the boat. The other two did not appear. After a while Martinez turned his boat around and left.

9 The Decision

Wednesday, October 17, 1962

Military aircraft begin moving into MacDill Air Force Base, not far from Tampa, Florida. Curious reporters ask if this has anything to do with Cuba. An Air Force information officer says, absolutely not.

Thursday, October 18, 1962

The USS *Enterprise*, back only six days from Mediterranean duty, hastens out of Norfolk Naval Base. Destination: unannounced.

Friday, October 19, 1962

A transport ship, the USS *Grant County*, appears off Key West, Florida. Several hundred marines and scores of vehicles disembark. The marines place their equipment—carefully hidden beneath tarpaulins—onto trailers, move across the island to Boca Chica Naval Air Station, and take up guard positions around its perimeter. Huge Globemaster cargo planes begin landing. Key West is the southernmost spot in Florida. Havana is less than a hundred miles away.

Other planes begin landing at Air Force bases around Florida—at Patrick, at Homestead, at McCoy.

The administration found it hard to preserve its secret. John Kennedy had ordered ExCom at their first meeting not even to tell their wives or secretaries. Rusk later told a CBS interviewer, David Schoenbrun, that, "senior officers did their own typing." "Some of my own basic papers," he said, "were done in my own handwriting." But the government could not maintain the charade indefinitely. Comic situations occurred—like the evening the State Department was giving Gromyko his dinner in the eighth-floor dining room. Reporters had gathered out front to catch anything newsworthy from those who came or went. At 7:30 ExCom was supposed to meet in George Ball's conference room on the seventh floor. When McNamara, Gilpatric, and McCone, who had just eaten together, arrived for their meeting, a newsman spied them.

"Are you going to dinner?" he asked, thinking that they were dining with Gromyko.

"Yes," they quickly declared, and walked inside. The reporter should have wondered, but did not, what these three would have been doing at such a diplomatic affair.

Gradually the number of people privy to the secret increased. Each member of ExCom turned to his own staff for advice. They in turn brought in others. At the Pentagon and the State Department there were by Friday probably almost a hundred individuals who knew what was afoot. Outside official circles, others also began to find out.

Mac Bundy later asked important participants how many had in fact told their wives. Most, including John Kennedy, had. Some wives who had not been told became upset at their husbands' secret all-night sessions.

A conference of intelligence experts from Great Britain, Canada, New Zealand, Australia, and the United States had long been scheduled. The foreign guests grew aware something momentous was developing. Senior American officials were coming late to sessions and leaving early, taking urgent phone calls, and failing to keep appointments. The visitors conferred with each other; it was a crisis, they agreed, but where? Berlin? Cuba? Laos? They kept their respective governments informed.

Reporters suspected something was brewing, and at least one newsman gained secret information. On Friday morning the Miami *News* printed the following "AP report" from Washington: "Yesterday, the White House said plans are being worked out for a U.S. quarantine on Cuban shipping." Details "probably won't be ready for announcement this week." The Miami *News's* Washington correspondent, Hal Hendrix, who had a number of contacts at CIA, was possibly the so-called "AP report." He was a well-known "friend" of the agency, and it often leaked juicy news bits to its "friends." But if so, who at the agency provided him with the story—and why? On Thursday night, when the "AP report" must have been written, no one in Washington could have been positive that a "quarantine" would be President Kennedy's decision. For that matter, ExCom did not even discuss using the word "quarantine" until Friday morning when an assistant attorney general *first* proposed it to several men at the State Department. Was some official (possibly a member of ExCom) leaking information to test popular reaction? Or even to force the issue? If the "AP report" was Hal Hendrix, why him? Was it because he worked for a Miami newspaper, a city filled with Cubans?

The Miami *News* was not the only paper to carry such stories. On Friday morning another report, written by a pair of journalists, Paul Scott and Robert S. Allen, referring vaguely to missiles in Cuba, appeared in several newspapers. How these two newsmen got their information is also unknown. One thing was clear: The secret was clearly beginning to spill over.

During the morning John Kennedy, on his way to the Midwest to campaign for local Democrats, took Ted Sorensen aside. He was displeased. The Joint Chiefs, along with several others, including Acheson, Bundy, and Rusk, had just been to see him. They had all pleaded for an air strike. The President told Sorensen that he and Bobby should guide ExCom to some sort of consensus (presumably in favor of a blockade) and to do it *soon*. Bobby should call him as soon as the group came to a firm decision.

ExCom met again that morning. They tiredly hashed over the same arguments, their mood sour. Sorensen waspishly reminded them that they had agreed on a blockade the night before and that their bickering was not helping his ulcer, nor was it "serving the President well." His goading had no effect; they were at a deadlock.

They agreed to break into their two contending groups, each to write a scenario for action. Acheson went with the air strike advocates but told them the President had only asked him to give general advice. He felt it inappropriate for him, officially unconnected to the government, to be drawing up military plans. This may have been his real reason for excusing himself, but one senses his feelings of relief to get away from the impasse. He had by now become annoyed at Robert Kennedy's moralistic "Pearl Harbor" analogies, and by the tedious repetitiveness of the arguments.

Ted Sorensen, meanwhile, retreated to his office to write two speeches—one if Kennedy opted for a bombing, the other for a quarantine. He started with the latter. As his superb mind focused on the matter, he began to realize that although he personally preferred a blockade, he could not see how it was going to work, how it would force the removal of the missiles. (The week offers no better example of the fact that many of those in favor of the quarantine only chose it because they could not face the idea of a bombing—not because they really wanted a blockade.) Sorensen quit work on the speech; he could not visualize it. He returned to ExCom that evening, stumped, and asked the rest of them to help him formulate his thinking.

It was an important moment. Faced with the specific question—How could one put the quarantine concept into a few persuasive sentences?—ExCom conceived a conceptual breakthrough. What they really wanted, it dawned on them, was not particularly a blockade by itself, but an action, less violent, less provocative than bombing, which would still show the Russians they meant business. Ball and McNamara and Robert Kennedy, among others, had latched onto a blockade earlier in the week because it had seemed to offer the *appearance* of action. Yet, until Sorensen sat down by himself to put their proposal into words, none of them had apparently thought through its implications. Now, late Friday, after several days of debating in the abstract, the blockade advocates realized that all they really wanted was a strong, symbolic act. A quarantine was as good as any, perhaps better, partly because they had already discussed a number of its problems. Since the President was pressing them, the fact that they had already done the basic preliminary planning was important. Now that they realized what they really wanted, they agreed that if the blockade did not jolt the Russians into withdrawing the missiles, the United States should immediately become more openly aggressive. *If the quarantine, as a show of determination, did not succeed, they would then resort to bombing,* possibly *even an invasion.*

Most members of ExCom, this late Friday night, now felt a sense of relief. They were Americans, trained to believe in compromise, and had just achieved a satisfactory marriage of two, apparently opposing, ideas. Some of the Joint Chiefs were still dissatisfied, and perhaps one or two others, but the consensus the President had wanted had been achieved.

Sorensen went back to work on the speech feeling much better. He finished about three in the morning.

John Kennedy had flown by helicopter from the south grounds of the White House to Andrews Air Force Base, and from there by Air Force One to Cleveland. Again the political rituals: the governor, the senator, the congressmen, the motorcade, a mass of flesh lining the route to view their handsome young President. He arrived at a side door of Cleveland's Sheraton Hotel, greeted its manager, then walked out the main entrance to face a huge mob jamming Cleveland's Public Square. According to a recent Gallup Poll his popularity had just dropped to 61 percent, the lowest it would ever be. But one could not perceive any such tepid mood in Public Square. Whistles and cheers detonated in the air as he stepped to the platform. A massive animal sound erupted from the crowd. Several hundred thousand smiling faces beamed up at their leader who, although they did not know it, would make a decision in the next few hours determining whether they would live or die. They felt joy just seeing him. They cheered and stomped their feet at every mundane thing he said. "These are the issues of the campaign," he shouted at them in the somewhat stilted manner he adopted for formal addresses, "housing [hurrah], jobs [huzzah], the kind of tax program we write in the coming session. . . ." The usual phrases. The words were not really important. His presence was to be a "draw," to bring out lots of voters to see local candidates now standing near him. The occasion hardly deserved a real speech. It was an exhibition, an extravaganza, like an all-star sporting event.

After receiving an autographed football from the student body of a local Catholic high school, Kennedy flew to Springfield, Illinois where he went to Lincoln's tomb and placed a wreath, standing silently for a moment as taps softly sounded. From there he drove—accompanied by Richard Daley's hand-picked senatorial candidate, Sid Yates—to the Springfield State Fairgrounds. At the livestock pavilion he spoke of farm matters. "In the last twenty-one months," he told a crowd, "we have not, by any means, solved the farm problem. But we have achieved the best two-year advance in farm income of any two years since the depression." (Foreign affairs went unmentioned throughout.) He flew on to O'Hare Airport in Chicago. It was late in the afternoon and drizzling lightly when he arrived. Pierre Salinger, with him that day, recalls: "JFK was gloomy as we drove from O'Hare to our hotel, the Sheraton-Blackstone. An anti-Castro picket in front of the hotel, carrying a sign, LESS PROFILE—MORE COURAGE, did nothing to improve his mood."

Salinger had hardly arrived in his room when the phone rang. The two columnists, Allen and Scott, were about to publish another story that American troops were to invade Cuba. As soon as Salinger hung up, the telephone rang again. A Chicago reporter named Carleton V. Kent said he had heard that paratroops were awaiting a signal to jump off to Cuba. Would Salinger like to comment? The press secretary told Kent he would call back.

Salinger went upstairs to the presidential suite. The President, with only an hour and a half before he had to leave for another speech, was taking this opportunity to relax and had already stripped to his underpants. When Salinger arrived, Kennedy was on the phone to Washington. Salinger noticed that as he placed the phone back in its cradle he looked tired and nervous.

The press secretary told him about the two calls he had taken downstairs. "Call Kent," the President said, "and tell him that report is all wrong. We are not planning to invade Cuba." He turned to O'Donnell, also in the room, and ordered him to call McNamara. The secretary of defense should ask Allen and Scott not to print their column.

This minor crisis out of the way, Kennedy settled down for a bowl of oyster stew. About 7:15 he left for a $100-a-plate dinner for Sid Yates. Richard Daley was an excellent political organizer and the banquet hall was packed to overflowing.

Afterward, Kennedy drove with Daley to a theater where he addressed the Democratic precinct captains, the stalwarts of Daley's machine. The mayor had been one of Kennedy's first supporters for the presidency. This evening's effort—speaking warmly to Daley's henchmen while America's military forces gathered in the night's darkness—may have gone far to pay the debt.

O'Donnell remained at the hotel to take incoming calls from Washington. During the course of the evening he talked with Rusk, Bundy, and Robert Kennedy. As he was sitting there Salinger returned. The press secretary still knew nothing specific.

"You're going to have to cut me in pretty quick," he told O'Donnell. "I'm flying blind with the press."

"All I can tell you now," O'Donnell replied, "is that the President may have to develop a cold tomorrow."

John Kennedy arrived back at the Sheraton about 10:30 and called his brother Bobby. It was almost midnight in Washington. Robert Kennedy no doubt told him that ExCom had reached whatever consensus was possible. The President agreed to return the next morning to the capital. He asked O'Donnell to notify Rear Admiral George G. Burkley, his government physician who often traveled with him, to come to the suite early tomorrow, prepared to diagnose a cold.

The next morning at 9:15, as Pierre Salinger was giving the press the President's itinerary—after a few more speeches in Chicago, Kennedy was to fly to St. Louis, to Albuquerque, and eventually on to Seattle—a messenger summoned him upstairs. The small crowd of reporters broke up and began to move toward the buses.

When the rotund press secretary arrived at the presidential suite, a coy one-act play transpired. John Kennedy, unshaven and in his pajamas, was in bed. Nearby stood O'Donnell, Dave Powers, and Admiral Burkley.

"I have a temperature and a cold," the President intoned

seriously. "Tell the press I'm returning to Washington on the advice of Admiral Burkley."

Salinger turned to go.

"Wait a minute," the President added. "Let's be sure we're all saying the same thing."

On a pad of Sheraton-Blackstone stationery he jotted: "Slight upper respiratory." He started to write "½," then crossed it out and put in, "1 degree temperature . . . Weather raw and rainy . . . Recommended return to Washington . . . Canceled schedule."

"There," said the President, tearing the page from the pad and handing it to Salinger, "tell them that."

The various actors played the comedy out to the end. Salinger went downstairs, got the reporters off the buses, and read them the bulletin. When Kennedy arrived at O'Hare to board the plane, he sported a hat, as if to baby his "cold." He hated hats; the last time he had worn one was on the day of the inauguration. (When Lyndon Johnson, campaigning in Hawaii, also returned to Washington because of a cold, a newspaper editor asked Salinger if an epidemic had broken out.)

Washington. 9:00 A.M. Saturday, October 20, 1962

ExCom met again in Ball's conference room. They went over Sorensen's draft, made only a few changes, and approved it. Robert McNamara turned to the telephone. He called the Pentagon and told them to harness up four tactical bomber squadrons. Since ExCom had just agreed on a blockade, a State Department man, overhearing McNamara, expressed real surprise at this order. McNamara told him: "If the President doesn't accept our recommendation, there won't be time to do it later."

It was sunny and cool in Washington as John Kennedy arrived. He emerged from the helicopter and rushed into the White House. The first thing he did was read through the proposed speech draft. He talked a few minutes with Sorensen, reviewing the blockade's pros and cons. Robert Kennedy later recalled that as his brother took a short swim, "I sat on the edge of the pool and we talked." Meanwhile members of ExCom were entering the White

House—by different entrances so as not to arouse suspicions. They were shown into the Oval Room.

At 2:30 John Kennedy arrived and the session opened. John McCone presented the most recent photographs and provided them with the latest intelligence information. He told them that at least some of the San Cristóbal missiles were now ready to fire, others would follow from day to day. He soberly noted that if the Kremlin learned the United States had discovered the missiles, they *might* assume America would go to war, and instantly order a nuclear attack. One could not *know* what the Russians would do. One could hope they would be rational, but maybe Khrushchev or someone else would crack. One must be very . . . careful.

Dean Rusk spoke briefly, summarizing the arguments for both sides. He favored a blockade, and his written summary which he now handed the President said so, but he apparently did not openly argue for it at this session.

McNamara then began. In a remarkably well-structured, cogent presentation he pointed out that the blockade would "maintian our options." No doubt the Kremlin would retaliate somewhere—probably, Berlin—no matter what action the United States took. This was a "cost" America would have to bear. (Khrushchev once said: "Berlin is the testicles of the West. Every time I give them a yank they holler.")

Mac Bundy, who by this time had supported almost every possible option, reiterated the arguments for an air strike. He noted that only a bombing would accomplish their goal. According to Robert Kennedy one member of the Joint Chiefs added that they might as well use nuclear weapons since the Soviets would undoubtedly use theirs.

When both sides finished their presentations, an awkward silence ensued. All eyes turned to John Kennedy. Roswell Gilpatric broke it. "Essentially, Mr. President," he said, encapsulating McNamara's arguments, "this is a choice between limited action and unlimited action; and most of us think it's better to start with limited action." Kennedy nodded understanding.

This moment was perhaps the most important of his presidency. He could so easily make a mistake. He was like an Old Testament judge. He had listened carefully and in silence to both sides. Which road—this one or that? Both had pitfalls. A misstep could be fatal—for himself and the world. He recognized that sooner or later he had to make a decision; he could not put it off indefinitely. Yet, even now, he refused to commit himself totally. He said he wanted to talk personally to the head of the Air Force Tactical Bombing Command to see if a "surgical strike" was absolutely impossible. Until he had talked to him, he would not make a *final* decision. ExCom could, however, tentatively assume he would choose the quarantine. He liked its limited approach and the fact that he could always opt for bombing later if the Russians refused to move.

"There isn't any good solution," he said. "Whichever plan I choose, the ones whose plans we're not taking are the lucky ones—they'll be able to say 'I told you so' in a week or two." "Whichever way we go," he added, "a week or two from now, everyone will wish they had advocated some other action, because all of them are full of dangers and disadvantages." But the quarantine, he concluded, "seems the least objectionable."

Having come to a provisional conclusion—awaiting a final verdict about bombing—the President opened up the meeting to a discussion about what diplomatic approaches to take. How about the UN?

Adlai Stevenson took the floor. He stated that the United States should be prepared to offer *something* in return for the removal of the missiles; the administration should develop some sort of bargaining position. Stevenson was a cautious man. He did not like unnecessary risks. As a child he had been taught to chew each bite a specified number of times. Faced by this crisis, he recognized that, at the very least, the Russians would make some counter-demands. As a prudent individual, he wanted to be prepared. Kennedy's speech, he suggested, should include a proposal for political negotiations, to go along with the blockade announcement and the threat of bombing. The United States would thus appear reasonable rather than belligerent. Kennedy could say, for instance, that once the Soviet Union removed its missiles, Washington would *discuss* the "demilitarization" of Cuba, by which the Soviets and Cubans would drastically reduce the island's recent arms buildup, and the United States would dismantle its military base at Guantanamo. Kennedy might add that Washington would also *consider* taking its missiles out of Turkey and Italy. Stevenson was not proposing a simple trade as he was later accused of doing. His idea was much more subtle. He was suggesting the *total* removal of the Soviet military from the Caribbean. To accomplish that significant goal he was willing to see the United States give up bases of debatable military value.

As he spoke, most of the others in the room listened angrily. Perhaps he expressed himself clumsily, because to many of them he seemed to be offering to "pay" Russia to take the missiles out—something they were determined the Kremlin must do for "free." From this moment on, some of them would consider him a coward. Their contemptuous reaction to him and his proposition would tarnish his last years. He would die in 1965 a bitter man. Here in the Oval Room this Saturday afternoon, the sunlight slanting against its yellow walls, Stevenson had found a stony audience. He was an aging man, encircled by ancient political opponents like Acheson and the young, tough New Frontiersmen. His proposals, while they may have indicated his courage, showed his lack of understanding of the administration's will. The rest of ExCom were as worried as he about "looking bad," but to them that meant looking weak, backing down anywhere in the world.

When Stevenson raised the possibility of what seemed on the surface to be a horse trade—the Turkish missile bases for the Cuban—he was entering a diplomatic snakepit. Douglas Dillon, who had been part of the Eisenhower administration, admitted: "Well, everyone knows that those Jupiter missiles aren't much good anyway. They were only put there during the previous administration because we didn't know what else to do with them, and we really made the Turks and Italians take them."

The Jupiters were liquid-fueled IRBMs, slow to fire, and rather sluggish in motion. They had been one of America's first rockets. In 1957, after the Soviets successfully fired Sputnik, NATO had voted to create a missile system in Europe. The United States had soon placed sixty Thors in Britain, thirty Jupiters in Italy and another fifteen in Turkey—just across the Black Sea from the U.S.S.R. A few experts like Averell Harriman had said all of these missiles were "counterproductive." All they accomplished was to bruise

Soviet pride and increase the influence within the Kremlin of the hard-liners. Less subtle analysts than Harriman had merely noted that the missiles were militarily inefficient and rather useless. (It is interesting to note, in light of much of the hoopla during the crisis, that the Soviet missiles in Cuba which the Kennedy administration called "threatening," "aggressive," and "offensive" were quite comparable to the "obsolete" Jupiters.)

Pressure had built to remove them. On February 11, 1961, a few weeks after John Kennedy took office, a Joint Congressional Committee on Atomic Energy suggested they be dismantled, and that henceforth Europe could be protected by Polaris submarines. A few weeks later, following a March 29th National Security Council suggestion, Kennedy demanded a review of the Turkish IRBMs. On June 22, 1961, the report was ready. It said that, in light of Khrushchev's recent "hard posture," dismantling the missiles "might seem a sign of weakness." At the same time General Norstad of NATO stated his opposition to their removal. He believed that the Greeks and Turks in NATO would be uneasy if the Jupiters were taken away. The Turks, he said, would feel particularly insulted. (John Kennedy would cynically say that "what the Turks want and need is the American payrolls those represent.")

Kennedy did not let the subject of the bases die. Even though officials in the State Department told him they believed it would be imprudent to remove the missiles, in August 1962 he decided to recall the Turkish Jupiters. For some reason no action was taken. Apparently Kennedy did not actually *order* their removal, and his generalized wishes were lost in the bureaucratic labyrinth; in mid-October the Jupiters were still there. Once the crisis had begun, the Turkish installations took on renewed importance. Their position so close to Russia seemed so much like the Cuban bases that a number of people considered a trade a simple solution. On Wednesday, October 17, even several hawkish members of the government had discussed making such a deal with the Kremlin. They would even have been willing to throw in three American air bases inside Turkey to sweeten the arrangement. On Sunday, October 21, almost every member of ExCom would agree that the United States might eventually have to give up its Turkish missiles to settle the crisis. (About this time John Kennedy would tell Ben Bradlee that personally he could sympathize with Khrushchev worrying about American forces just across his border. Kennedy would say he realized that Russia's troops in Cuba were comparable to the Americans in Turkey. But he warned Bradlee that this admission was not for publication. "It isn't wise politically to understand Khrushchev's problems in quite this way.")

Given the fact that so many adminstration members could see a clear relationship between the Turkish and the Cuban bases, why were Stevenson's suggestions leaped on so ferociously? All observers agree that Dillon, McCone, and Lovett—among others— attacked the ambassador's musings (or, at most, "proposals") as if he were Neville Chamberlain returning, umbrella in hand, from Munich. Was it the ambassador's tone? Was he posturing, or pontificating, or moralizing? He *had* developed an annoying tendency to purse his lips, like a disapproving schoolmarm, when making a point. He did use the word "wise" to describe his suggestions, thereby implying that other methods would be "unwise."

Maybe Stevenson had become the group's lightning rod. Dillon and McCone and Lovett, Republicans, may have indirectly been warning the President against any sign of weakness. It would have been unpolitic to tell Kennedy bluntly not to waver. They— unconsciously—may have used this convenient occasion (and this irritating individual) to raise their caution flags. The President may also have himself been using Stevenson, allowing the UN ambassador to present ideas which he, the President, could reject. Then, in choosing the blockade, Kennedy could appear as if he was taking a middle-of-the-road stance.

Another possibility, and in some ways the most believable, is that almost all of the men in the room had been working sixteen- to twenty-hour days on this problem. They were tense and exhausted. After agonizing effort, they had finally come down to two possibilities which they had just presented to the President. Here was Stevenson, in this case the outsider from New York who had attended few of their meetings, offering something totally different. To some of them, it might have seemed rank unprofessionalism—a quality they detested.

(Later on, as reporters tried to piece together the events of the crisis, two journalists, Charles Bartlett and Stewart Alsop, would write an article for the *Saturday Evening Post*. The article would emphasize how several unnamed ExCom members were saying that Stevenson had proposed a "sell-out." When Kennedy would hear that the *Post* was going to publish the Stevenson story, he would ask Bartlett about it. Bartlett recalls the President's reaction: "He sort of shook his head. That was the only real comment that he made.")

After the Stevenson episode, the meeting broke up. The President and his brother, along with Kenny O'Donnell and Ted Sorensen, stepped out on the second-floor balcony and stood looking through the dusk, the trees around them girdled in soft yellows and browns.

"Well," said Kennedy ruefully, "I guess Homer Capehart is the Winston Churchill of our generation."

They talked about Adlai Stevenson. Robert Kennedy was scornful.

"He's not strong enough or tough enough to be representing us at the UN at a time like this." (Bobby was his father's son and he still carried political wounds from the Democratic Convention of 1960 when Stevenson had almost taken the nomination from his brother.) The attorney general proposed that John McCloy or Herman Phleger—interestingly, both wealthy lawyers and Eisenhower Republicans—supplant Stevenson in the coming UN negotiations.

"Now wait a minute," O'Donnell remembers Kennedy saying. "I think Adlai showed plenty of strength and courage, presenting that viewpoint at the risk of being called an appeaser. . . . Maybe he went too far when he suggested giving up Guantanamo, but . . . I admire him for saying what he did."

Later that evening O'Donnell ran into Stevenson at a party. "I know that most of those fellows," the ambassador sighed, "will probably consider me a coward for the rest of my life for what I said today, but perhaps we need a coward in the room when we are talking about nuclear war."

O'Donnell assured him that after the meeting President Kennedy had spoken well of his courage. This may have made the UN ambassador feel somewhat better. (One wonders how he felt a few days later when Kennedy did send John McCloy to "help" him at the UN.)

John Kennedy called Jacqueline at Glen Ora, the Kennedys' Virginia farm, 35 miles from Washington. The two of them often spent Sundays there with the children. This weekend she was there. The President told her he would be unable to leave the city and asked if she would mind returning. Everything was closing in on him and he wanted his family close.

Livingston T. Merchant had twice served as American ambassador to Canada. He had recently retired and settled in Washington. He was at Princeton that day, watching the Tigers play Colgate. After the game he went to dinner with some acquaintances. When he returned to his hotel he found a message: Phone the State Department immediately; ask for either Dean Rusk or George Ball. He put through the call. Could he come to the State Department tomorrow morning? he was asked. They wanted him to take a special message to Foreign Minister John Diefenbaker in Canada. They couldn't tell him the specific message over the phone.

Walter (Red) Dowling, the ambassador to West Germany, was in Georgia visiting his mother. He also received a call from the State Department: He should return to the capital immediately.

Dean Acheson, spending the weekend at his cozy Maryland farm, answered his telephone. It was Dean Rusk. The President, Rusk said cryptically, had decided not to take the action Acheson had preferred, but he would very much like him to go see De Gaulle. The President had remembered what Acheson had said about warning the French leader in "an impressive way." Kennedy had decided that a visit from the ex-secretary would show the proper respect. Would Acheson be willing to come to State early tomorrow morning to get final instructions?

Acheson remembers thinking about something he had once heard Oliver Wendell Holmes say—that "we all belonged to a club which was the least exclusive in the world and the most expensive," the United States of America.

"I guess," Acheson said to Rusk, "if I belong to that club I better do what I'm asked to do. Sure, I'll go."

"Well," Rusk said, obviously relieved, "you don't mind that your advice isn't being followed?"

"Of course not, I'm not the President, and I'll do whatever I can."

The President called his friend, the British ambassador, David Ormsby-Gore, and asked him to come by for lunch the next day.

For two or three days Gore had suspected that something was up. He now assumed he was about to be let in on the secret.

Newsmen were also getting the scent. They were noticing that certain important officials were failing to show up at parties or were leaving abruptly in the middle of them. Lights were staying on very late at the Pentagon and State Department. And John Kennedy's health looked suspiciously good for someone suffering a severe cold. Reporters began to haunt government buildings, prowling the corridors. Sharp-eyed editors grew aware of reports from various places around the country that certain military units were moving.

Pierre Salinger received half a dozen inquiries. The Virginia *News Pilot* wondered if there was any connection between all the activity at Norfolk Navy Yard and the President's cold. The AP asked about various movements of Marine battalions. The *Herald Tribune* called Salinger, and CBS, and the Washington *Post*.

James Reston pieced it all together. He checked his story with George Ball, then Mac Bundy. They each pleaded with him not to write it.

Max Frankel of the *New York Times* was also set to go with what would have been a rather accurate piece. As he was hammering it into shape, he called the White House for confirmation but failed to reach the President. Meanwhile, at a party in Washington, Stevenson whispered to Kenny O'Donnell that he had heard that the Washington *Post* and the *New York Times* were about to crack the story.

O'Donnell went into the bedroom and phoned the White House.

"I suppose everybody at the party is talking about it," Kennedy grumbled. "This White House is like a sieve." (A few minutes later, talking to Salinger, the President would broaden his complaint: "This town is a sieve," he would growl.) One can hear in his plaint the echoes of so many Presidents, particularly recent ones, who have wanted to control information—out of embarrassment, out of a childish love of suspense and surprises—and usually basing their positions on the grounds of "national security."

"Sieve?" O'Donnell replied. "You did very well to keep a story like this one out of the papers for the last five days." O'Donnell suggested that someone should call the two papers and ask them to hold the story.

Kennedy announced he himself would phone. He now returned Max Frankel's call. Did Frankel, he asked, *know* what the administration was about to do? No? Well, as Commander in Chief, he had just ordered a blockade of Cuba. But he didn't want the Russians to find out about it until everything was ready. They might do something drastic. Couldn't the paper sit on the story, just for a day or so? Would Frankel ask his publisher and call him back?

Several *Times*men debated the issue. Perhaps James Reston, who also worked for the paper, took part in the conversation. They reminded each other that at the time of the Bay of Pigs they had held back information. That invasion had been a disaster. Had they not been partly culpable for the debacle, accomplices in the crime?

They called the White House. They asked Kennedy if he would give them his word that he would, in Frankel's words, "shed no blood and start no war during the period of our silence." He agreed.

Frankel later reminisced sadly: "No such bargain was ever struck again, though many officials made overtures. The essential ingredient was trust, and that was lost somewhere between Dallas and Tonkin."

On Friday the Pentagon sent orders to two different Marine units: one at Cherry Point, North Carolina, the other all the way across the country at Camp Del Mar in southern California. They should prepare to move immediately. By late Friday night both were ready.

On Saturday rain began falling on Camp Lejeune, North

Carolina. Marines stood around in parking lots, cursing the weather and dingbat generals in Washington. In California the fog hung low and thick over the Marines in their combat gear.

Late Saturday afternoon the word came down. Both units were to move out. They were not told where. As they scrambled into the trucks that would take them to waiting planes, they speculated among themselves.

Admiral Alfred Gustave (Corky) Ward was a calm man, one of those soft-spoken, affable people who never got rattled. He was short and stocky with dark hair and eyes. He still retained the heavy Southern drawl he had taken with him from his birthplace in Mobile, Alabama. An intelligent man and hard-working, he had graduated thirteenth in his class in Annapolis and had earned a master's degree in electrical engineering from M.I.T. If you wanted something done, you turned to him. He took charge and was steady under pressure. He had won two Bronze Stars during World War II.

About noon on Saturday he received orders to fly to Washington. He was told about the blockade and that he would lead it. When he arrived in the capital, George Anderson, chief of naval operations, outlined the plans. Large ships coming from the Atlantic, Anderson said, could only reach Cuba by a handful of specific navigable channels. Destroyers could easily block off those routes. The Navy would use nineteen ships—seventeen destroyers and two cruisers. They would not really need that many, but the numbers might impress the Soviet Union. They also considered it prudent to make sure a large number of ships were already at sea in case of war. The aircraft carrier *Wasp* with five screening destroyers was to cruise nearby.

At a Washington party that evening Walter Lippmann, the most respected columnist in America, told a friend that the United States was on the brink of a war.

10 Preparations

Secretary McNamara gives orders to all nuclear units that they should load their weapons. Polaris submarines begin deep runs toward the Soviet Union. SAC planes circle in the air, crisscrossing the Atlantic, their bomb-bay doors *closed*, an indication they are carrying full loads. Other SAC crews wait on the ground never far from their planes. It is the greatest alert in SAC history.

The nation's ICBMs go on alert: ninety Atlas missiles and forty-six Titans almost seem to pulsate, ready for firing. Nikes and Hawks ring Florida.

America's military machine to "Defcon (Defense Condition) 3." (Defcon 5 stands for peacetime condition; Defcon 2 means a unit is fully mobilized for war; Defcon 1 means it is at war.) *SAC, with most of the nation's nuclear weapons, is at Defcon 2.*

Deep in the Pentagon's War Room, behind a green door, electronic consoles blink brightly. Vast lighted maps reveal every American outpost around the globe. Each Marine unit, each nuclear submarine, each Titan missile is flashed against one screen or another. Here and there in the room are unobtrusive Klaxon horns. If they should sound, President Kennedy has just signaled Defcon 1. According to plans, one of the individuals in the room will instantly step forward, keys in hand, and unlock several padlocks on a small red box. Inside he will find plastic bags containing the proper coded message being sent at that moment to SAC bases around the world.

An Air Force captain later remembered about this period: "When I went down to the command post I had a feeling I never had before. I wondered if I would see my wife and kids again. I felt we were near to war."

The land around Fort Hood, Texas is sandy and harshly rolling. It is the home of the 1st Armored Divison, "Old Ironsides." Fort Hood is a grim spot. Barracks sprawl line upon dreary line. Much of the year the place is hot and windswept—dry, crushing hot. Most GIs hate it. The nearby town of Killeen, rich from its proceeds off lonely soldiers, has no open bars. Outside the town's municipal boundaries huddles a tawdry, unwashed quarter, the only place nearby where one can freely buy liquor.

The 1st Armored Divison is ordered to the East Coast to prepare for a possible invasion of Cuba. If the quarantine does not succeed, they will charge in, more than 15,000 of them, four tank battalions and six mechanized infantry, with artillery and other assorted elements. The Army loads the division on thirty-six trains, some more than 150 cars long. Four other Army divisions will soon join them.

The Navy prepares its blockade force. Tankers leave immediately; their captains are told they will receive further orders later. Destroyers begin to set out from Norfolk and Key West. If they do not have enough crewmen, they "borrow" men from other ships being overhauled. They are to slip out quietly; they are under orders not to place the usual announcements on local radio and television stations that crewmen on leave should return to ship.

The Navy asks for interpreters who know Russian in case Soviet ships are stopped at sea. The government combs all its language schools in the region and comes up with nine men who are rushed aboard various ships. Most blockade vessels are also equipped with special photographic teams, tape recorders, riot guns, and hand grenades. The Navy is able to put together these odd assortments and get most of the ships underway amazingly fast. By Monday evening, when the President will give his speech, many of them are already in place near Cuba.

The United States begins to clench its military fists. All across the world America prepares for battle.

The USS *Essex,* already at Guantanamo Bay, lies quietly in the harbor, dark waters lapping her sides. The hot Caribbean air, heavy with humidity, hangs over her decks. It is 3:30 on Sunday morning. Below, sailors toss in their sleep. *Essex* is a carrier, recently equipped with highly sophisticated surveillance devices.

Suddenly breaking the stillness comes a shrill piping: "Reveille, reveille, all hands. . . ." Within seconds the engines turn faster and the *Essex* gets under way. She heads out of the harbor and stands offshore. Her orders are to provide protection for several thousand Marines about to arrive at the base.

Only an hour before the Marines arrive has the base commandant found out they are coming. When they land, the Marines pour off their planes in a rush. They immediately begin to build bunkers along the rim of the base. Church congregations in Guantanamo that Sunday morning are sparser than usual.

On Monday the Navy evacuates Guantanamo's American civilians, mostly women and children. Shortly after 10:00 in the morning, the base headquarters begins notifying them—by radio and telephone mainly, but also by word of mouth—to get ready to go. Evacuees are told they can bring one suitcase each. They are to carry immunization cards and an emergency payment authorization. Housewives are to tie their pets outside in the yard, to put house keys on their dining-room tables, and to stand in front of their homes with their children to wait for buses which should arrive in a few minutes.

This same announcement goes to all the base's schools. Children are immediately released and run gaily home, shouting excitedly as they reach their front doors, "We're being evacuated!" This is sometimes the first their mothers have heard about it.

One Navy wife later tried to recreate that day: "My husband was apparently calm but soaked with perspiration. . . . He helped me get my big suitcase from the closet shelf.

"I put in two pairs of slacks, underwear straight from the clothesline [Monday is wash day in the Navy], a suit, a wool skirt, two sweaters, a flashlight, some pictures of my husband, a little sentimental jewelry, important papers and documents and a few items that cannot be justified as either useful or irreplaceable." (In this she was quite normal. In such times people often grab curious, unimportant items. Later, when asked why, they do not know.)

"For some strange reason I felt compelled to defrost the refrigerator, although I made a mess of the job by allowing the drain to run over and spilled the water all over the floor.

"I poured a little over a quart of milk into a pan and put it out for the cat. I hope my cat will be able to forage a living. . . .

"I felt as if I were enacting some terrible, compulsive dream. I cried, of course."

Within minutes, buses (most of them school buses) begin picking people up, rushing them to the docks. Pregnant women, due to give birth before December 1, are evacuated by air. Six planes fly 379 of them to Norfolk, Virginia. One lady, Louise H. Kittleson, has been scheduled that very day for a cesarean at the base's hospital. Her plane detours to the closer facilities at Cherry Point, North Carolina. She arrives in time. At 9:17 that evening Anne Louise Kittleson is born.

Meanwhile thousands gather at Guantanamo's dock area. The first to arrive is a civilian male who, as soon as he heard the news, has run all the way. Forty-five minutes later the first buses arrive.

The sky is clear and sunny. The temperature hovers at 91°, the humidity at 65 percent. As thousands of women and children gather by the ships, the baking sun boils tempers. Direct sunlight becomes so blinding, the Navy lines everyone up under a tin-roofed supply shed. But beneath it, the air lies leaden. The temperature inside it becomes awesome. Babies, hundreds of them—the youngest only four days old—start to cry. Older children yank their mothers' arms and make demands. Many women, some in their teens, sob uncontrollably.

Some scenes at the docks are poignant. One husband and wife—he on the dock, she aboard ship—feel too proud to shout to each other across the distance. They simply stand quite still, looking at one another until she is ordered below.

One woman kisses her husband goodbye, not knowing when she will see him again, war quite possibly only hours away. Her parting words to him are: "Don't forget to take out the garbage."

At 3:05 the first of four evacuation ships leaves Guantanamo. Less than two hours later the last pulls away. They are carrying 2,430 passengers, as well as their regular crews. Some ships are so crowded, women have to share bunks in eight-hour shifts. *Upshur*, the largest ship, carries 580 women, 25 men, 168 teenagers, 735 younger children, and 195 babies under two years old. Just before the vessel pulls up her gangplanks, a truck rushes to dockside bringing the last important items to put on board: a load of diapers.

The four ships draw up into a convoy. In the heat and the rolling seas, some passengers become seasick. The ships' crews try to make things as agreeable as possible. They show movies three times a day and provide books and games. Yet the situation is not pleasant. As the convoy sails north, the temperature drops. By Thursday it is 35 degrees. Most evacuees have only tropical clothing. A naval supply ship brings some warm clothes but it is not enough to go around.

The *Upshur*, since it is fastest, finally takes off on its own and arrives first. As it pulls into Norfolk late Thursday night, a cold dank wind blows in off the sea. The passengers, tired and chilled, stand by the railing looking down on the dock where a thirty-five-piece Navy band plays, "Sailing, Sailing, Over the Bounding Main."

The evacuees are led to barracks, fed, checked over, and given winter clothing. One by one they walk out into the night.

Washington. Sunday morning, October 21, 1962

General Walter C. Sweeney, Jr. went to the White House early. It was cloudy, and there was a light mist in the air, a last reminder of Hurricane Ella as she drifted out into the Atlantic. General Sweeney was chief of the Tactical Air Command. If the government decided to bomb the missiles, he would be in charge. The President asked him if he could guarantee knocking out all the Cuban missile sites. No, the general replied, he could only promise 90 percent effectiveness; nor, he added, could he promise that bombing Castro's twenty airports, many in heavily populated areas, would not result in a large number of casualties. The President thanked him and the general left. Sweeney's reply confirmed Kennedy's tentative decision of the day before. The blockade promised to be the "best" approach.

Up to this point John Kennedy had often been tense and irritable. Now he seemed to relax. During the next two days he remained calm, almost tranquil. It was as if the decision had been painful and dragged out of him. Now that it was made, now that the logistics of the operation had begun, he appeared imperturbable. Observers would marvel at his coolness. His composure steadied those around him.

About 9 o'clock that morning, Pierre Salinger came to Kennedy's office to ask him about church. "You always go on Sunday," Salinger said. "If you don't go today, the press is going to draw its own conclusions."

"Don't worry," Kennedy said, "I'm going."

Just before 10 the Kennedys left for mass at St. Stephen's. Maybe he was still hoping to keep reporters off the trail with a show of normality. Perhaps he wanted divine guidance.

During that Sunday, to confuse newsmen who were convinced something was going on but could not be sure where, the State Department sent three different prominent officials to the White House: Averell Harriman (assistant secretary of state for Far Eastern Affairs), Martin Hillenbrand (from State's German desk), and Phillips Talbot (assistant secretary for Near Eastern affairs).

Harriman did not like his decoy job. "How long do I have to sit here?" he reportedly grumbled.

Sixteen newsmen, scheduled to observe Operation PHIBRIGLEX 62, flew into Roosevelt Roads, Puerto Rico. They expected to see a large fleet and thousands of Marines, but these were nowhere around. A briefing officer blamed the hurricane. The fleet, he said, had gotten scattered all over. It should be ready by early Monday morning. Meanwhile, he said, the reporters might as well relax.

That evening, after dinner in the officers' mess, a group of reporters sat in the lounge, playing poker.

Early Sunday morning Livingston Merchant arrived at State. He was told he should leave the next day for Ottawa. His task would be delicate. He was to tell Canada's leaders about the developments in Washington. Prime Minister John Diefenbaker did not much like Kennedy and had been rather prickly about the whole subject of the United States. But Canada was very important to America's plans. In 1957 the two countries had signed a joint defense agreement creating NORAD (North American Air Defense System). In an emergency the separate components of both nations would join together. Since the Cuban crisis was such an "emergency," Diefenbaker's cooperation seemed now essential.

Dean Acheson also arrived early at State. He had come directly from his Maryland farm, without extra clothes, money, or passport. While he was being briefed, several high officials at State chipped in and raised about fifty dollars for him. He then rushed to his P Street house and packed; his secretary brought him his passport. A limousine sped him to the airport where he climbed aboard a large Air Force jet. As the plane roared down the runway, heading for Europe, he found himself one of only eight passengers. Red Dowling (flying back to West Germany to tell Chancellor Konrad Adenauer) and Acheson represented the State Department. The other six passengers were three CIA agents, each with a set of photographs (one for England, one for France, and one for West Germany), and three armed guards to prevent unauthorized persons from catching any glimpses of the pictures. Acheson wryly remembered about the flight that as the men on the plane stood around a table looking at the photographs the three guards became nervous. Every time one of the plane's Air Force officers walked through the compartment, the guards quickly covered the pictures. Acheson was amused, but one has to sympathize with those military escorts, ordered to protect the photographs *with their lives*, having to deal with striped-pants diplomats acting so nonchalant about "highly classified secrets."

It was dark when the plane touched down at the SAC base near Newbury, England. A cold wind whipped across the runway. Waiting there was David Bruce, the American ambassador to England. Bruce told Acheson he had two "interesting things" in his raincoat pockets. He promptly produced a bottle of scotch and they had a drink together.

As to the other "interesting thing"—"Put your hand in my pocket and see what's there," Bruce said mysteriously.

Acheson did so and felt a revolver. "Why?" he asked, stunned.

"I don't know," Bruce responded. "I was told by the Department of State to carry this when I went to meet you."

"There was nothing said about shooting me, was there?" Acheson asked.

"No. Would you think it's a good idea?"

Acheson briefly described the Cuban situation to Bruce, then told him the ambassador should see Macmillan tomorrow. He should go in with the CIA man, the photographs, and the guard, and officially inform the prime minster.

Dean Acheson and Dowling then flew on. It was after 3 in the morning when Acheson, sixty-nine years old, climbed wearily into bed in Paris.

Robert Lovett, just two years younger than Acheson, flew into Washington late Sunday morning on an Eastern Airlines shuttle to attend another ExCom meeting. He was supposed to go first to Robert Kennedy's house for lunch. He had been told that someone would meet him at the airport, and he looked around for that person. Lovett had served his government since the days of Franklin Roosevelt. He could be charming and witty but was also known as a very tough man. He had been traveling—embarking and disembarking—for well over fifty years now, ever since his father, a wealthy lawyer and judge, had sent him off from Texas to the Hill School in Pennsylvania to acquire polish. By now, at this point in his life, in this crisis, just one among many he had seen, he was merely "serving his country," to use an old phrase, caught up once more by the stimulating, exciting nature of Power.

He espied his welcoming committee. It was a sight he would always remember. Standing near the main doorway was a smiling, gay Ethel Kennedy (wife of Robert), accompanied by a small daughter dressed in an Uncle Sam suit so he could see them easily. Mrs. Kennedy asked if he would accept them as an escort in lieu of Bobby. He replied gravely that their companionship was not a hardship, but a boon. The three of them—the old man, the vital young woman, and the girl—left the airport together.

Years later, Lovett recalled with a trace of nostalgia the lunch that day at Bobby's house in McLean, Virginia: "I never saw a finer looking group of children in my life than the platoon of young

Kennedys which surrounded the porch on which we gathered."

David Ormsby-Gore arrived at the White House for luncheon.
He and the President discussed the missiles. Kennedy, after listing
a few of the alternatives, asked the British ambassador what *he*
would do in the circumstances. Blockade, Ormsby-Gore replied.
The President smiled.

The two sat for a while on the Truman balcony. When Kennedy
left for his meeting, the ambassador went to his office and
contacted Macmillan, telling him of the latest developments.

John Kennedy rather liked Macmillan. Dave Powers, when
asked to account for it, once said, "Maybe it's because they both
speak English." Later that evening, when Kennedy's own message
finally arrived in London, it emphasized the importance of the two
governments' working cooperatively. "I found it," Kennedy's
message said, "absolutely essential, in the interest of security and
speed, to make my first decision on my own responsibility, but
from now on I expect that we can and should be in closest touch."
He mentioned "the dangers we will now have to face together."

At 2:30 that afternoon the President convened an ExCom
meeting in the Oval Room. Models of frigates rested on the
fireplace mantel. Pictures of seaships lined the walls. The nautical
scene seemed appropriate.

Dean Rusk reviewed what the State Department had been
doing: writing personal letters to forty-three separate heads of
government; putting together two resolutions, one for the OAS,
another for the UN; drafting a Quarantine Proclamation; and
outlining instructions for all American embassies around the world.

Kennedy then asked Admiral Anderson to describe what
progress the Navy had made in blockade planning. The chief of
naval operations told them what he and his colleagues had agreed
on the night before. Kennedy, the ex-Navy man, quizzed Anderson quite closely on the specific procedures American ships would
use in the quarantine. How, for instance, would they stop an
oncoming vessel?

First, Anderson replied, they would use international signals to
tell the foreign ship to halt. If that did not work, they would fire a

shot across the other ship's bow. If the foreign vessel still sailed on, the American ship would shoot its rudder, crippling it. The foreign ship would not sink but would have to stop.

"You're certain that can be done?" Kennedy asked Anderson, a dubious smile on his lips. "Yes, sir!" the Admiral crisply replied.

Anderson was a highly intelligent, handsome man. He stood 6 feet 2 inches and weighed just under 190 pounds. His skin was tanned from years at sea; his eyes crinkled deeply at the corners from peering into the sun. He had been a crackerjack naval aviator. It had long seemed almost inevitable that he would eventually lead the Navy. Yet, his detractors considered him a little weak and not totally honest. They found him a touch hypocritical. A deeply religious Catholic, trained in Jesuit schools, he gave out frequent directives about the necessity of avoiding obscenities. Yet he was known in the service for his fund of extremely dirty stories.

Anderson later remembered a comment Kennedy made to him just as the meeting broke up and they were leaving the room. "Well, Admiral, it looks as though this is up to the Navy."

"Mr. President, the Navy will not let you down."

That evening a new, somewhat insipid play, *Mr. President*, opened on Broadway. It was about a decent and noble chief executive, filled with patriotism and hatred for Communists. This particular "Mr. President" showed the Kremlin who was boss.

11 A Television Event

A nondescript French car picked up Dean Acheson, took him to a spot near the Elysée Palace, and deposited him across the street, so as not to attract attention. Acheson slipped unobserved through a doorway, went down some stairs, then moved by winding passages toward the palace. It all reminded him of something out of Dumas. He turned to Sherman Kent, the CIA man just behind him, and said, "Porthos, is your rapier loose in its scabbard? I think some of the cardinal's men may be lurking here."

A few minutes later he entered De Gaulle's office. The general rose from his desk and waited while the American crossed the room. As they shook hands, De Gaulle said gravely in French, "Your President has done me great honor by sending so distinguished an emissary." Acheson, unable to find a reply, simply bowed. The general motioned the American into a chair and returned to his desk. He sat, folded his hands, looked right at the ex-secretary, and said "Je vous écoute" ("I am listening").

Acheson handed him a letter from Kennedy along with the main part of the speech to be given in Washington a few hours later.

The French president read through them, then looked up. "In order to get our roles clear," he said, "do I understand that you have come from the President to inform me of some decision taken by your president—or have you come to consult me about a decision he should take?"

"We must be very clear about this," Acheson responded. "I have come to inform you of a decision which he has taken." Acheson added that the United States would not take any belligerent steps, unless the Russians tried to rush the blockade.

"That is a wise step." De Gaulle said.

Acheson asked the French president whether he wanted to see the photographs.

De Gaulle waved his hand. "Not now." he said, "these will only be evidence. A great nation like yours does not act if there were any doubt about the evidence, and, therefore, I accept what you tell me as a fact without any proof of any sort needed. Later on it would be interesting to see these, and I will see them, but let's get the significance of the situation before we look at the details of it. Do you think the Russians will attempt to force this blockade?"

"No, I do not."

"Do you think they would have reacted if your President had taken even sharper action?"

"No, I do not think they would have done that."

"I don't either," the old general said.

They both agreed that the Russians might, but probably would not, retaliate in either Berlin or Turkey. Then De Gaulle asked, "Suppose they don't do anything. Suppose they don't try to break the blockade. Suppose they don't take the missiles out. What will your President do then?"

No one in Washington had prepared Acheson to answer this question, but he said something about how the United States would tighten the blockade and "bring Cuba to a standstill."

"That's very good," the French president nodded.

Acheson continued. "If we have to go further, why, of course, we'll go further."

"I understand," De Gaulle said.

The general now asked to look at the photographs. His eyesight was weak, and he peered at the gray dots with a magnifying glass.

"C'est formidable! C'est formidable!" he said. "From what height were these taken?"

"65,000 feet," Acheson replied.

"We don't have anything"—he caught himself, not wanting to admit France trailed in any area of human endeavor. "Well, I'm not very familiar with photography but this seems quite remarkable to me." He looked very closely at the pictures.

The proud old Frenchman turned to Acheson. "You may tell your President that France will support him in every way in this crisis."

London

Harold Macmillan liked President Kennedy and felt sympathy for his problem. Maybe because of this, or because they were both leaders of countries with imperial histories, his first reaction, as he later admitted, was to tell the American President, "to seize Cuba and have done with it." Great powers like Britain and the United States, he believed, should not have to suffer in silence the petty mewlings of the Castros and Nassers of the world. But he thought better of this advice and assumed a more temperate tone.

He considered the Cuban situation quite serious but he did not agree with Kennedy that Britain should mobilize her military forces. For one thing, such a move would be unpopular with his countrymen. Englishmen had lived for years within range of Soviet missiles. They had become used to them, and might find it rather amusing to see Americans so flustered at the prospect. They would not, moreover, be pleased that Washington would threaten world peace over a situation which the British had come to accept as a fact of life.

Macmillan also recalled the origins of World War I. When the Russians had begun to mobilize in 1914, the Germans had decided they had better do so too. This in turn had frightened the French . . . and so on. These 1914 preparations for war had actually helped lead to it. Mobilization now, Macmillan thought, might *cause* the Soviets to react and therefore bring about the thing they all wished to avoid.

David Ormsby-Gore agreed with Macmillan. Although a close

friend of John Kennedy's, he secretly telegramed London that, personally, he could "not believe that the missiles so far landed contributed any significant military threat to the United States."

Macmillan's real concern was Berlin. He wanted Kennedy to stand firm there, not to trade it—or any other position—for Cuba. Europe was important; Cuba was not.

Ottawa

Livingston Merchant met with Prime Minister Diefenbaker late in the afternoon. He officially told the Canadian leader about the Cuban missiles and what the United States intended to do about them. He showed Diefenbaker the photographs. The prime minister listened quietly, not particularly impressed. That evening, when told that NORAD wanted the Canadian Air Force placed on Defcon 3, he adamantly refused. His cabinet, he said, would meet the next morning; he would ask them. His minister of defense pleaded unsuccessfully with him to change his mind. (The next morning Diefenbaker was still opposed. On general principles he did not like going along automatically with the United States. Also, like Macmillan, he feared that rash mobilization might precipitate some Soviet reaction. Eventually, on October 24, Canada's minister of defense did finally persuade him.)

The United States was not exactly alone in this crisis, but not a single major allied leader was willing to go to the brink over Cuba.

Washington

All morning President Kennedy met with various officials and tied loose ends together, checking over the speech, talking about Berlin.

As one meeting broke up, he looked out the window and saw his daughter Caroline. Each weekday she and several other children had nursery school at the White House. At this moment the children were playing on the south lawn under the watchful eye of their teacher, Alice Grimes. Kennedy watched the scene a moment, then on impulse opened the doors, stepped out on the portico, and clapped his hands to get his daughter's attention. She failed to rush to him as she usually did; she seemed engrossed in play. The President returned to the Cabinet Room and sat down to another meeting.

A few minutes later Caroline flung open the door. "Daddy," she said anxiously, "I would have come sooner, but Miss Grimes would not let me go."

The President looked at her. "That's all right, Caroline," he said softly.

The little girl, satisfied and happy, whirled around and left. The men in the Cabinet Room turned back to their discussions.

At precisely noon Pierre Salinger made a phone call to the person representing all three news agencies. The President, he said, would like to have network time at 7 o'clock that evening to speak on a matter of "the highest national urgency." It was the first time Salinger had ever used that description. The network man said he would call back shortly.

While Salinger awaited a response, he gave White House reporters a news briefing. He mentioned the request he had just made.

"Do you think they will give it to you?" one reporter asked dryly.

"I have a feeling they will," Salinger responded.

The newsmen left and called their headquarters. The report about the President's coming speech made the 12:30 news on many radio stations. By early afternoon crowds began to gather at the White House fence. Some carried signs of one sort or another; others just stood silently, peering in through the high spikes. They did not know what Kennedy might say, but they appeared to feel a sense of foreboding, of crisis.

Kennedy phoned his predecessors—Truman, Hoover, and Eisenhower—about his decision. He also called several prominent individuals like George Meany of the AFL-CIO whose help he might need if the situation took a sudden turn for the worse. Politicians began phoning the White House. One congressman asked Sorensen, "Is it serious?" "Yes," Sorensen replied. The President's brother, Ted, campaigning in Massachusetts for the Senate, also called. "Should I give my campaign dinner speech on Cuba?" he asked. "No," Sorensen answered.

At 3 o'clock the full National Security Council convened to review everything one last time before "P" hour, the designation for the moment Kennedy's speech would begin.

A few minutes after 4, the President had a meeting—scheduled long beforehand—with Milton Obote, the handsome young prime minister of Uganda. Kennedy, at first impatient at this interruption, gradually grew involved in his conversation with Obote, as the two discussed Uganda's education system and its economy. This strange interlude, sandwiched between grim decisions, a break in the tension, must have been rather pleasant for the President. Kennedy was gracious and charming to his guest, and when the meeting ended after forty-two minutes, he seemed quite relaxed. He walked Obote out onto the driveway of the West Wing and warmly said goodbye. (Later the Ugandan would marvel at the President's coolness.)

As his guest's Cadillac pulled away, the President spun around to reenter the White House. Nearby reporters, who had been gathering all day, hungered for any tidbit. Kennedy smiled aloofly at them and started to pass through. One newsman blurted out: How are things going, Mr. President?

"It's been an interesting day," Kennedy calmly replied, and walked inside. (One senses he accompanied Obote outside in order to show the press his self-control.)

The President then held a brief formal Cabinet meeting, simply informing them what was about to occur.

At 5:30 he met with seventeen congressional leaders. Things had been going smoothly all day; the harmony now ended.

Starting Sunday, Pierre Salinger and Lawrence O'Brien had contacted certain prominent politicians, asking them to come to a meeting at the White House. Congress was not in session and most were out campaigning or on vacation.

Mike Mansfield was in Florida resting. Larry O'Brien tracked him down. "I'm at a place that I can't get away from," the senator said. O'Brien promised to arrange transportation. The following day Mansfield flew by helicopter to the air base in Tampa where he met Senator George Smathers of Florida. The two politicians were sped to Washington by Air Force jet.

The Air Force also brought Congressman John McCormack back from Boston and House Republican leader Charles Halleck from a pheasant-hunting trip in South Dakota.

Elections were only two weeks away and some politicians were reluctant to return unless the matter were urgent. If it were, however, they could always tell voters later that the President had rushed them to the White House to give him advice. Senate minority whip Thomas Kuchel was in San Diego when he received the White House call. At first he was not at all pleased with the prospect of cutting into his campaign, but he finally relented. (As it turned out, he probably benefited politically from a picture of him, taken a few minutes later, climbing melodramatically into an Air Force jet.)

Senator J. William Fulbright had been campaigning in Arkansas for several months. The White House sent the newest presidential plane, so new that Kennedy himself had not yet flown in it. It also stopped in Atlanta to pick up Senator Richard Russell and Carl Vinson, chairman of the House Armed Services Committee. As the plane whizzed them north, the three politicians debated why the White House had called. They speculated that maybe it was Cuba.

House Democratic whip Hale Boggs turned out to be the hardest to contact. He was fishing 30 miles out in the Gulf when a plane circled overhead and dropped a plastic bottle near him. Inside was a message:

Call Operator 18, Washington. Urgent message from the President.

Lawrence O'Brien

Boggs pulled his boat over to a nearby oil rig. He put on a life jacket and inched carefully up a 150-foot ladder. At the top was a waiting helicopter which rushed him to a nearby air base. There they jammed him into a tight flight suit, strapped him into a two-seater plane, took away a sandwich he was still holding, and jetted him to Washington.

Kennedy's meeting with the politicians started pleasantly enough. He opened it by grinning at Everett Dirksen of Illinois. "Well, tonight you're going to get reelected."

Dirksen laughed. "That was a nice speech you gave for Sid Yates in Chicago. Too bad you caught that cold making it." The group chuckled.

The President then went over what they had learned. Robert McNamara, who had stayed behind after the Cabinet meeting, told the politicians about the missiles.

Richard Russell was unsatisfied with Kennedy's plan. He felt it was a half-hearted measure, unlikely to accomplish anything. The thing to do, he said somewhat tartly, was invade Cuba and get rid of Castro as well as the missiles.

Much to Kennedy's surprise, Fulbright, prestigious chairman of the Senate Foreign Relations Committee, backed his Georgia colleague. Fulbright had been the only prominent Democrat to oppose the Bay of Pigs affair a year earlier. At that time he had said: "The Castro regime is a thorn in the flesh; but it is not a dagger in the heart."

(Fulbright's apparent about-face was not a total reversal. Castro's Cuba, he believed, was now threatening the United States. This threat should be removed. Fulbright also considered a blockade *more* dangerous than an invasion. The blockade might put the United States into the position of having to fire on Russian ships. Invading Cuba seemed less provocative because that way American troops might only have to face Cubans while the Russians could stand aside.)

Fulbright's logic had some merit and so did Senator Russell's, but Kennedy did not want to hear any opposition. As with his Cabinet and De Gaulle, he wanted to "inform" the politicians, not "consult" them. He had not had to face any opposition on this decision all week. Now, here were Dick Russell and Bill Fulbright, who should have been his allies, opposing him. Everything was set. He was going to announce the quarantine within a few minutes. Their opposition was a rude shock and he did not like it.

"Last Tuesday," he said, trying to keep his temper under control, "I was for an air strike or an invasion myself, but after four more days of deliberations, we decided that was not the wisest first move, and you would be, too, if you had more time to think about it." (McNamara added that the military still needed ten more days before it would be ready to invade. It is interesting that no one mentioned bombing; apparently its attractiveness was rapidly disappearing.)

Dirksen, the Senate minority leader, said he would go along with the administration. Congressman Halleck, House Republican leader, concurred, but added that he wanted it on the record that Kennedy had merely *told* them what he was going to do; he had not asked them. (After they left, Kennedy blurted out, "Oh, sure, we support you, Mister President. But it's your decision, not ours, and if it goes wrong, we'll knock your block off.")

As the session broke up, Senator Hubert Humphrey asked to borrow a phone. He called his wife Muriel. "I'll have to stay on a few days," he told her. "Have I got any clean shirts and socks here?"

Kennedy, gamely trying to end the meeting on a light note, said, "Hubert, if I'd known the job was going to be this tough, I would never have beat you in West Virginia."

"Mr. President," Humphrey replied, "it was *because* I knew it was this tough that I *let* you beat me."

Deep down, Kennedy was angry. As he left the room, rushing to change before his TV appearance, he uncharacteristically muttered to Sorensen who strode along next to him, "If they want this job, they can have it—it's no great joy to me."

Donald Wilson, assistant chief of USIA, was acting as its head while Edward R. Murrow convalesced from major surgery. Wilson was responsible for making sure Kennedy's speech had a wide international audience—especially in Cuba. Monday morning Wilson had contacted Newton Minow, head of the FCC, tracking him down in New York where Minow had gone to give a speech. The FCC chairman, Wilson said, should fly back right away. "I couldn't tell him on the phone what it was," Wilson later recalled, "but it was more important than anything." (One feels an electric current running through Washington at this moment. The administration was playing an exciting game for high stakes. It was a never-to-be-forgotten thrill to be able to call someone and say that, although you could not specify what you wanted, *it was more important than anything*. What you were doing was Important. Almost without exception, the main participants nostalgically recall when the cots were moved into their offices. These beds almost became status symbols, dividing those who counted from those who did not.)

When Minow flew back, Wilson explained what he wanted. He had chosen nine specific radio stations, many of them in Florida, and wished to get them ready to link up with the White House without their owners being aware of it until the last moment. Would this be all right with the FCC? Minow checked and decided it was legal.

By that evening the White House telephone operators had everything arranged, all nine calls stacked up. At 6 Pierre Salinger picked up his phone and began. He had a written statement he read aloud to each owner, one after the other. The situation, he said, was a matter of "national emergency." Would the owner agree to having the government use his station? Wilson sat across the room from Salinger, holding another phone. As each owner said, yes, Wilson whispered this response into his receiver and that particular station was instantly hooked up.

Across town at the State Department forty-six representatives of America's official allies (NATO, SEATO, and CENTO) received a background briefing by George Ball. As the meeting ended, some stayed to watch the President's address on a nearby television. Just before 7, a savings and loan commercial came on the air. An announcer intoned, "How much security does your family have?" The ambassadors roared.

Meanwhile Dean Rusk was confronting Soviet Ambassador Dobrynin. (That afternoon there had been a slight panic in Washington when the administration received news Gromyko would make an "important announcement" at 3:30. Was the Kremlin about to jump the gun? Did the Russians know what was going on in Washington, and were they intending to get their own announcement in first? It turned out that Gromyko, about to leave New York to return to Russia, merely wanted to make a farewell speech.)

When Dobrynin arrived at the State Department, vigilant newsmen watched his face. The Russian smiled pleasantly at them and went in. Rusk immediately got to the point. He handed the ambassador a copy of the speech Kennedy was about to make, and also a sober personal message from Kennedy for Khrushchev which included the following ominous statement: "I wish to point out that the action we are taking is the minimum necessary to remove the threat. . . . The fact of this minimum response should not be taken as a basis, however, for any misjudgment on your part."

When Dobrynin left Rusk's office, the usually amiable ambassador tried to smile at reporters but could not. His face was gray and his shoulders sagged. What happened? reporters wanted to know. "You can judge for yourself soon enough," he answered grimly. Did he receive a document? they asked. He merely held up a manila envelope for them to see, and walked away.

Moscow

At the very moment Dobrynin was entering Rusk's office, Foy Kohler was handing the same two messages to Nikita Khruschev.

Berlin

East German guards at highway checkpoints between Berlin and West Germany began intensive scrutiny of papers and automobile trunks. Civilian traffic along the highway slowed almost to a crawl.

Havana. 5:40 P.M.

Fidel Castro ordered an alert. For days now, his government had sensed something was going on.

"When we saw certain movements in Washington," he later recalled, "the convocation, the special meetings, certain measures, we understood by instinct, by smell, that something would happen." The Cuban newspaper *Revolución* that very morning had featured a map on the front page, showing where American planes were gathering in the Florida keys.

Vietnam

A battle was taking place in the Plain of Reeds near the Cambodian border. South Vietnamese spokesmen said their forces had killed eighty guerrillas and had captured twenty-nine others. The situation, they said, was under control.

Washington

While Kennedy was changing clothes, network technicians took over in his office. They placed canvas on the floor to protect the rug. They removed furniture to make more room for their equipment: three television cameras, various microphones, and a set of heavy lights. Against one wall, they placed chairs for a small group of reporters chosen to observe the speech. They cleared the President's desk and spread brown felt over it to reduce the glare. The only item remaining on it was an eight-inch lectern, also covered with brown felt. They put a large screen behind the desk to block off the French doors and highlight the President's face. Finally, they put two pillows on Kennedy's black leather chair to make him appear taller. TV cables and electric lines littered the floor.

Technicians were still bustling about, checking the angles and voice levels, when John Kennedy returned. He sat behind his desk while they adjusted the lights and focused the cameras. With only a few minutes to go he retreated to the Cabinet Room to read through the speech a last time. At 6:59 he reentered and sat down. Evelyn Lincoln came toward him with a hairbrush, but he motioned her away. He turned toward the cameras.

Here was a near-perfect television event. In many ways this moment had been contrived. All the secrecy of the past week had been aimed at this point. Preparations had been made; a great nation's vast military machine had begun moving into place. Then the public had been notified that the President was about to reveal a Dramatic Secret. Attendance at New York theaters dropped noticeably that evening, as people apparently stayed away to see what Kennedy would announce. Tens of millions turned toward their televisions. One can argue that the entire operation was a media event, that it would have been handled differently, perhaps less theatrically, had television not existed.

In London Harold Macmillan and in Paris the military heads of NATO turned on their radios.

Rolando Martinez was bringing his boat toward the beach where he had dropped off the eight commandos. He had come back every night looking for the two men who had not returned, hoping they might still be alive. This evening he had arrived at dusk. Suddenly his radio crackled. President Kennedy, an announcement said, was about to make an address.

Across America somber passersby stopped in front of stores featuring television sets in their windows.

In Brookfield, Connecticut the radio announcer, Donald Baron, heard the UPI machine in his station's outer office clang furiously.

"Ladies and gentlemen, the President of the United States."

"Good evening, my fellow citizens," Kennedy began. The United States, he said, had discovered "offensive missile sites" in Cuba even though the Russians had recently denied bringing such "offensive weapons" to the island. This Soviet action was "a deliberately provocative and unjustified change in the status quo." Therefore, he continued, his voice almost methodically dull, his government was taking a series of "initial" steps. It was calling for meetings of both the OAS and the UN. It was placing certain military units on alert. It was instituting a quarantine. He indicated quite clearly that if a missile were fired from Cuba toward "any nation in the Western Hemisphere" (the Latin American experts at State had suggested this nice wording), the United States would counterattack against the Soviet Union.

He warned Americans, "many months of sacrifice and self-discipline lie ahead . . . months in which both our will and our patience will be tested." But, with God's help, America would prevail.

At 7:17 he finished. The cameras clicked off. He sat for a moment behind his desk, his face sagging a bit from exhaustion or tension. Then he stood up, handed Mrs. Lincoln his copy of the speech, and left.

USS *Essex.* As soon as Kennedy finished speaking, an announcement about what he had said was made aboard the aircraft carrier. A huge cheer arose from within its bowels.

In Portland, Oregon an eleven-year-old girl left her living room, went to her bedside, and began to pray.

At Jacksonville, Florida the audience at a symphony concert spontaneously stood and started to sing the national anthem.

In a New York bar a man stared a long time at the TV, then said, "God bless you, Jack."

In the Little Havana section of Miami, excited Cubans stopped a police car to ask the officer if he had heard the news. The policeman later told a reporter, "They sure are happy." Cuban emigré leader Sanchez Arango went on Miami TV and said optimistically: "This is the beginning of the end for Castro. We are very happy. The President is a wonderful man."

At Madison Square Garden a crowd of 8,000 Conservative party members booed the President. The quarantine, they said, was "too little, too late." They demanded an immediate invasion of Cuba. Delegates shouted, "Fight! Fight!"

The security around the President became very tight. Motorcycle policemen constantly cruised the White House grounds.

The Benjamin Franklin Bridge near Philadelphia was closed to pedestrians because of fear of sabotage. For the same reason, New Jersey state policemen increased security at the Wanaque Reservoir.

Briefings began at the State Department. Ed Martin talked to OAS representatives. Dean Rusk went to State's International Conference Room where he reviewed the situation for the fifty-six representatives of the so-called "nonaligned nations," most of them from Africa or the Near East.

Robert McNamara talked to the press at the Pentagon. He told them what he could about the quarantine and the military alert. The United States, he said, was prepared to go to the brink on this one.

The next step was up to the Russians. Would they decide that *their* reputation for toughness required them to take a firm stand or to make some forceful move? Most high officials in Washington assumed so. John Kennedy himself rather expected the Russians to bomb America's Turkish bases or to blockade Berlin. If either happened, John Kennedy would take, as he had just promised, "whatever action is needed." The United States had drawn a line in the sand. The fate of civilization now lay in the hands of one man, an individual the CIA characterized as unstable—Nikita Khrushchev.

Dean Rusk mused about the modern world. "In the old days," he said, "you could have a confrontation or a showdown, you could go to sleep and you'd wake up in the morning, and you'd be there, and the city would be there."

Now, that was no longer true. The men in Washington went to bed that night wondering whether they would indeed "wake up in the morning."

PART THREE

It was very clear that the United States took
the chairman right to the brink of nuclear war and he
looked over the edge and had no stomach for it.

FOY KOHLER

12 A Spectrum of Reaction

Any impressionistic portrait of American opinion about this crisis would display a rainbow of colors and tones.

After they heard the news, three Marine deserters returned to their battalion, hoping to be sent to Cuba. On the other hand, Linus Pauling and his wife called Kennedy's speech "horrifying."

At the University of Miami a student leaped upon a chair in a dorm lounge. "Are we going to beat Russia?" he bellowed. "Hell, yes!" a crowd of students shouted back. At Rutgers University in New Jersey, an audience of 2,500 stood and cheered a performance by the Leningrad Philharmonic. And, although the Stanford University student newspaper wanted to "Invade Cuba," the Harvard Crimson accused Kennedy of a "frenzied rejection" of diplomacy.

At the University of Michigan a graduate student named Tom Hayden, president of an organization called SDS (Students for a Democratic Society), announced an anti-blockade rally. Pacifist groups like the Women's International League for Peace and Freedom joined Hayden's call. On the afternoon of October 24, several hundred demonstrators assembled on the Michigan campus, planning to walk to town where they would hold a silent vigil. An opposition group began to gather nearby. As the "peaceniks"

191

began their march, their opponents screamed curses at them and threw rocks and eggs.

At the campus of Indiana University fifteen demonstrators carrying anti-quarantine signs were confronted with about 2,000 foes. Fistfights began.

The pollster, Samuel Lubell, discovered that three out of five Americans believed that "some shooting" was inevitable. According to a Gallup poll taken October 23, one out of five Americans thought the quarantine would lead to World War III. Gallup also found that 84 percent (of those who knew about the situation) favored the blockade; only 4 percent opposed it. This latter figure is misleading. It would seem to indicate overwhelming support for the quarantine. In fact most people probably only felt relieved by the simple fact of action, by America's show of open opposition to Castro and to the Soviet Union. The Cold War had always been a heavy burden requiring infinite patience and self-control. Most Americans, without internalizing all the implications of Kennedy's speech, were buoyed by the possibility of releasing some of the frustrations they had pent up in recent years.

Many of those questioned by pollsters or reporters responded by saying, "We've been pushed around long enough"; or, "We had to draw the line somewhere." Those polled by Gallup frequently said, "It should have been done a lot sooner." In truth the major recurring complaint was: "It was long overdue."

Not many Americans openly feared nuclear war, but a number of them did become agitated during the crisis. A young father of three in Illinois mapped out a route to fresh water in Canada, piled blankets and food in his basement, and bought rifle shells to hold off his less foresighted neighbors.

In East Lincoln, Nebraska a malfunctioning air raid siren went off around midnight. Citizens scurried into their cellars.

Donald Baron, the radio announcer in Connecticut, refused to leave his station. He called his young bride and told her he did not know when he would be home. He figured the Russians would retaliate somewhere and it might mean war. It would be dawn soon in Moscow, he said; the Kremlin might try something at any moment. He told her not to worry and hung up. Baron wanted to know what was going on everywhere around the world; he hovered over the UPI wire service machine which was constantly typing out news bits. If war began, he wanted to be first on the air with it. Normally his radio station went off early in the evening, but he received permission from its owner to stay on and keep it open. Throughout the long night—and the next day—and the night after that, he played records and read spot announcements from the tearsheets. He felt no fear, merely a delicious sense of exhilaration, of being in at the beginning of something momentous.

But his eyes grew red and his fingers clumsy. His voice over the air lost its radio announcer's resonance and began to slur almost drunkenly. What at first had seemed exciting became drudgery and boredom. The UPI ticket kept repeating the same stories. He had only a few bright moments, like his announcement that major fighting had just broken out in the border area between India and China. Maybe this was the beginning, he vaguely hoped. He finally gave up after thirty-six hours on the air and went home to bed.

At the American embassy in Uruguay, the diplomatic community drooped into gloom. One official there was heard to mutter: "It's *On the Beach* time," referring to a recent movie about the nuclear destruction of mankind.

In Miami, only a few miles from the Cuban missiles, the mood remained rather calm. Hardly any tourists checked out of the hotels. In general Miamians acted only as though a minor hurricane were coming. A Miami judge, W. R. Culbreath, did panic, however; he took his two children out of school and fled with them a thousand miles inland to a small town in Missouri where he stayed with friends.

In Los Angeles, far out of range of any Cuban MRBMs, housewives stampeded supermarkets. One somewhat stout lady bought a large supply of food for her underground shelter, including among her purchases two cases of Metrecal. A North Hollywood grocer named Sam Goldstad said about the panic buyers: "They're nuts. One lady's working four shopping carts at once. Another lady bought twelve packages of detergents. What's she going to do, wash up after the bomb?"

The truth was, if it came to world war, not much could be done for most of the population. After a brief bomb shelter bubble a year earlier, interest in the subject of civil defense had declined. In December 1961 when the Department of Defense issued its pamphlet, "Fallout Protection—What to Know and Do About Nuclear Attack," few people asked for it.

In the spring of 1962, McNamara's department had announced a plan which would cost $6 billion to locate "shelter spaces" in metropolitan areas. The government would choose certain buildings—schools, for instance—designate them as shelter areas, and stock them with supplies. Kennedy had asked Congress for $700 million to begin this plan. But this program had finally gotten started only about October 1, three weeks earlier. The Pentagon was forced to announce that America only had enough shelter spaces for 112,000 people.

On Tuesday evening, during a Pentagon news briefing, when Robert McNamara mentioned the civil defense program, newsmen in the room roared with derision.

Early Tuesday morning American pilots at Cecil Field in Jacksonville, Florida climbed into their jets, revved their engines, and took off. Within minutes they were flying over water. The sky was overcast, the sea a little choppy. Whitecaps frothed a few feet beneath their wings. They were flying low and fast to avoid Cuban radar. Within minutes they were roaring over the island's beaches, flying directly toward the missile sites. They were speeding so fast, traveling almost 1,200 miles an hour, that by the time the Cubans were aware they were coming they were gone. The planes were actually over the island only four or five minutes. They were reconnaissance planes, taking close-ups of the installations. Some of the pictures they took showed men below racing fruitlessly toward their Czech anti-aircraft weapons. SAMs were useless against low-level flights, and the American jets went by so fast that anti-aircraft teams did not have enough time to aim their guns. The Cubans did, however, fire flak at them and several U.S. planes did return to base with small holes in their wings—but that was all.

The Russians on the island responded to these flights by attempting to camouflage their missiles. They stretched tarpaulins and nets over the rockets, and daubed paint or mud across the canvases. This was the first time they had tried to conceal their missiles from the air.

Cubans in general became convinced American Marines were about to storm the beaches. By late in the week they could see the hulking dark shapes of American landing craft just a few miles off their island, awaiting orders from Washington.

Havana telephone operators began greeting callers with a cheery "Patria o muerte!" The director of the CDR (the civilian watchdog committees) exhorted the nation:

> Down with Yankee imperialism!
> Long live the international proletariat!
> Long live the solidarity of Latin American peoples!
> Long live "Máximo Líder" Fidel Castro!
> Death to the invader!

And so on.

The population prepared for invasion. Isidro Rodriguez guarded his factory, not leaving it for three days. Blanca Rivero was given a gun (a Santo Domingan one she recalls) to protect her jewelry store. Lookouts mounted the beach pillboxes and watched the gathering American invasion armada. Many Cubans went to service stations and filled five-gallon cans with gasoline. Some of them wanted it in case fuel became short, but others swore that if the United States invaded they would personally douse their own homes and burn them to the ground. They would, they said, leave nothing but ashes for the Yanqui attackers.

Havana sprouted tanks in the streets and anti-aircraft guns in the public squares. Barbed wire and sandbags ringed the major buildings.

Teresa Mayans, like many young women, was a *miliciana*. On Tuesday she began standing guard at one of Havana's public buildings. She stood for many hours every day, her feet wide apart, a rifle in her hands, her small son hidden behind her skirt. She covered him and herself with olive oil which, she understood, would repel napalm. She expected another Hiroshima. Much of the time, as she stood guard she cried—not so much for herself but for her boy.

For two days, Carlos Alfonso sat in the entranceway of a government building. He held his rifle upright between his knees so that when he started to fall asleep his forehead hit the barrel and woke him up.

Another young Cuban, Gabriel Capole Pacheco, in his enthusiasm decided to volunteer for the militia. He suddenly found himself guarding an arsenal. His first night on duty he heard a noise. He became so afraid he wet his pants and hid behind a coconut palm. He took his machine gun, pointed it into the darkness, and pulled the trigger. He began to cry for his mother.

Tuesday evening it began to sprinkle in Havana. On Wednesday the temperature dropped and cold winds whipped across the island. A torrential rain began to fall, splashing against the faces of young boys in the militia guarding their island from American Marines with machetes in their belts.

On Tuesday evening Fidel gave a speech. For an hour and twenty minutes (brief by Castro's standards) he urged his nation to hold off the invader, to fight in the trenches. At first he seemed tired and perhaps a little uncertain. His TV studio audience, made up of government officials, many dressed in militia uniforms, appeared glum. But gradually Castro warmed up. He called Kennedy a pirate. He read passages from the presidential address and wiggled his brows and shook his head. By the end of his speech he had grown relaxed and was occasionally laughing. The officials at the studio now looked quite jovial.

The most striking thing about the Cuban reaction was its remarkable calmness. On the surface, at least, there seemed little hysteria. There occurred some minor panic buying of such Cuban staples as rum and cigarettes, but the government clamped down and hoarding ceased. Castro felt some concern about the possibility of internal uprisings and sabotage, and he had a few suspected dissidents arrested. But compared to the days of the Bay of Pigs, the Cuban nation remained amazingly quiet.

Washington. Tuesday morning, October 23, 1962

The day started well. Officials who had had a restless night, wondering what action the Kremlin might take, awoke to discover that, thus far at least, nothing had happened. Kennedy's speech had not triggered an immediate, violent reaction. Everything remained peaceful in Berlin and Turkey. Intelligence had learned that the Kremlin had canceled all Soviet military leaves and had begun holding hurried meetings with its allies, but the Russians had not yet mobilized their forces. Discussions between the two powers were still possible—and as long as the two sides kept talking there was hope.

Dean Rusk slipped into George Ball's office early in the morning and found him asleep on the couch. Rusk woke him up and grinned. "We have won a considerable victory," he said. "You and I are still alive." John Kennedy was also smiling as he arrived at his office. At the first White House meeting of the day, Robert Kennedy noticed "a certain spirit of lightness—not gaiety certainly, but a feeling of relaxation perhaps." The attorney general, later looking back at this morning, used about the same words that Rusk had. "We had taken the first step," he reminisced; "it wasn't so bad, and we were still alive."

During the course of the day, however, the pressure started to build again. The administration had only crossed the first hurdle. The Kremlin might still blockade Berlin at any moment. And, more ominously, the real test would come the next day when Soviet ships entered the quarantine zone. American intelligence had pinpointed every Soviet merchant ship crossing the Atlantic and Pacific, heading toward Cuba. They knew approximately where each was and how fast each was moving. Simple arithmetic indicated when the ships should arrive at the blockade line. A few of these Soviet ships probably carried missiles. Would they push on, forcing the Americans to fire? American planes had also detected a Russian submarine coming toward the line. Would it try to escort the merchant ships through?

American intelligence redoubled its efforts all around the world. What was happening at this border crossing or that airfield? The tiniest change might indicate war was about to begin. The United States had to be prepared to move fast. Simultaneously, one did not want to become too jumpy. America might overreact to some inconsequential action and initiate the very war it wanted to prevent.

The President had recently read Barbara Tuchman's book *The Guns of August*, covering the beginning of World War I, telling how European leaders stumbled into that war. Not a single major leader, according to Tuchman, had wanted that war, and yet it had begun. Bad communications, mistakes, stupidities on all sides had brought it on. John Kennedy talked about the book with his brother Bobby, Ted Sorensen, and Kenny O'Donnell. He recalled for them something the German chancellor had later said when asked how the war had started: "Ah, if we only knew."

O'Donnell remembered Kennedy saying, "I wish we could send a copy of that book to every Navy officer on every Navy ship right now," cynically adding, "but they probably wouldn't read it."

Robert Kennedy would later recall the four of them agreeing that the United States and the Soviet Union might totter into war over such abstractions as "security," "pride," and "face." The President, according to Bobby's recollections, was very sensitive to this possibility and wanted to avoid it. One wonders whether John Kennedy was perceptive and honest enough to see that in a way he himself was pushing the world closer to destruction because of "security, pride, and face."

The best news of the day for the White House was the OAS vote. The administration had hoped, not very optimistically, that it could win the necessary fourteen votes, two thirds of the OAS membership. During the all-day meeting one delegate or another would step out for a moment to receive instructions from his home government. The telephone line from Bolivia was so staticky that the Bolivian representative could not hear a word. He finally took personal responsibility and voted in favor of the main resolution. The Uruguayan government, made up of a seven-member junta, failed to convene fast enough to send instructions to its representative so he decided to abstain. At 4:45 the OAS took the crucial vote. Astonishingly, it was unanimous (with the temporary abstention of the Uruguayan delegate who later recorded his vote as 'aye'). Brazil, Mexico, and Bolivia refused to support a clause authorizing the use of armed force (presumably an invasion or bombing) to stop the missiles from becoming "an active threat," but all twenty governments agreed that the Soviet missiles were unacceptable and approved Kennedy's quarantine. If the Russians had counted on Latin American divisions, the Kremlin must have been shocked by the vote.

During the next few days anti-U.S. riots took place in six Latin countries. And in Venezuela saboteurs attacked American-owned oil companies, blowing up several transformer stations and some pipelines. The CIA believed these actions were carried out by local Communist groups to protest the blockade.)

At 7:06 Tuesday evening President Kennedy signed the quarantine proclamation—to go into effect the next morning at 10. By this time his cheerful mood from earlier in the day had disappeared. He was unsmiling, even grim, and wordlessly left the room as soon as he had signed his name. He was worried about the quarantine. Tomorrow American and Soviet forces would bump against each other at sea. Would they clash?

13 The Quarantine

Moscow. October 24, 1962

A cold rain glistened on the cobblestones of Red Square. Winter was approaching. Muscovites bundled up, pulled their collars high on their necks, and covered their heads.

During the morning a crowd gathered outside the American Embassy. Demonstrations in Russia were often engineered but this one seemed genuine. It consisted mainly of several hundred children about ten or twelve years old. They were enjoying themselves. They laughed and called back and forth. "Hands off Cuba! Hands off Cuba!" they chanted, wide grins on their faces. "If you touch Cuba," they yelled, "we'll knock your teeth in." They linked arms and sang, "Viva Cuba. Viva Cuba." A handful hurled ink bottles at the yellow walls of the embassy.

Russian adults angrily watched the demonstration. A round-faced grandmother grimaced. "These demonstrations are stupid," she said. "What are all these children doing?" Militiamen finally shoved the children away. "Go home," one soldier said, "and get your homework done." When asked their own opinion of the Cuban situation, the adults tended toward sadness. "I don't care what happens to me," one ballerina sighed. "I just don't want my little son to die." Another Muscovite, tears in her eyes, told an

American reporter, "Americans don't know what war is. If you had experienced war the way we did, you would not always threaten us with war." An elderly woman stated, "Your friend Kennedy is lucky he's not here. We'd tear him to pieces." (Later in the day a group of about 3,000 adult demonstrators gathered outside the embassy. They were more organized and more malicious than the children.)

What was the reaction of Russia's leadership to Kennedy's hard line? Kremlinologists watched the comings and goings of Soviet leaders, checking out who was with whom and if they seemed happy. The experts concluded that a small Kremlin group was making the decisions—just as ExCom was doing in Washington—and that harsh arguments had split the leadership. Most likely, they believed, the Kremlin (like the Kennedy administration) was divided between hawks and doves.

Khrushchev himself seemed to have lost prestige. A fascinating little item which may have signified much bobbed to the surface on October 25. The Presidium of the Ukrainian Supreme Soviet announced that the town of "Khrushchev" was now to be called "Kremges." This change seemed to connote that Khrushchev's reputation and power were declining. Perhaps the premier was even in danger of being ousted.

Tuesday night Khrushchev took some Rumanian leaders to *Boris Godunov*, being performed by an American troupe at the Bolshoi Theater. After the show he warmly congratulated basso Jerome Hines. First Deputy Premier Anastas Mikoyan, called back from vacation, was also at the post-show party. The wily first deputy was all smiles with the Americans. He even proposed a champagne toast to their beautiful women.

An American businessman named William Knox, the president of Westinghouse International, was in Moscow, invited there to give the Russians advice about international patent procedures. On Wednesday afternoon Khrushchev acted out an odd little drama. The Soviet leader asked Knox to visit with him. The sixty-one-year-old American came to Khrushchev's Kremlin office. He noticed it was a long, narrow room with plain wooden walls. Ruffled yellow curtains covered the windows. A large desk dominated one end. Not far away was a conference table surrounded by

chairs and covered with green baize. Khrushchev often did his
work at this table, with two telephones, one green and one yellow,
next to his elbow. An engraving of Lenin was on the wall at one end
of the room; one of Marx was across from it.

When Knox—a slim, balding, pipe-smoking gentleman—
arrived, Khrushchev got up from his desk and came across the
room to meet him. He escorted the American to the conference
table. He indicated that the interpreter should sit at one end; he
and the American would sit on either side, facing each other. Knox
later remarked about their conversation: "Khrushchev was calm,
friendly and frank—without any histrionics—although he did appear very tired."

The Russian premier stressed the importance of negotiations.
He noted that he had been "very pleased" with the progress of
talks several weeks earlier between Gromyko and Dean Rusk. He
said he thought President Kennedy might be taking a hard line
because of the coming elections. Eisenhower, he said, would have
taken a more mature, reasoned approach. (It is interesting to note
that privately Eisenhower also thought Kennedy might be posturing for political reasons.) "How can I deal," Khrushchev complained, "with a man who is younger than my son?"

The Russian leader's only real threat involved the blockade.
The United States, he warned, might stop one or two or even three
Soviet ships, but eventually he would lose patience. He would
order his submarines to sink an American ship, either at the
blockade line or somewhere else.

After three hours the interview ended. As he was leaving, Knox
pointed at the picture of the bearded man and said, "Who is that?"

"Why, that is Karl Marx."

"I didn't know Marx was a Cuban," Knox said lightly.
Khrushchev thought this was hilarious and burst out laughing.

It was UN Day in New York City. The actor Paul Newman gave
awards to winners of an essay contest on the United Nations. The
Leningrad Philharmonic played Tchaikovsky and Beethoven.

The Soviet UN representative, Valerian Zorin, met with a
number of African and Asian delegates. Many were frightened by
the Cuban situation and asked Zorin what the Russians would do.
"The Americans are thoroughly mistaken," he told them, "if they

think we shall fall into their trap. We shall undertake nothing in Berlin, for action against Berlin is just what the Americans would wish." The Soviet Union, he added, would do everything it could to preserve peace.

The Africans and Asians were angry at Kennedy. They thought he was pressing the world toward war. They talked to U Thant, acting secretary general, and pleaded with him to intervene.

Wednesday afternoon U Thant sent a message to both world leaders, asking the Soviets to suspend arms shipments to Cuba and the Americans to stop the blockade for two or three weeks. In the interim, he suggested, discussions could begin.

In London a naval attaché at the Soviet Embassy contacted his friend, an osteopath named Dr. Stephen Thomas Ward. The British government, said the Russian, was the only hope for world peace. It should call for a summit conference to meet in London. He suggested that Ward—something of a high-class pimp with important connections—contact people at the top. The Russian was probably speaking for his government.

Many Englishmen criticized Kennedy's stance. Of those who knew about Monday night's speech, 30 percent totally opposed the American position; many others only supported it grudgingly. The conservative *Daily Mail* of London said that: "President Kennedy may have been led more by popular emotion than by calm statesmanship." The *Daily Telegraph* considered the blockade "greatly mistimed." The *Guardian* suggested that "what is sauce for Cuba, is also sauce for Turkey." Thousands of angry demonstrators surged around the American Embassy in Grosvenor Square, chanting "Viva Fidel, Kennedy to hell." London police arrested 134 of them.

Bertrand Russell, the ninety-year-old philosopher, telegramed both sides, appealing for caution. Khrushchev replied first. "The question of war and peace," he said, "is so vital that we should consider a top-level meeting. . . . As long as rocket nuclear weapons are not put into play it is still possible to avert war."

Later in the week Kennedy responded to Russell's charge that America's "desperate action" threatened human survival. "I think," Kennedy's message sharply said, "your attention might be directed to the burglars rather than to those who have caught the burglars." The old philosopher disdainfully pointed out the flaw in Kennedy's logic. How could the Russians be "burglars" if the Cubans invited them? It was a point well taken. Kennedy's reply to Russell *had* implied a kind of American "right of domain" over the Western Hemisphere which Russia had entered like a "burglar." Kennedy's response had smacked of pomposity—or worse.

Russell remained shrill and angry. He dashed off a leaflet warning Englishmen they were about to die, "because rich Americans dislike the government Cubans prefer."

But much of British public opinion swung in favor of the United States when on Wednesday Kennedy reluctantly authorized the American Embassy to release photographs of the sites. The pictures had already been shown to reporters in Washington and foreign diplomats, but until now the administration had refused to allow their release.

Although the first photos were grainy and almost impossible to decipher, the reaction in England was immediate. English newspapers headlined them as absolute proof of Kennedy's claims. Maybe it was the sheer physical fact of the pictures. The American President might describe Cuban missiles, but presidents had been known to lie. Photographs, one suspected, told the truth.

Once they had been released in England, American reporters demanded from Pierre Salinger that the administration show them in the United States as well. Salinger agreed and convinced the President. Eventually the USIA would distribute them around the world.

The quarantine was not so much a single line, 500 miles from Cuba, as it was an interlacing web that stretched from the Soviet Union all the way to Havana. This network involved spies at the Bosporus and the Baltic Sea, and planes over the Mediterranean, out of Greenland, from the Azores, from Roosevelt Roads, from Florida, and even out of Guantanamo Bay in Cuba.

A vacation cruise ship, *Victoria*, sailing from Jamaica to Port Everglades, happened to pass Cuba several hours after Kennedy's speech. Although at 11 o'clock at night and pitch black, an American naval plane flew very low overhead, and panned it with searchlights from one end to the other.

A reporter, Gene Miller, from the Miami *Herald* decided to see the quarantine for himself. On Tuesday he chartered a twin-engine seaplane and flew out into the Florida straits. Thirty-five miles south of Key West he encountered an American destroyer, lined up at precisely 24 degrees latitude, chosen by the United States as the southernmost limit for sightseeing. As Miller's plane approached, the destroyer's fore and aft turrets revolved toward him and zeroed in. Miller turned his plane and flew east. Thirty-five miles away he came across another destroyer. The quarantine was set.

During the next several days blockading ships would follow suspicious vessels to find out where they might be going. The destroyer, *J. R. Perry*, began tailing two Russian fishing trawlers, one towing the other. *Perry* kept them in sight, taking pictures. The men aboard the American ship grew rather tense, however, as the trawlers sailed straight toward Cuba. The *Perry* was only six miles from Havana when it received orders to pull away.

The quarantine web was not perfect. Three Cuban refugees arrived in Miami on Wednesday, totally unaware of the blockade. They had slipped away from the island on small boats before Kennedy's announcement. They had been at sea ever since and had seen nothing.

The blockade line was not a wall. It marked off a sector. Ships inside the outer line when the blockade started were allowed to continue. Only those entering it after 10:00 A.M., October 24th were liable to being stopped. Task Force 136, commanded by Admiral Ward, guarded the five main channels. Ward put a cruiser at each tip of the arc and placed destroyers in between.

A few days later Task Force 137 appeared south of Puerto Rico, to cover that section. This fleet was comprised of seven ships—one from the United States, and two each from Venezuela, the Dominican Republic, and Argentina. This new force was mainly for show since American surveillance knew that nothing suspicious was coming by the southern route. But Task Force 137 was a public relations success. An international fleet, representing the OAS, signified a diplomatic coup for the United States.

The total number of quarantine ships—including the aircraft carriers—was sixty-three. If one also counted all the ships preparing for a Cuban invasion, the United States had 183 ships involved in the Cuban operation. Moreover, since American vessels had had to withdraw from their North Atlantic patrols, and since Canadian and British ships had filled in for them, the fleets of both these Anglo-Saxon countries were aiding America's cause.

Thirty thousand American military men—pilots and sea-men—were directly involved in locating incoming ships. Hundreds of thousands of others prepared an invasion. The Cuban crisis was assuming massive proportions.

Washington was concerned that the Soviets might try to bring missile supplies in by air. Intelligence knew that since the Russians owned no planes capable of flying heavy objects nonstop from the Soviet Union, any cargo planes would have to pause somewhere along the way—Scotland perhaps, or Newfoundland. The United States quickly persuaded Britain and Canada to prevent the Russians from bringing missile parts in by way of their airfields. This meant that the only satisfactory alternatives for Soviet planes would now be in Africa, most particularly the large airports in Morocco, Senegal, and Guinea.

On October 24, Moscow asked Guinea for permission to land long-range jets. Guinea refused. Its leftist president, Sekou Touré, told the American ambassador, William Attwood, that Guinea was nonaligned and would stay that way. Senegal and Morocco, perhaps under some pressure from France, also refused landing rights to Russian jets.

When Kennedy announced the quarantine, twenty-three Soviet ships were en route to Cuba. Most of them were far from the island, some as distant as the Baltic. Only nine were within 1,500 miles of the island. Of seven Soviet ships capable of carrying missiles, three were presently on their way to Cuba: the *Bolshevik Sukhanov*, due there in about ten days; the *Leninsky Komsomol*, already within the quarantine zone and carrying IL-28s on her decks; and the *Poltava*, which would arrive at the quarantine line within a matter of hours.

Washington. October 24, 1962

Tension hung over the White House. At 10:00 A.M. the quarantine would go into effect. What would the Soviets do? An intelligence report that morning said, "we think it probable" that the Kremlin would risk a confrontation at sea to put pressure on Washington to lift the quarantine. (On Tuesday evening a Russian general named Vladimir A. Dubovik announced at a Soviet Embassy party in Washington: "Our ships will sail through." Whether he had been ordered to say this to frighten the administration is unknown.)

Early Wednesday morning John Kennedy talked with his brother Robert. "It looks really mean, doesn't it?" He sighed. "But," he added, obviously trying to convince himself, "there really was no other choice."

"I just don't think there was any choice," the attorney general agreed, and pointed out, "if you hadn't acted, you would have been impeached."

John Kennedy apparently didn't say anything for a few seconds, then said, "That's what I think—I would have been impeached."

At ExCom's 10 o'clock meeting the tension was palpable. Two Soviet ships, the *Gagarin* and the *Komiles,* were within sight of the blockade line. "There wasn't one of us in that room," one man later recalled, "who wasn't pretty sure that in a few hours we'd have to sink one of those Russian ships." If that happened, Paul Nitze later said, "it seemed highly doubtful that Khrushchev would hold still without further action." One thing might lead to another very fast now; the situation could escalate into war within minutes.

The American government geared for the worst. The Damage Assessment Center pressed into full operation. In underground sites beneath Washington, men and computers awaited a nuclear attack. In case of war their duty was to analyze attacks on the Soviet Union, to see which targets had not been obliterated, and also to keep track of which American resources remained untouched and useful.

The President's naval aide, Tazewell Shepard, was placed in charge of the evacuation of key personnel. Certain individuals received pink identification cards, allowing them to be sped, along with John and Jacqueline Kennedy, to a secret location outside Washington. Those receiving such cards included members of the Cabinet, as well as administration staff people like O'Donnell, Salinger, and Evelyn Lincoln. One of the hardest moments for them came when they had to tell their wives (or in the case of Mrs. Lincoln, her husband) that they would be leaving them behind. Helen O'Donnell asked her husband, Kenneth, "While you're safe with the President under a rock somewhere, what am I supposed to do with your five children?"

At first, each spouse was handed a packet of information, telling her to make her way across the Potomac to a place outside Washington near Quantico, Virginia. This plan had obvious flaws. With a maximum warning of only eighteen minutes, few would be able to get out of the city, to say nothing of traveling all the way to Quantico—especially in the kinds of traffic jams one could expect. Also, the instant war began, civil defense regulations would place restrictions on civilian traffic. After having this problem pointed out to him Tazewell Shepard handed out a correction to the original packet. Everyone, he said, should assemble at a spot in northwest Washington relatively accessible to most families of staff members. They were not to bring any personal belongings (to save room) or food (which would be supplied). They would gather inside the fenced-in Reno Reservoir, and then make their way by motorcade to the hiding place in Virginia. One can imagine the nightmarish scene: wives of officials with small children in tow trying to make their way by car or foot to the reservoir. Washingtonians not lucky enough to have pink identification cards, seeing the others passing through the gate guarded by military police, would suspect what was going on, and would try to force their way in. A crowd of sobbing, shrieking people would probably gather at the fence. Some would try to hang onto incoming or outgoing cars. The rest is best left unimagined.

Neighbors of Dave Powers, knowing he would be one of those flown out of the city, stayed up late each night to see if he came home. When he turned off his lights and went to bed, they relaxed and could fall asleep.

The civil defense plan for federal employees grew complicated. Even middle-rank officials in the Department of Agriculture received special passes allowing them into the department's own shelter, stocked that week with water, survival wafers, and medical kits.

Individuals handled the tension in different ways. John Kennedy at first wanted his wife and family with him, then changed his mind and asked Jacqueline to leave town for the duration. She refused. He spent a lot of time with her, more than usual, and read to Caroline. His son John, still quite small, had a cold that week and a fever of 104 degrees. The President looked in on him frequently. Kennedy invited friends for dinner most nights and he swam almost daily with Dave Powers.

Some men played poker: Pierre Salinger, for instance, and Art Buchwald, David Brinkley, and the ABC reporter John Scali. They, and others who later joined them, became a kind of club. *Sports Illustrated* would dub them the "Cuban Missile Crisis Poker Club."

Llewellyn Thompson, usually a man of iron self-control and coolness, late that week told his wife Jane in a moment of nervousness, "I may not come home tomorrow."

A Russian press officer in New York said to an American, "This could well be our last conversation. New York will be blown up tomorrow by Soviet nuclear weapons." In Canada, even long after the crisis was over, officials kept packed suitcases in their offices.

One of the most moving recollections of the participants was that of Robert Kennedy. During ExCom's 10 o'clock Wednesday meeting, as the group awaited word from the quarantine line, a report came in that a Soviet submarine had just positioned itself between the *Gagarin* and the *Komiles*. The President's face turned gray and haggard. He put his hand over his mouth and opened and closed his fist spasmodically. The two Kennedy brothers looked at each other. "For a few fleeting seconds," Bobby would later recall, "it was almost as though no one else was there. . . . Inexplicably, I thought of when he was ill and almost died; when he lost his child; when we learned that our oldest brother had been killed; the personal times of strain and hurt. The voices droned on but I didn't seem to hear anything."

A professor of psychology at Yale has called the attorney general's reaction "momentary dissociation." It was, he says, "a typical anxiety reaction," similar to those felt by soldiers in combat and patients on their way to major surgery.

When Robert Kennedy's mind returned to the present, he became aware that the secretary of defense was describing how the Navy would handle a submarine. The aircraft carrier *Essex*, equipped with both Iconorama tracking gear and subchasing helicopters, would move up to the Soviet vessel. *Essex,* using her hull-mounted sonar, would signal the sub to come to the surface. If the Russian refused, one of the carrier's helicopters would drop a small explosive in the water near the sub which would be thus urged to come up. Those listening to this explanation understood the gravity of the implications. Although the Soviet submarine would remain relatively unharmed, the United States would have openly fired on a Russian military ship.

"Isn't there some way," the President said, "we can avoid having our first exchange with a Russian submarine? Couldn't we pick something else?" No, said McNamara, there was no way to ignore the submarine.

"We must expect," the President resignedly said, "that they will close down Berlin—make the final preparations for that."

Then, at 10:25, a messenger slipped into the room and handed a piece of paper to CIA Director McCone. He read it and turned to John Kennedy. "Mr. President, we have a preliminary report which seems to indicate some Russian ships are stopping."

The news could mean anything. ExCom waited for more information. At 10:32 a second note arrived. McCone read it and declared, "The report is accurate, Mr. President. Six ships previously on their way at the edge of the quarantine line have stopped or have turned back." (The Russian ships, scattered all over the world, had in fact halted the afternoon before, long before Kennedy's quarantine had officially gone into effect. American intelligence, with the entire Atlantic and Pacific to cover, had apparently not become aware of this until their dawn flights on Wednesday. It had then taken several hours to piece together the general pattern.)

Dean Rusk nudged Mac Bundy and said quietly, "We're eyeball to eyeball and I think the other fellow just blinked." This statement became the most famous line of the crisis. It seemed to sum up so much. Perhaps unintentionally. In a way Rusk was implying that the United States was in an almost childish staring contest with the Soviet Union, or at least in a competition over which was "tougher."

The real issue—Would the Kremlin remove its missiles?—was in no way decided. In a sense the great weakness of the quarantine had been revealed: It had had no effect on the activity going on at the Cuban sites. In fact, as the week progressed, construction actually accelerated. Soviet troops even began working in the dark under floodlights.

Arthur Schlesinger, Jr. has recalled that in 1960 Kennedy had praised the credo: "Keep strong, if possible. In any case, keep cool. . . . Never corner an opponent, and always assist him to save face. Put yourself in his shoes." That is precisely what the President now did. He imagined Khrushchev's discomfort, probably at this moment surrounded by angry hawks. He felt empathy for the Kremlin leader's predicament. To take the heat off the Russian, to give him time to think, Kennedy ordered the Navy not to intercept any Russian ships. At this moment, the *Essex* was probably almost on top of the submarine. He ordered it to hold back. "Send that order in the clear," not in code, he said. He wanted no mistakes.

Intelligence had not suspected that Russian subs were in American waters until October 17 when an American plane spotted a Soviet submarine-replenisher, the *Terek,* near the Azores. From then on they searched ever harder for Russian submarines. The Navy, anxious to test out its ASW (anti-submarine warfare) techniques and equipment, searched out any subs which might be in American waters. Once they found one, they stayed on its tail. Diesel-powered subs, the kind the Russians had, have to surface occasionally to recharge their batteries. Now, every time one came up, an American vessel would be nearby, asking if it needed any assistance. The American then would politely request that the Russian leave the area. Ultimately the Navy would root out at least six Russian submarines. American intelligence noted that these ships had long been at sea and badly needed repainting.

A question never answered was, What were the submarines doing there? They had obviously been under way for some time, long *before* Kennedy's quarantine speech. Had they been spying on the American coastline? Were they coming to Cuba, to a submarine base about to be erected there? (In the early seventies rumors spread that Soviet nuclear submarines were stationing themselves in Cuban waters. Each was capable of firing long-range nuclear warheads at the United States. Nixon's government did not like the situation, but did nothing concrete about it. Although this presumed nuclear danger was the same or worse than 1962, a decade had made a big difference.)

On Wednesday evening, Robert McNamara drove to the Pentagon to check on the quarantine. He knew that the President and the attorney general (both ex-Navy men) were concerned that the Navy might be overanxious and might press the Soviet ships too hard. McNamara and Gilpatric went to the Navy's command center, called Flag Plot. Inside this huge room dominated by maps and charts the secretary of defense confronted Admiral Anderson. Both men were tired and irritable. Neither much liked the other.

On one wall McNamara saw a projection of the Atlantic. He noticed an American ship marker off by itself. "What's it doing there?" he asked. Anderson whispered to McNamara that it was sitting directly over a Russian sub. (One wonders why he couldn't openly tell the secretary; it could hardly have been a secret to the others in the room.)

McNamara continued to bark questions. The admiral tried to reassure him. The Navy, Anderson said, knew how to run blockades. They had been doing it since the days of John Paul Jones. McNamara grew impatient; he would not be put off. "We must discuss it," he snapped. He began to ask increasingly sharp, detailed questions. McNamara liked to control events, and control comes from a total understanding of details.

Historically the government has generally stayed out of the Navy's way, and Anderson accused McNamara of "undue interference in naval matters." The secretary of defense did not give up. Were there Russian translators aboard each ship in the quarantine? "I don't know," Anderson said, "but I have faith in my officers." Find out, McNamara ordered.

The other thirty men in Flag Plot watched the byplay closely. Finally McNamara asked the admiral what a ship's captain would do if a Russian refused to describe his cargo. Anderson, by this time furious, picked up a *Manual of Naval Regulations* and waved it in McNamara's face. "It's all in here," he said (and in fact it is).

"I don't give a damn what John Paul Jones would have done,"

McNamara said, his red-rimmed eyes glaring at the admiral. "I want to know what you are going to do, now."

Anderson attempted once again to pacify him, but finally said, a touch patronizingly, "Now, Mr. Secretary, if you and your deputy will go back to your offices, the Navy will run the blockade." McNamara strode out; he had made his point. (He would also have the last word: A few months later, Admiral Anderson failed to be reappointed chief of naval operations. He would be sent off as ambassador to Portugal.)

Exactly what this scene meant is uncertain. Was McNamara concerned about the Navy in general, or, more specifically, about Admiral Anderson himself? McNamara's statement demanding to know what *Anderson* was going to do seems to indicate the latter. Kenneth O'Donnell later wrote that, "One prominent officer of Irish-American ancestry," rather obviously Anderson, had been heard to utter in the Plot Room earlier that day, a "loud four-letter obscenity" when it became obvious that the Russian ships had stopped. McNamara had not heard about this incident, but he was aware of Anderson's general attitude and was concerned.

The admiral's resentment at White House interference seems to have been somewhat isolated. Admirals Ward and Dennison both later said they had considered it was wise of President Kennedy to keep tabs on the quarantine.

Wednesday afternoon about 4 o'clock Henry Luce, owner of Time-Life, Inc., came to the White House at Kennedy's invitation. Luce observed that the President looked tired. During their conversation, lasting about half an hour, Kennedy asked the publisher several times whether he thought the United States should invade Cuba. (Obviously the President did not have total faith in the quarantine which was still in its first day and had already achieved a certain effect.)

Late that afternoon Kennedy chatted with the foreign minister of Portugal about Portugese problems, talked privately to Senator Fulbright, then brought the rest of the congressional leaders up to date in a forty-five-minute meeting.

At 6:30 Kennedy went to the Situation Room for news about the quarantine. The Navy had already warned him that just because some Soviet ships had stopped, it did not prove they would all retreat. They might be gathering together to form a convoy, to be escorted to Cuba by submarines.

At 8 o'clock the President went upstairs to dinner. Among his guests was Charles Bartlett, the reporter. Bartlett suggested that, since the Russian ships had apparently pulled back, perhaps the group should celebrate.

No, Kennedy said, not yet. Almost anything might still happen. "You don't want to celebrate in this game this early."

Later that evening, after Bartlett had left, a secret message arrived in Washington from Nikita Khrushchev. The quarantine, the Russian said, was unacceptable. "You are doing all this not only out of hatred for the Cuban people and its government, but also because of considerations of the election campaign in the United States." Khrushchev said that the Kremlin had instructed its ships not to retreat but to continue on.

Kennedy called Bartlett at home. "You'll be interested to know," he said, obviously under great strain, "I got a cable from our friend and he said those ships are coming through, they are coming through tomorrow."

ExCom. (*National Archives*)

Joint Chiefs of Staff: (*from left*) Earle G. Wheeler, Army; Curtis E.
LeMay, AF; Maxwell D. Taylor, Chairman; George W. Anderson, Jr.,
Navy; David M. Shoup, USMC. (*USAF*)

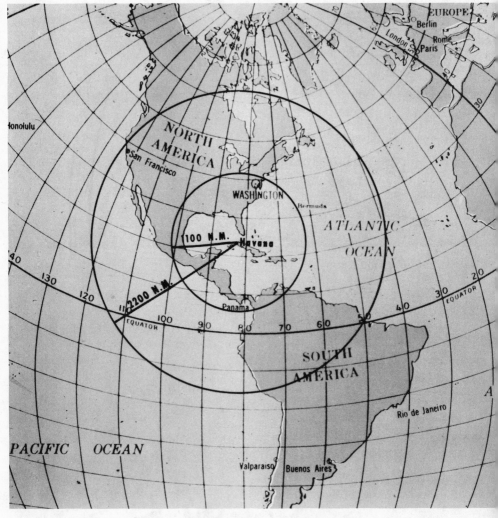

Range of missiles. (USAF)

John F. Kennedy and Milton Obote,
October 22, 1962. (*National Archives*)

Adlai Stevenson at UN.
(*National Archives*)

San Cristóbal, low level, October 23, 1962. (*USAF*)

Soviet ship, *Kasimov*, with IL-28s in crates; one crate is open.
December 15, 1962. (*U.S. Navy*)

Americans boarding the *Marucla*; USS *Joseph P. Kennedy, Jr.* in the rear. (*U.S. Navy*)

Marine on line at Guantanamo Base, 1962. (*USMC*)

Major Rudolf Anderson, Jr. (*USAF*)

A small gun emplacement
on a Cuban beach today:
the end of an era.

14 *The Ends of the Rope*

New York. Thursday, October 25, 1962

"Today," Adlai Stevenson told the Security Council, "we must address our attention to the realities of the situation." The Soviet Union, he said, had accused the United States of threatening the peace. "This is the first time, I confess, that I have ever heard it said that the crime is not the burglary but the discovery of the burglar." (This sentence is so similar to the note the White House sent Bertrand Russell that perhaps the same person wrote both.) If some people, Stevenson went on, were still unsure whether Cuban missiles did exist, "we shall gladly exhibit photographic evidence to the doubtful." The United States had had to do something about the missiles, for inaction "would have discredited our will."

Was the quarantine, Stevenson rhetorically asked, too strong a measure? He told a delightful story he attributed to Lincoln. A man, he said, was once confronted with a charging hog and stabbed it to death with a pitchfork. The owner of the animal was irate. Why, the owner wanted to know, had not the gentleman used the pitchfork's blunt end? And why, the man replied, had not the boar attacked him with *his* blunt end? Here was Stevenson, the Illinois lawyer and politician, at his best: quietly witty, sincere, the homey Lincoln story.

The representative from Cuba declared that America's position was a bluff. The United States, he said, had "no valid proof" of any nuclear threat against the Western Hemisphere.

Valerian Zorin, the Soviet delegate, sat in the presidential seat. (Each month the position of presiding officer revolved; this month was his turn.) The Russian looked grim, his underslung jaw tight as he replied to Stevenson's speech. Among the points he made was a comment that although Kennedy claimed to have evidence of the missiles, the President had failed to show any to Gromyko when the two talked. "Why?" Zorin asked—and answered, "Because no such facts exist. The government of the United States has no such facts in its hands except these falsified information of the United States Intelligence Agency which are being displayed for review in halls and which are sent to the press. Falsity is what the United States has in its hands—false evidence." The scene which then occurred may be the most famous incident in United Nations history.

Adlai Stevenson replied to Zorin. "Well, let me say something to you, Mr. Ambassador—we do have the evidence. We have it, and it is clear, and it is incontrovertible, and let me say something else—these weapons must be taken out of Cuba!"

Stevenson scornfully told Zorin that the Soviets had been lying about these offensive weapons for many weeks now. "Let me ask you one single question: Do you, Ambassador Zorin, deny that the U.S.S.R. has placed and is placing medium- and intermediate-range missiles and sites in Cuba? Yes or no? Don't wait for the translation. Yes or no?"

The Russian ambassador had been staring straight ahead, listening to the calm, antiseptic voice of the interpreter. He looked up at Stevenson, slightly startled and obviously annoyed.

"I am not in an American courtroom, sir," he replied, "and therefore I do not wish to answer a question that is put to me in the fashion in which a prosecutor puts questions. In due course, sir, you will have your reply."

Stevenson: "You are in the courtroom of world opinion right now and you can answer yes or no. You have denied that they exist, and I want to know whether or not I have understood you correctly."

Zorin: "Would you please continue your statement, sir? You will have your answer in due course."

Stevenson (melodramatically): "I am prepared to wait for my answer until hell freezes over, if that is your decision." (The watching audience of fascinated delegates and guests burst into good-natured laughter at this line. It was so marvelously theatrical. Even Zorin smiled slightly, a trifle uncertainly.) "I am also prepared to present the evidence in this room."

Zorin (acting as president of the Security Council): "I call on the representative of Chile."

The Chilean (delighted to join in the humiliation of one of the UN's most humorless bullies, did not let Zorin off the hook): "I did not expect the incident which has just occurred, Mr. President, but since it has occurred, I would prefer to yield the floor to you and ask for the floor again when you feel it is necessary or after you have been good enough to reply to the question put to you by the United States representative. Therefore, that being the case, I am quite willing to yield the floor to you." (more laughter)

Stevenson: "I have not finished my statement. I asked you a question, Mr. President, and I have had no reply to that question. I will now proceed, if I may, to finish my statement."

Zorin (his face flushed with anger, but apparently relieved): "By all means you may proceed."

Stevenson: "I doubt if anyone in this room, except possibly the representative of the Soviet Union, has any doubt about the facts. But in view of his statements . . . if you will indulge me for a moment, we will set up an easel here in the back of the room where I hope it will be visible to everyone."

Two aides came forward with an easel and about a dozen large photographs on posters. The aides placed them against the back wall, near a huge mural symbolizing individual freedom. People crowded around as the aides pointed at changes in the landscape near, for instance, San Cristóbal. Stevenson continued, his voice droning slightly like a professor covering some obscure point which he knew too well. Zorin glared stonily ahead, hardly turning to see the show behind him.

Had Stevenson, as some believe, set Zorin up? The presentation could hardly have been spontaneous. He had with him the easel, the aides, the pictures, and specific notes about them. Perhaps he meant to show them afterward in a side room, but had taken the obvious opening provided by the Russian. Or possibly he knew his antagonist so well that he figured Zorin (or the Cuban ambassador) would give him an opportunity.

Why did the Soviet ambassador bring up the subject? While the pictures were being shown he certainly looked foolish. He himself had said, before Stevenson began, that the photographs had been splashed across the newspapers all day, and even out in the UN corridors. Why did he say "no such facts existed"? Why did he leave himself open to Stevenson's ploy? The most reasonable explanation, until other evidence comes along, would seem to be that Zorin had put together his speech a day or two earlier—before the United States released the pictures—and that he was too bureaucratically cautious, too lazy, or too unimaginative to change it. (He would within weeks be withdrawn from New York.)

When Adlai Stevenson finally finished his talk, Zorin snidely questioned the authenticity of the pictures. The Soviet representative noted that at the time of the Bay of Pigs, Stevenson had also brought in photographs—and that those had been faked.

One wonders whether Stevenson winced; that previous occasion had been one of the most humiliating events in his life. But he had an immediate answer: "I wonder if the Soviet Union would ask its Cuban colleague to permit a United Nations team to go to these sites," and check them.

"And now I hope that we can get down to business, that we can stop this sparring. We know the facts and so do you, sir, and we are ready to talk about them. Our job here is not to score debating points. Our job, Mr. Zorin, is to save the peace. And if you are ready to try, we are."

Stevenson, toward the end of his life, admitted as he said, that he had "gone too far" that day in the UN. He had gotten carried away and played the television prosecutor with too much juice. He had used a diplomatic forum for a rather adolescent show. During the next several days, he received a great deal of congratulatory mail, but he felt a trifle ashamed of his performance. The following year when he met Khrushchev in Moscow, the Russian grumbled to him: "Stevenson, we don't like to be interrogated like a prisoner in the dock."

Why the charade? Why did Stevenson do something so out of character, so . . . ungentlemanly? Who was he hamming it up for? The UN?—where he may have been caught up in the contagious mood of jibing at the sour Zorin. The American electorate?—which had rejected him in 1952 and 1956. Or, most probably, the tough young men in Washington who obviously thought him soft? Perhaps he unconsciously wanted to show them how tough he could be. If so, it worked. Kennedy, watching the show on television, said: "I never knew Adlai had it in him. Too bad he didn't show some of this steam in the 1956 campaign."

The President was more impressed by Stevenson's performance than the ambassador himself. John Kennedy understood the importance of the confrontation with Zorin better than Stevenson. This whole crisis was a *public* test of wills. It was Good Theater in which the cast of characters and the audience intermixed. The man from Illinois had publicly indicated America's determination. As far as White House goals were concerned, Stevenson's theatrics fit in perfectly, much better than "proper" diplomatic behavior.

Ships continued to move toward the blockade line. ExCom debated how to treat them. American intelligence actually knew the cargoes most of them carried, especially now that sixteen of the twenty-three Soviet ships had turned around and were heading home. Since the quarantine was not only to prevent missiles from getting to Cuba, but to show the Soviet Union Washington's anger, ExCom felt it important to confirm the justice of its position.

During the quarantine's first two days, ExCom allowed a British ship on its way to Jamaica to pass through, then a Greek tanker, the *Sirius,* on its way to Cuba, and an East German passenger vessel, the *Voelkerfreundschaft* with almost 500 passengers aboard. An interesting incident occurred when a Swedish ship, the *Coolangaata,* carrying nothing but potatoes and other foodstuffs, entered the quarantine zone and ignored all signals from an American destroyer. The Swede pressed haughtily ahead. Although it was under charter to the Soviet Union and had picked up its cargo for Cuba at Leningrad, the United States decided to let it go through, too. Polish and Czech freighters were also approaching the line.

A Soviet tanker, the *Bucharest,* like other Russian ships, had stopped in the Atlantic on Tuesday. But on Wednesday it started up again. ExCom could plot its path and knew when it would arrive at the line. It would be the first *Russian* ship to do so, and some in ExCom firmly believed it should be stopped and boarded—as a sign of Washington's determination. Others said it would be wise to give Khrushchev more time. The President listened to both sides and decided to let the tanker pass. He saw the matter in terms of Khrushchev's problems within the Kremlin. Throughout this week he tended to do this, to personalize this issue around the Soviet leader. This sensitivity to the problems of the Russian politician was one of his chief contributions to the discussion. He did not think in terms of the "Soviet Union" or "the Kremlin"; he thought about what Khrushchev *the man* would do. When he decided to let the *Bucharest* push through, he thought about Khrushchev: "We don't want to push him to a precipitous action—give him time to consider. I don't want to put him in a corner from which he cannot escape."

Early Thursday morning the USS *Gearing* contacted the *Bucharest* by radio. What, the American asked, was it carrying? The question was crucial. The United States knew quite well that the tanker's cargo was oil. But would the Soviet ship respond? Would it give any sort of answer, or would it sail through the line like the Swedish vessel? When the *Bucharest* acknowledged the call and answered that it carried only petroleum, the White House had won another small victory. By replying to *Gearing's* query, the Soviet Union had indirectly recognized the existence, and in some ways the legality, of the quarantine.

Meanwhile in New York City a State Department representative was briefing politicians. Dean Rusk, with President Kennedy's permission, had set up five regional meetings around the United States. Congressmen and governors could go to any one of them and receive the latest information. The number of those attending these briefings varied between about 70 and 110. Some politicians used them as forums to reach voters back home just before the elections. At the New York City meeting, for example, Republicans made a number of partisan comments about the White House's Cuban policies. Finally some Democrats began to shout at them to sit down and be quiet. Afterward, as the politicians straggled out, Congressman James Van Zandt, a Republican from central Pennsylvania, hoping to be elected to the Senate and obviously wanting his name in the papers, stopped and talked to reporters. He told them of the *Bucharest* incident (about which he had just been informed). This was news: The first time a Soviet ship had come to the quarantine, the United States had allowed it to pass through without boarding. The White House seemed to be backing down somewhat. The reporters happily rushed off to call their offices.

ExCom was in the midst of discussions when someone came in and told them what Van Zandt had done. John Kennedy, who had once told his fiancee, Jacqueline, that his chief flaw was irritability, became furious. How dare Van Zandt release that information to the press?

The matter rapidly blew over. The Defense Department was scheduled to give out the *Bucharest* story in a few minutes anyway. Yet the President's reaction was typical of his desire to control every aspect of the situation, of his almost blind craving to keep the issue quiet. He is recorded as becoming angry on perhaps a dozen different occasions during the crisis. In most cases the cause was someone giving out unauthorized information.

ExCom's debates about the *Bucharest* did convince the President that eventually he would have to stop a ship coming into the zone. Since it might be dangerous to try to halt a Russian vessel or even an East European one, either of which might ignore the summons and force a confrontation, ExCom and the President finally agreed on what seemed the perfect solution: *Marucla*.

The *Marucla* was built in Baltimore during World War II as a Liberty ship christened the *Ben H. Miller*. After the war its history grew murky. By 1962 it was owned by a Panamanian company, chartered by a Russian organization, and it flew a Lebanese flag. Its crew consisted of thirty Greeks, aged sixteen to fifty-nine, and one Italian. On July 10, 1962, it had left Santos, Brazil with a cargo of cotton, heading for Ventspils, a Latvian port on the Baltic. It had taken on a load of Russian goods, added some more in Riga, and set sail for Cuba on October 3. Its cargo now consisted of sulfur, asbestos, electronic measuring instruments, lathes, emery powder, cardboard, truck parts, and twelve trucks. *Marucla* was a classic old freighter, the stuff of Joseph Conrad and Jack London. She was a lumbering sea whore with an international, mysterious aura. She was a perfect target for the quarantine. She was flying a neutral flag and tied to neither side. Stopping her could irritate no one of any importance.

A radar plane, circling the Atlantic looking for submarines, kept an eye on her. As she approached the line late in the afternoon of October 25, an American destroyer, USS *John R. Pierce*, began to follow her, waiting for further orders. Night had almost fallen by the time Washington reached the decision that *Marucla* would be the test case. Now, because of darkness, boarding her had to be put off until the next morning. At headquarters an admiral named Wallace Morris Beakley made a suggestion to Corky Ward. Task Force 136 included a destroyer, the *Joseph P. Kennedy, Jr.*, named after the President's brother killed during World War II. Admiral Beakley said it would be a nice touch to use this particular ship, if possible, to board the freighter. (The President later said dryly, "I suppose everybody will say that I sent the *Kennedy* in there deliberately to give our family some publicity.")

The *Kennedy* had also had an interesting history. The President's sister Jean had originally christened it. His brother Bobby had served aboard it in 1946 when, ironically, it was stationed in Cuba at Guantanamo Bay. Its crew had recently presented John Kennedy with a wooden model of the ship. (He had placed it in the Fish Room.) They also had given him a leather-bound folio of pictures of the ship and signatures of the crew. Its skipper, Commander Nicolas M. Mikhalevsky, had been born in Sevnica, Yugoslavia only four years after his Russian parents had fled St. Petersburg at the time of the revolution. In addition to English and Yugoslav, Mikhalevsky spoke both French and Russian fluently.

At 5:43, Thursday evening, Mikhalevsky received orders from Admiral Ward to proceed toward the *Marucla*. It was dark by the time *Kennedy* joined *Pierce*. As the two American warships steamed along just 2 miles behind the freighter, Mikhalevsky prepared the boarding party. He himself would, of course, not be leaving his own ship, so he reviewed with those who would board the freighter how a "visit-and-search" should be conducted. They should wear whites and carry no weapons. The leader of the boarding party would be *Kennedy's* executive officer, Lieutenant Commander Kenneth C. Reynolds. Accompanying him would be an interpreter (a naval ensign named Edward Mass); a French translator just in case (an enlisted man who would stay on *Marucla's* rusty deck with a radio communicator, describing everything back to *Kennedy*); and Lieutenant Commander D. G. Osborne, executive officer of the *Pierce*. Osborne had served several years in the Merchant Marine and knew from this experience a fair amount about merchant ships and their cargoes. The Russian translator, Ensign Mass, had a father in the construction business and might be able to determine the quality of any machinery found in the holds.

During the night the *Kennedy* radioed *Marucla* to prepare for boarding the next morning. The Greek skipper, Georgios Condorrigas, readily agreed. He told the Americans what cargo he was carrying and said if they wanted to examine it that would be fine with him.

At first light the flag man aboard the *Kennedy* hoisted the international signal: OSCAR NOVEMBER ("Stop"). Unexpectedly, *Marucla* continued. No doubt the Greeks could not see the flag in the darkness. Then *Kennedy* signaled with a flashing light: REQUEST YOU STOP. I INTEND TO BOARD YOU. REQUEST YOU ADVISE WHEN YOUR SEA LADDER IS READY. *Marucla* signaled she was prepared. As dawn broke over the Atlantic waters, the old freighter stopped dead. On her port side was the USS *Joseph P. Kennedy, Jr.*; on the starboard side lay the USS *Pierce*. (The three ships were lying to, several hundred miles due east of President Kennedy's vacation home in West Palm Beach, Florida.)

At 6:32 a whale boat set off from *Kennedy* and picked up Osborne. At 6:51 the boarding party climbed aboard the freighter. For the next two hours a little play took place aboard the "Lebanese" vessel. Several of the Greeks escorted Commander Reynolds and his party up to the ship's bridge where Condorrigas met them. The Greek spoke good English, was pleasant and cooperative, though not at all obsequious. He told them he had heard about the American quarantine. He offered them coffee while they poked through his papers. The ship's log was of no use to the boarding party since it was written in Greek. The Americans examined the ship's cargo manifest, its charter, its certificate of health, and so on.

The boarding party asked to see the cargo. Accompanied by Condorrigas, the Americans wandered around the ship. They examined some trucks lashed to the decks. Commander Reynolds asked that the Number 4 hold be opened. He picked that one because according to the manifest it contained "electro measuring instruments" and "truck parts." If the ship carried any contraband, it would likely be here. The Greeks moved deck cargo off the hatch covers and pulled them back. The Americans peered down into the hatch at a huge mound of boxes, Russian stenciling on their sides. Since there was no easy entrance to the hold, the Americans merely observed the pile from above and said O.K., the Greeks could close the hatch.

At 9 o'clock Reynolds radioed back to *Kennedy* that he recommended that the *Marucla* be allowed to proceed. He told the Greek captain that he regretted the delay and wished him good luck.

Washington. Friday, October 26, 1962

The *Marucla* incident was over. The United States had demonstrated its will. The quarantine plan had worked. Friday morning McCone told ExCom that all the Soviet dry cargo vessels were on their way home; they were not stopping to convoy or pick up submarine escorts. The only Russian ships continuing toward Cuba were tankers. If the *Bucharest* were any example, the Russians had decided not to force the blockade. Apparently there would be no conflict at sea. The military supply line to Cuba had been cut off.

McCone noted, however, that the Russians were still building the missile sites. More installations were being completed; the IL-28s were being assembled.

What, ExCom wondered, should they do now? Were they back exactly where they started? Dueling with Zorin at the UN and the

Marucla at sea had accomplished little if the missiles were allowed to remain.

By Friday morning the possibility of a Cuban invasion loomed as a very real and frightening possibility. At the beginning of the crisis, over a week before, everyone had agreed that an invasion should only be a last resort. It seemed now, however, to be approaching. On the Guantanamo Bay perimeter several thousand poncho-enshrouded Marines squatted numbly in trenches, drenched in torrents of rain. Ringing Cuba, another 25,000 Marines were almost set as a landing force. Over 100,000 Army troops in Florida were ready to follow. The carriers *Enterprise* and *Independence* had closed with the island. Cruiser captains had already received their orders about where to start firing.

McCone warned them it would not be easy. Castro would retreat into the hills and would have to be blasted out. As Kennedy himself said, it would mean "a very bloody fight." Kennedy asked for the names of every Cuban doctor in the Miami area, to send them immediately to Cuba to provide medical assistance when the attack began.

The 101st Airborne was to take Mariel Bay and head inland toward San Cristóbal. Che Guevara had stationed himself at Mariel with almost a division of Cuban soldiers, and near the missiles were Soviet troops. (American intelligence had estimated that the Russians only had 5,000 regular soldiers in Cuba. The numbers in fact were at least 20,000, perhaps as many as 40,000. They were well armed, possibly with nuclear field weapons.) A shooting confrontation between Americans and Russians would certainly become very difficult to stop. The weight of their deaths would press upon both leaderships. The two governments would probably find it politically impossible to extricate themselves. The Russians at the missile sites might even fire their MRBMs at the United States.

Kennedy gave preliminary approval to a leaflet to be dropped on Cuba. On one side it showed a low-level photograph of one of the San Cristóbal installations. On the other it carried a brief statement, in Spanish, blaming the Russians for putting Cuba into mortal danger.

As soon as Kennedy approved the design, a USIA press service director flew to Fort Bragg, North Carolina to begin production. The USIA man, Ray Mackland, apparently somewhat bureaucratically officious, was jumpy about this project. For one thing, it was secret. When he arrived at the Fort Bragg Psychological Warfare Section, he discovered that some of the plant's labor force, made up largely of unskilled Southern black civilians, lacked the proper security clearances. He insisted that only soldiers should prepare the leaflet. He hung around, making himself so obnoxious that the center's chief of staff finally excluded him from the pressroom.

The largest problem with the leaflet arose from the photograph, which was to use one whole side, all the way to the edge. The Army man pointed out to Mackland that this would require eight separate cutting operations of a guillotine paper cutter for each leaflet. And the USIA wanted five or six million of them. Mackland refused to allow any changes in the design since the President had already approved it. The operation therefore took days.

When the leaflets were finally ready, they were loaded into canisters and hooked beneath some fighter planes in Florida. If an invasion came, they would snow down all over the island, presumably weakening the Cuban will to resist.

The pace of events stepped up.

The Special Group (Augmented) met in Room 2B913 of the Pentagon. They discussed plans for toppling Castro's regime.

A professor named Zbigniew Brzezinski telegraphed his friend Arthur Schlesinger, Jr.: "Any further delay in bombing missile sites fails to exploit Soviet uncertainty."

A newsman asked Lincoln White, the State Department's press officer, what the United States might do if the quarantine did not work. White, following normal procedures, pointed out that the President had already answered that question in his quarantine speech on Monday night: "Should these offensive military preparations continue," the President had said, "further action will be justified." When Kennedy heard about White's response, he was angry. The Russians, Kennedy thought, might believe that he himself was indirectly threatening them. He called White and shouted at him. Kennedy's nerves were apparently growing raw. His period of tranquility was obviously over.

The State Department prepared a message for Castro to be sent via a complex conduit: from the American ambassador in Rio de Janeiro to the Brazilian government; from Rio to Brazilian ambassador Luis Batian Pinto in Havana. The State Department suggested that Batian should tell Castro that time was getting short for Cuba, that Russia was trying to trade the island for some American bases in Europe, and that Cuba was being used and betrayed. Ambassador Batian, according to the State Department message, should also say he was "confident that the OAS would not accept an invasion of Cuba once the missiles were removed and that the U.S. would not risk upsetting hemispheric solidarity." (This message, promising that the United States would not invade Cuba if the missiles were withdrawn, comes rather close to the guarantee that President Dorticós had asked for early in October.)

John Scali was ABC's diplomatic correspondent. His prominent nose and high-domed head had become well known to television viewers. As an experienced reporter, he maintained close relations with men in the State Department. He kept in frequent contact, for example, with the State Department's intelligence director, Roger Hilsman. Throughout the early part of the week he kept in constant contact with Hilsman—as well as a number of other officials.

In Washington Alexander S. Fomin was officially listed as a counselor at the Russian Embassy. Fomin, a blond man of medium height in his late forties, was known to insiders as a colonel in the KGB, probably the head of the Kremlin's American intelligence operation. Rumors also had it that he was a personal friend of Khrushchev's. In the fall of 1961 Fomin had asked John Scali to meet him at a restaurant called Duke Ziebert's. Their conversation there has gone unrecorded, but Scali later admitted having half a dozen such meetings with Fomin. (The newsman would claim that as a diplomatic correspondent he often met with foreign diplomats. Yet a newsman normally grooms "sources" by such meetings, and Scali could hardly assume that a KGB colonel would provide much information. One may speculate that the Russians were using this connection as a pipeline through which they could relay information to the United States. John Scali was a militant anti-Communist, but a reliable and somewhat unimaginative recorder of information. Because of these characteristics, and because of his contacts and his reputation for honesty, the Kremlin could use him to transmit messages accurately. He may not have done so before this crisis; they may have merely been setting him up.)

On Thursday afternoon Scali was at his reporter's desk at the State Department, eating a bologna sandwich. The phone rang; it was Fomin. Would Scali, the Russian asked, have lunch with him immediately? The newsman said he was busy, but Fomin urged him to come. "It's very important," he said. "Meet me at the Occidental in ten minutes."

The KGB agent was already there, sitting at a small table against the wall, when Scali arrived. The Russian arose, shook hands briefly, and sat down. He looked haggard. "The situation is very serious," he said. "Something must be done." Scali told him the Kremlin should have thought of that before it put the missiles in Cuba.

A waiter came by. There was an awkward moment as the two ordered while trying to appear normal. When the waiter left, Fomin leaned across the table and whispered, "Perhaps a way can be found to solve this crisis." The Cuban UN delegate, he said, may have suggested a solution. (Presumably Fomin was referring to President Dorticós' speech of several weeks earlier.) If the United States pledged not to invade Cuba, the Russians would dismantle the bases and promise never again to introduce such "offensive" weapons to Cuba. The UN could even inspect the sites. "Would you," he said, "check with your high State Department sources?" "It is very important," he said again. He gave Scali two telephone numbers, one at the Soviet Embassy, the other at his home. Call me, he pleaded, at any time.

It was about 4 o'clock by the time Scali got back to State. He typed up a five-paragraph memorandum of the conversation, exactly as he recalled it, rushed it into Hilsman's office, and gave it to the intelligence chief. He briefly reviewed what had happened and left to prepare his segment of that evening's ABC broadcast. It must have been difficult for him two hours later on the air not to mention that incident.

Meanwhile, Foy Kohler, at the American Embassy in Moscow, had just contacted Washington, saying that he would be sending along, starting about 6 o'clock, an extremely long message from Khrushchev to the President. (It was so long that the American Embassy, in the process of informally translating it, transmitted it in four separate sections, which arrived in Washington between 6 and 9 o'clock.) It looked, noted Kohler, like a breakthrough. Dean Rusk called a meeting of ExCom's central core to come to his office at State: McNamara, Robert Kennedy, Llewellyn Thompson, Mac Bundy, and a few others. As they waited for the first part of Khrushchev's note to come in, they read Scali's memorandum.

Between 6 and 7 o'clock the first and third parts of the Soviet premier's message arrived. ExCom saw some correlations between them and Fomin's proposals.

"Dear Mr. President," Khrushchev's message opened, "I have received your letter of October 25. From your letter, I got the feeling that you have some understanding of the situation which has developed and a sense of responsibility. I value this." War, he said, was "our enemy and a calamity for all the peoples." "We must not succumb to intoxication and heady passions, regardless of whether elections are impending in this or that country." Khrushchev assured Kennedy that the weapons in Cuba were not "offensive," but admitted that their governments were clearly not going to agree on this. These two sections of the note then rambled slightly, but closed with an apparent proposal: "If assurances were given by the President and the government of the United States that the U.S.A. would not participate in an attack on Cuba and would restrain others from actions of this sort, if you would recall your fleet, this would immediately change everything." He was not speaking for Castro, he said, but he thought the Cubans would be happy to have peace.

The men at the meeting read the note carefully. It smacked of Khrushchev himself, not some committee. As Dean Acheson later said, one could almost imagine the Russian, pacing his narrow office, his stubby legs walking back and forth, dictating to a secretary. The message was not panicky, but it showed genuine concern. McNamara, Bobby, and Mac Bundy left immediately for the White House. The message was already being received there in the Situation Room. They wanted to see what the President thought of it.

As soon as Scali finished his segment of the evening news, he sped back to State, arriving at 6:45. Hilsman escorted him upstairs in the private elevator, and when he knocked on the door, Rusk stepped out of the room. He handed Scali a note he had written out on yellow, lined paper a few minutes before. The reporter should tell the Russian:

I have reason to believe that the USG [United States government] sees real possibilities and supposes that the representatives of the two governments in New York could work this matter out with U Thant and with each other. My impression is, however, that time is very urgent.

Apparently Dean Rusk then took Scali to the White House to get the President's approval for this approach. As the two men waited outside Kennedy's office, Rusk off to one side, Pierre Salinger noticed the newsman. All week Salinger had been trying to keep reporters away from the President. Now it appeared that one was trying to sneak in for a private interview. "What the hell are you doing here?" Salinger shouted.

Rusk stepped forward. "It's O.K., Pierre, I brought him here."

Kenny O'Donnell, who had run out of his office when he heard Salinger's commotion, took Scali and Rusk in to see the President. Kennedy listened to the story about the meeting with the KGB man. Kennedy knew by this time of Khrushchev's message. He agreed with Rusk that Fomin's proposal was an acceptable basis for settlement of the crisis. "But don't use my name," he said. "That's against the rules. Give them the impression that you talked to me, but don't say so. Tell them you've gotten a favorable response from the highest authority in the government."

Scali went on to the Sheraton and Rusk returned to the State Department to await the next sections of Khrushchev's letter. The secretary of state called Acheson and asked him to come over. As they waited for the rest of Khrushchev's message, they sat in Rusk's office sipping scotch.

The second and fourth parts came in between about 8:30 and 9. Only a madman, Khrushchev continued, would initiate a war of total destruction. He appealed to Kennedy not to use the blockade too harshly. "We and you ought not now to pull on the ends of the rope in which you have tied the knot of war, because the more the two of us pull, the tighter that knot will be tied, and a moment may come when that knot will be tied so tight that even he who tied it will not have strength to untie it, and then it will be necessary to cut that knot. . . . Let us not only relax the forces pulling on the ends of the rope; let us take measures to untie that knot. We are ready for this."

At the Sheraton, Fomin and Scali drank coffee. The television newsman repeated Rusk's note almost word-for-word from memory, keeping it hidden in his pocket. The Russian asked twice if this came from high sources in the government. Fomin was concerned that he not look foolish to his Kremlin superiors. Scali reassured him.

The Russian changed the subject. Since the two governments were in apparent agreement about UN inspectors of Cuban bases, how about a UN inspection of American military bases in Florida and in the Caribbean to ensure that the Americans disband their invasion force. Scali angrily pointed out that this was something new. The Russian shrugged and agreed. He said he was just "a small fry" and was only asking.

Scali responded that he himself was only a reporter, but he imagined that such a scheme would be politically difficult for the President, faced as he was by pressure to invade Cuba now.

Fomin assured Scali that this information would be passed on immediately "to the highest levels."

The two men stood up. The Russian picked up the thirty-cent check and walked to the cashier's booth. He looked through his pockets for change. When he could not find any, he became so agitated and impatient, he dropped a five-dollar bill on the counter and walked away. The two men stood in the outer lobby a minute. Fomin said he would contact the American soon, and rushed off.

Scali spent the next forty-five minutes or so typing up the conversation as he remembered it. He contacted Hilsman at a Korean dinner and asked him to return to his office. When the intelligence man arrived, Scali told him about the latest episode. Hilsman decided they had better talk to Rusk again. Once more they went upstairs. Rusk listened quietly, then thanked the reporter. "You have served your country well, John," he said. "When you report this," he added, "remember, eyeball to eyeball they blinked first." (Apparently, the secretary of state liked his colorful little metaphor.)

Rusk ordered Hilsman and his staff to prepare an analysis of both Khrushchev's letter and Fomin's proposal, then returned to his meeting. Dean Acheson, still there, was about to leave. The old ex-secretary was concerned. The State Department people, like Rusk and Thompson, appeared too relieved, almost euphoric, as if the crisis were over. Acheson himself was not so willing to come to an agreement with the Russians. Khrushchev, he thought, seemed rattled. Now was the time to put on more pressure. They could probably get the Soviets out of Cuba altogether.

About 10 o'clock ExCom gathered again at the White House. They reviewed the new developments. Fomin's suggestion of a UN inspection, added to Khrushchev's message, seemed to suggest an acceptable package. They speculated that about 1 o'clock that afternoon Fomin had probably received orders at his embassy to contact someone in the American government. It was about that time that Khrushchev had probably begun dictating his message to Kennedy.

ExCom went to bed. George Ball later said that they felt "a vast sense of relief."

Acheson was right. They *were* overoptimistic.

15 *At the Brink*

Saturday morning, October 27, 1962

Rudolf Anderson, Jr. climbed slowly into his U-2. The sky was clear, hardly a cloud in sight. The recent rains had passed toward the east. A warm breeze blew softly. Anderson's mission was to fly over eastern Cuba taking pictures of Nipe Bay. American intelligence still suspected the Russians might be turning this area into a submarine base.

Washington

As the participants gathered for Saturday morning's ExCom meeting, most felt quietly optimistic. A memo written by Walt Rostow represented the prevailing mood. It noted in Friday's events "a greater willingness . . . for Moscow to disengage from the Cuban crisis without extracting any net advantage and barely saving face." The self-satisfaction expressed by Rostow's memorandum was part of the reason, no doubt, for the shocked reactions ExCom was about to feel, and the black gloom and pessimism that followed. They had lived through Monday night (when they thought the Russians might attack at any moment), and Wednesday (when the quarantine had gone into effect). Yesterday a breakthrough had come. It had looked like they had won. They had cleared all the hurdles unscathed and were almost at the finish line.

The first disturbing sign came that morning when J. Edgar Hoover called Attorney General Robert Kennedy and told him the FBI had heard that "Soviet personnel in New York were apparently preparing to destroy all sensitive documents." Burning documents is an action diplomats take only when the enemy is breaking through the gates.

McCone opened ExCom's meeting as he always did, reviewing the CIA's latest intelligence report. Each man in the room was handed a stapled pamphlet labeled:

Central Intelligence Agency
Memorandum
[CIA SEAL]
THE CRISIS
USSR/CUBA
Information as of 0600
27 October 1962

It was a fascinating document. Its first two pages contained a point-by-point summary of its contents. It then provided (a) a map of Cuba with the locations of each missile; (b) a view of the Atlantic with the positions at sea of every relevant ship; and (c) several sections describing the situations in Cuba, in the Soviet Union, and in the other European Communist countries. The CIA had given ExCom such a report every morning since early in the crisis. McCone had begun each meeting by going over the summary, noting the key phrases, reading them out loud. He did this slowly and solemnly. He considered these readings extremely important. This document was the summation of America's knowledge.

McCone led off Saturday's meeting by disclosing that a Soviet tanker, the *Grozny*, was about to reach the quarantine line. The ship, carrying ammonia, was bound for a nickel refinery at Nicaro, Cuba. What should be done about it? Should it be allowed to pass like the *Bucharest*? Yesterday Khrushchev had sent a message to U Thant, replying to a plea from the UN acting president that both sides avoid a confrontation at sea. The Soviet leader had said he had just "ordered the masters of Soviet vessels bound for

Cuba . . . to stay out of the interception area." But now here was the *Grozny*, pressing forward without stopping. Perhaps the Russians had decided after all to take a tough stand.

McCone also told ExCom that the Cuban MRBM installations would be completed this very day, and that the Russians were erecting bunkers for nuclear warheads. They were even sprucing up the living quarters for their troops, building barracks to take the place of tents. Apparently they expected to be here indefinitely.

Then, a report came from downstairs in the Situation Room. A message from Khrushchev to Kennedy was being broadcast openly over Radio Moscow. It took about fifteen minutes for the Russian announcer to finish reading it; the members of ExCom probably had fragments of it in their hands soon afterward. Its tenor was different from last night's note. This one was more controlled, less erratic. It had the clipped tone of a state document produced by a committee. More significantly—much more significantly—it added a major new element. Before the Soviet Union would remove its missiles, the United States not only had to guarantee not to invade Cuba and to prevent Cuban emigrés from doing so but it also had to promise to remove its Turkish bases.

The Russians undoubtedly had been aware that the respected American columnist, Walter Lippmann, had suggested such a swap in his Thursday column. Maybe they had assumed Lippmann was sending up a White House trial balloon. For Moscow to suggest an exchange was hardly shocking. Despite ExCom's flap a week earlier over Stevenson's proposals, the American government had for several days been giving serious consideration to a trade. On Wednesday George Ball had drafted and sent duplicate telegrams to the American Embassy in Turkey and the American NATO delegation, saying that State considered it "possible that a negotiated solution for removal of Cuban offensive threat may involve dismantling and removal of the Jupiters." The telegram had asked them to smooth the way, to "prepare carefully for such contingency," without harming Turkish relations.

The American ambassador to Ankara had responded that the Turks would be enraged. They did not consider themselves "stooges" of the United States, as they felt Cuba was of the Soviet Union.

Thomas Finletter, the American NATO delegate, had replied with an interesting suggestion. He proposed that the American government tell the Turks it would replace the Jupiters by putting Polaris submarines near Turkey; and that the United States would also set up an international naval force of Turks, Italians, Americans, and possibly Greeks. The State Department had immediately decided Finletter's ideas were worth pursuing and by Saturday had already begun preliminary discussions of the proposal.

The disconcerting thing, then, about this new Soviet demand was that the Russians had not mentioned it previously; Khrushchev's apparent offer of the evening before had seemingly been cast aside. ExCom was confused. What did the change mean? Had something happened in the Kremlin? Had there been a coup? Had Khrushchev been overthrown? Were hawkish members of the Presidium forcing a tougher stance?

Llewellyn Thompson, who had been rather confident all week, became uncertain. He suggested that maybe all the Kremlin wanted was to get something they (or at least Khrushchev) could use to save face, but he was unsure.

Dean Rusk was no more decisive. As usual he offered no suggestions, merely alternatives. And his words and his syntax stumbled. Rusk had clearly grown weary to the point of exhaustion. Surrounded by tennis players and touch football addicts, the decline of his physical stamina had become apparent to all.

John Kennedy was infuriated by this new Kremlin overture. America's Turkish missiles had become a heavy weight, pulling him down. Because of them, Kennedy either had to give in to this Soviet demand and look weak, or refuse and possibly bring about a war. He stood up, trying to keep his temper under control, and went out to the rose garden to walk around a moment, to release his fury in physical movement. Kenny O'Donnell joined him. As the two paced up and down, the President talked about "those damn missiles" in Turkey. Had he not, he muttered, repeatedly suggested their dismantling? (At one point during the course of this day, he reportedly screamed, "Get those frigging missiles off the board.") In truth he had never really *ordered* their removal; an unconscious awareness of this fact may have made him feel guilty and therefore doubly angry. He finally calmed down and returned.

ExCom then discussed what reply they should make to Moscow. They could come to no agreement. Nor could they decide what to do about the *Grozny*. They could not even agree whether or not to utilize Donald Wilson's USIA leaflet and had to defer that decision. Obviously they were going nowhere. They broke for lunch just before noon.

The President spoke privately to McNamara and Rusk. He wanted them to consider very carefully the possibility of a swap. He did not wish to irritate or frighten his NATO allies, so any withdrawal would have to be done cautiously. He told Gilpatric to go down to Bundy's office and work out some sort of scenario to take the missiles out of both Turkey and Italy.

Roger Hilsman came in from State about 1:30 to drop off a note for Bundy. As he entered the White House grounds, he had to drive past two or three hundred demonstrating YAF members. They carried signs saying: "Invade." They passed out flyers accusing opponents of the blockade of being "Communist Fifth Columnists." Yet, when a reporter asked their leader's reaction to a Cuba-Turkey trade, recently discussed on the radio, the young man said, "Sure, we'd go for that."

Hilsman was on his way back out of the White House when a guard told him to return, that an urgent call awaited him. When he got to the phone, he was told of a frightening new development. Hilsman became dizzy and had to sit down. He had been thirty hours without sleep. This latest news seemed too much to accept.

That morning a U-2 plane had taken off from Elieson Air Force Base in Alaska, apparently on a routine mission for the Atomic Energy Commission, checking the atmosphere over the North Pole for signs of Soviet nuclear testing. On his flight back the pilot made a navigational error and began flying over the Chukotka Peninsula in the northeast corner of the Soviet Union. He put through an emergency call over unscrambled radio for navigational directions. Soviet radar picked him up and Russian fighter planes climbed after him in hot pursuit. One can imagine the absolute horror in Moscow as Russian generals watched an American blip enter Soviet air space. For a long, awful moment they must have assumed that an attack had begun, that the plane was on a preliminary reconnaissance mission. One can empathize with their feelings. Their fingers must have inched toward the fatal buttons.

To make matters worse, American fighters took off from Alaska to escort the U-2 home. This action created a new terrifying possibility. Soviet fighters could not fly high enough to attack a U-2, but they could close with American fighters. This raises a question: Since the American planes could have had no hope of reaching Siberia in time to save the U-2 from a Russian attack, why did they fly toward the Soviet Union? Would these war planes actually have purposely entered Soviet air space, even to steer a U-2 home? Was someone in a high position at Air Force headquarters—LeMay perhaps—trying to create an incident? The answer is almost certainly, no. Most likely, without even considering the consequences, the Air Force was only following standard operating procedures: Lost planes must be guided back to base.

Robert McNamara was meeting with the Joint Chiefs at the Pentagon when he received word of the incident, or at least the first stage of it. The calm, controlled secretary of defense reportedly turned white and yelled almost hysterically, "This means war with the Soviet Union!" And he rushed from the room to call the White House.

Luckily the U-2 pilot got his bearings and turned toward home. Both groups of fighters broke off and returned to their respective bases. The incident was over. It was probably about this time that someone reached Roger Hilsman at the White House.

After he hung up, the intelligence man found Kennedy standing by Evelyn Lincoln's desk. Hilsman breathlessly told the President the story. Kennedy took it calmly. (Presumably McNamara had just notified him.) By now the situation in Alaska seemed under control. Kennedy's only comment, dryly referring to the fact that he had ordered all such flights canceled, was: "There is always some son-of-a-bitch who doesn't get the word."

As intensity built at the White House, normality and sanity elsewhere prevailed.

According to the *New York Times*, on Saturday afternoon, Army's "forces, endowed with depth, speed and crushing ground power, were convincingly superior" to George Washington University's football team. Adam Yarmolinsky of the Defense Department watched the game as a guest of his friend, Cyrus Vance, a general counsel at Defense.

As the world slipped closer to the edge, much of America spent a typical October afternoon, playing or watching football. It was Navy Day in Norfolk, Virginia where the Naval Academy "Middies" defeated the Panthers of the University of Pittsburgh. Several hundred spectators, guests of the Navy, had been among those who had evacuated Guantanamo. They saw a sophomore quarterback named Roger Staubach go 8 for 8 in passing.

In Florida that evening, not far from Cuba, 4,500 spectators cheered the North Miami High School Pioneers to victory over their arch rivals from Pompano Beach.

Two Soviet planes intercepted an American T-29 aircraft as it was leaving Berlin. The Russians made three passes by the Americans. United States intelligence suggested that the Kremlin could be working up to at least some sort of air harassment around the German city.

Early Saturday morning, Castro began to lose his nerve. He announced that *his* anti-aircraft guns—not the SAMs which were still being manned by Russians—would start shooting at low-flying American reconnaissance planes. If Cuba did not stop them, he said, eventually these flights could provide cover for a surprise air strike. Castro's point was valid, especially since he knew an attack was at most only days away. Cuban anti-aircraft guns did start firing at some American planes flying in at about treetop height. None of them was seriously damaged.

Simultaneously, a more sinister event occurred. Soviet soldiers at a SAM site near Nipe Bay spotted Rudolf Anderson's U-2 plane overhead, and fired a missile at it. Anderson's aircraft plummeted out of the sky and crashed into the jungle. The plane split apart like a crushed cigar. The major died instantly.

Exactly why they shot down Anderson is unknown. One might posit a theory that some individual Russian at the SAM site had lost control over his emotions and pushed the button. This seems unlikely; each SAM installation had 250 men working at it. It would be almost impossible for one man to do much unaided. Possibly a handful of conspirators at the Kremlin, in order to damage negotiations for peace, had instructed that particular SAM commander to open fire. Maybe Khrushchev himself had ordered a single attack, as a kind of gamble, to shock Kennedy into backing off. Or perhaps this particular installation had just been completed and had automatically opened fire, following standard regulations.

SAC knew its U-2 plane was down but at first was not sure why. They speculated that the plane might have malfunctioned, leading to "pilot hypoxia" (oxygen deficiency). They did not, however, really think it was a malfunction. Anderson, they knew, had gone down near Banes, right next to a SAM site. SAC relayed this news to the White House.

Kenny O'Donnell tells the story that when John Kennedy first heard about Anderson's plane, he asked McNamara to find out whether the pilot had a family. The President was later swimming in the pool with Dave Powers when he received the reply: Anderson was the father of two—a son, Rudolf III, age 5, and young James, age 3. As Kennedy hung up the phone he looked stricken. "He had a boy about the same age as John," he told Powers.

Much more important than the life of this one young father was the possibility that this event might trigger a war. "We are in an entirely new ball game," Kennedy said. He knew quite well that four days earlier he and ExCom had agreed that if a U-2 were fired on, America's bomber and fighter planes would immediately destroy a SAM site. The Tactical Air Command could fulfill this assignment within two hours of a presidential command. With the news about Anderson, Kennedy must have felt almost compelled to order a retaliatory attack.

By late afternoon the pressure was growing immense.

Adlai Stevenson talked to reporters and other diplomats. He mentioned that if the Russians continued work on their missile bases, the United States would bomb the sites. It was the first time any major governmental spokesman had *openly* mentioned this possibility.

In Cuba Fidel Castro talked to one of his officials calling from

Rome. The man asked if he could return home to be with all of them in this moment of crisis. No, Castro wryly told him, someone had to be alive to tell the story of the Cuban revolution.

Looking back at this time, eight months later, Harold Macmillan would tell the House of Commons: "The week of the Cuban crisis—and I have been through some in peace and war—was the week of the most strain I can ever remember in my life. . . . During that week, as the pressure developed and built up to a climax on Friday and Saturday, the strain was certainly very great."

In 1968 Robert McNamara would describe the crisis: "The world was faced with what many of us felt then, and what since has been generally agreed, was the greatest danger of a catastrophic war since the advent of the nuclear age."

At the State Department, meanwhile, Dean Rusk and his crew were meeting in George Ball's office, trying to make some sense of it all. In the middle of the afternoon, Rusk called John Scali and asked him to come over right away.

The newsman arrived at 3 o'clock. Rusk stepped out of his meeting for just two minutes. In light of the attack on Anderson's plane and also the morning's public message from Moscow, Rusk suggested that Scali contact Fomin again to find out what was going on.

Scali called the Russian and said he wanted to see him right away in the Sheraton lobby. The American newsman was seething; he suspected that he had been used. He was afraid that if they met in the coffee shop again, he might completely lose his temper and be overheard. When Fomin arrived, Scali went with him to an empty banquet hall on the mezzanine. There they whispered harshly back and forth, their quiet voices echoing slightly in the empty room.

"What happened?" the American said angrily.

Fomin acted jittery and nervous. The Kremlin, he said, probably had not received the message he had sent yesterday following their conversation; or at least they had not gotten it before they put together this morning's proposal. Maybe his message had been delayed because of heavy cable traffic.

Scali exploded. It was "a stinking double-cross," he said.

But, Fomin said defensively, the idea of trading missile bases was not new. Walter Lippmann had himself proposed it.

"I don't care who suggested it," Scali responded, "whether it was Walter Lippmann or Cleopatra. It's totally unacceptable. It was unacceptable yesterday; it's unacceptable today. It will be unacceptable tomorrow and ad infinitum." If the Russians wanted to bring up American bases, they could do so as part of some Geneva disarmament talks.

"Don't get excited," Fomin pleaded. The proposal he had made yesterday was still valid, there had been no double-cross.

Scali said he could no longer believe him. A U-2 had just been shot down over Cuba by a Soviet-manned anti-aircraft missile.

Fomin's face turned white. "Oh, no," he said tiredly.

"If you think the United States is bluffing," Scali threatened, "you are part of the most colossal misjudgment of American intentions in history. We are absolutely determined to get those missiles out of there. An invasion of Cuba is only hours away."

The KGB man appealed to the American to trust him. He and Dobrynin were merely awaiting a reply to the message they had sent yesterday. As soon as it came in, he would call.

Scali was still angry when they parted. He returned to State but found Rusk and most of the others had left for another ExCom meeting. He dictated a two-page memorandum on his conversation with Fomin, left immediately in a State Department limousine for the White House, and turned the memo over to the decision makers.

The Joint Chiefs met with ExCom that afternoon. The attacks on American planes settled the issue as far as they were concerned. They stated, and apparently almost everyone else agreed, that bombers and fighters should be sent the next day to destroy the SAM sites. They reminded the rest of them of Kennedy's promise. The hawks at the meeting also urged Kennedy to destroy the MRBM and IRBM installations too—by Monday at the latest—if the Russians did not start dismantling them immediately. The United States could begin an invasion on Tuesday.

The President listened to all the proposals. Perhaps the attack on Rudolf Anderson had been a mistake, he thought, an isolated event, the act of a madman. He decided to give the Russians another chance. Another reconnaissance mission would fly tomorrow morning—without a fighter escort. It would probe Soviet intentions. If it were fired on, he would instantly order a counterattack. If not, there might still be a chance to persuade Khrushchev by diplomatic means to back down. "It isn't the first step that concerns me," Robert Kennedy recalls his brother saying, "but both sides escalating to the fourth and fifth step—and we don't go to the sixth because there is no one around to do so."

(Graham T. Allison, a Harvard historian, states that some military men were shocked by the President's unwillingness to bomb. According to Allison, some in the Pentagon thought that "the President had cracked and folded.")

In case the United States did decide to attack Cuba and in case the Russians then retaliated against America's Turkish installations, Kennedy ordered the atomic warheads on the Turkish missiles be defused. He himself wanted to give any go-ahead before they could be fired. As he told Bobby that day—still pondering Barbara Tuchman's book, *The Guns of August*—"I am not going to follow a course which will allow anyone to write a comparable book about this time, *The Missiles of October*. If anybody is around to write after this, they are going to understand that we made every effort to find peace."

Kennedy was aware that tomorrow or the next day he might have to order an attack. He told McNamara during the evening to have General Sweeney of the Tactical Air Command come see him early next morning.

ExCom's discussion turned to the question of how to react to the two Soviet messages. The State Department had worked out a note stating that any trade was unacceptable.

Robert Kennedy disagreed. Maybe it was the politician in him. Sometimes threats and pressure work; sometimes the best approach is to pretend you haven't heard the nasty things a voter or a reporter or a political opponent has just said. You smile and reach out your hand. There are times when this method works best.

The attorney general spoke sharply against State's draft on the grounds that it was too negative. He spoke so sharply that the President, apparently in exasperation, finally said to him, "If you disagree so violently, go draft one yourself."

Bobby took Ted Sorensen, the superb wordsmith, into an adjoining room and together they banged out a new tack. Instead of replying to the most recent message, they ignored it as if it never came. They "accepted" what was essentially the Fomin offer: (1) Washington would promise not to invade Cuba; (2) the Kremlin would remove the missiles; and (3) a UN team would inspect the sites.

It was a brilliant stroke. Any good salesman knows how important the word "yes" is. Instead of saying, "No, we will not trade bases with you," Robert Kennedy proposed that the White House say, "Yes, we accept the offer you gave us yesterday."

Bobby and Sorensen brought their draft back to the meeting. The others were tired and grumpy and perhaps willing to accept almost any way out. They agreed to this new draft.

The time was about 7:15. The President said that they should all take a break. They could eat dinner, relax a while, and be back at 9 that evening. Meanwhile he would see that this message was typed and sent immediately to Moscow. He would simultaneously release it to the press.

As the others trooped out, Dean Rusk, Llewellyn Thompson, and the two Kennedy brothers discussed the Kremlin's possible reactions. They agreed that Bobby should immediately go to see Dobrynin and personally explain the situation to him. (Several times that week the attorney general had privately conferred with the Russian ambassador, carrying secret messages back and forth. According to Khrushchev's memoirs, a few days earlier Robert Kennedy had gone in a state of exhaustion to see Dobrynin. The American had pleaded with the Soviet ambassador to persuade Khrushchev to back down, telling him that the pressure on the White House from the hawks was growing. Khrushchev recorded Bobby as saying, "I don't know how much longer we can hold out against our generals." This statement seems rather overblown, but the attorney general may have actually said it, or at least something quite like it, perhaps to put pressure on the Kremlin. Soviet officials were privately saying similar things about *their* generals.

On the other hand Bobby may have said it and meant it. He never did get along well with the Pentagon. Besides, pressure from the hawks was building. Scali had in fact said almost the same thing to Fomin on both Friday and Saturday.)

Robert Kennedy now called Dobrynin and made arrangements to meet him at the Justice Department. When the two men sat down, the attorney general gave the Russian the President's message. He also verbally emphasized something not written in the note. Russia, he declared, was about to force the President's hand. Soviet troops were continuing to build the missile installations, even after Washington's warnings. It almost seemed as if Russia were totally ignoring America's demands. Furthermore, this very day the Russians had shot down an unarmed U-2. The Soviet Union had moved to the brink. The White House, Robert Kennedy stated ominously, was out of patience. Either Russia make an immediate commitment within the next twenty-four hours to remove the bases or, the attorney general said, "we would remove them."

This was a classic ultimatum. Robert Kennedy was giving the Russians both a deadline and a threat of what would happen if they failed to meet it.

Dobrynin asked the attorney general what the Americans planned to do about their own bases in Turkey. Robert Kennedy replied by admitting something ExCom had never agreed on. He said that under the present circumstances—the political situation inside the United States and America's relations with her allies—his brother could make no deal. He later revealed that he told Dobrynin that "President Kennedy had been anxious to remove the missiles from Turkey and Italy for some time. He had ordered their removal some time ago, and it was our judgment that, within a short time after the crisis was over, those missiles would be gone, four or five months."

Assuming that Robert Kennedy's later recollections about this conversation were accurate, this statement to Dobrynin about the Turkish bases is significant. If the attorney general had received permission from the President to make this kind of remark, then John Kennedy had clearly backed down in his absolute refusal to consider a swap. If, on the other hand, Bobby was merely offering

Dobrynin a personal opinion, the statement may only have been a typical lawyer's proposal: "Look we can't make any promises, but if you do this. . . ."

Whichever of these two possibilites it was, it probably appeared to the Russians that the White House was suggesting a deal. Here was the President's own brother and closest advisor stating that the United States would remove its Turkish missiles "within a short time." We do not know, of course, what went on in the Kremlin during the next twelve hours, but Robert Kennedy's indirect promise may have helped tip the scales, allowing Khrushchev to save face. It is possible that the Soviet leader could now declare to his more hawkish opponents that his Caribbean venture, his Cuban gamble, had not been a failure after all. It had wrought important American concessions.

Meanwhile in Washington that night, ExCom's 9 o'clock meeting was brief, lasting less than an hour. They discussed some possible steps they might take next. The United States could, for example, put petroleum on the quarantine's prohibited list.

The men at the White House were aware, however, that the time for subtle pressures might be past. When America's U-2s flew over Cuba the next morning, Soviet SAMs might again fire at them. In that case the United States would immediately counterattack with a bombing attack. Even if the SAMs remained quiet, American troops were still about to attack Cuba—that is, if Russia did not very soon back down. McNamara suggested that the President call up from the air reserve twenty-four squadrons of troop carriers. These 14,000 men would help carry the invasion force. An announcement to that effect was immediately given to the press.

The Kremlin could hardly mistake the signs. John Scali and Robert Kennedy had both just warned the Russians that time was running out. Now the White House was calling up an air reserve unit designed almost solely for attack. All week long the American military had been building up their forces in Florida, at Guantanamo, and in the waters off Cuba. An assault on Cuba—and the Soviet troops stationed there—loomed.

Late Saturday, just after midnight, the State Department sent a telegram to all its ambassadors stationed in NATO countries. The ambassadors should inform those governments that the Cuban situation "is increasingly serious and time is growing shorter." The United States, the ambassadors should say, might soon have "to take whatever military action may be necessary to remove this growing threat."

War was now only hours away.

16 *To Live with Goats*

The men of the Politburo, as always, made their decision in secret. We can only imagine what bickerings may have occurred. Were some Kremlin leaders in favor of pushing ahead, of defying the United States, ignoring its threats? Did some of them lambaste Khrushchev himself? Did a few panic as war inched near? What kinds of arguments did each side—assuming that there were indeed opposing sides—raise to support its position? Which of the several dozen American actions had the greatest impact on their discussions? We do not know. All we can be certain of is that sometime during these next few hours, while darkness blanketed Washington, the Kremlin decided to step back from the brink.

John F. Kennedy had won. While he and the rest of America's leaders were still asleep, the crisis passed.

Robert Kennedy woke up early. He had promised his daughters to take them into the city to see the horse show. He was at the armory when he received a call from Dean Rusk. Khrushchev had just sent a message to the President. The Soviet government was backing down. It had agreed to dismantle its missile installations and take them home.

As word of the new development spread across town that morning, the members of ExCom felt great relief. Donald Wilson of USIA later said, "All of a sudden this huge burden was lifted and

I felt like laughing or yelling or dancing. . . . It was a marvelous morning. I'll never forget it as long as I live."

A Pentagon general also remembered that day. "There was great euphoria right at that moment," he said, "and all over town you could meet any number of people who could tell you at the drop of a hat how good we all were—that here we had really discovered how to do it, that this was crisis management at its best." (Maybe the New Frontiersmen were proud of themselves because they had apparently made up for their Bay of Pigs failure.)

John Kennedy talked with Bobby. He suspected he might be at the high point of his administration, that he might never achieve this kind of victory again. He said to his brother, referring to Abe Lincoln, "This is the night I should go to the theater."

During the next several days letters and telegrams came to the White House. Dean Acheson, for instance, commended the President on his "leadership, fairness, and judgment." (Privately, Acheson thought Kennedy had been awfully lucky, but good manners required congratulations.)

Daniel Moynihan, senator from New York, has, however, called this moment, a "defeat." The Kremlin, according to Moynihan, should have expected "a lot of trouble with the United States—and real trouble" for putting their missiles in Cuba. Although the Russians did take their missiles away, Moynihan complains, Kennedy allowed them to retain their influence with Castro's government. One wonders what other course the senator would have wanted Kennedy to pursue. Apparently Moynihan would only have been satisfied had the United States invaded the island—or in some way totally humiliated the Russians. Few have agreed with him.

At Sunday morning's ExCom meeting John Kennedy took a statesmanlike stand. Rather than increase the pressure, he ordered all U-2 overflights canceled, and he told the Navy not to stop any ship at the quarantine line. (McCone had just told them that the *Grozny* had halted short of the line the evening before.) Later in the day the President also directed the Navy to prevent any operations by Cuban exile units and mentioned Alpha 66 by name. (On October 30, the Special Group [Augmented] ordered a halt to all its own sabotage operations.) Kennedy warned ExCom that they

should not crow about an American "victory" or a Soviet "capitula-
tion." He recognized what a ticklish position Khrushchev had just
put himself in by backing down. Kennedy did not want to weaken
Khrushchev's standing so much that the Kremlin's hawks took
over. The United States would have to deal with the Russians on
many other issues—a test ban treaty, for example—and it would be
unwise to infuriate them. Kennedy's position was mature and
rational. He might not be achieving everything he wanted in
Cuba—such as the ouster of Castro—but winning "everything" in
Cuba mattered little if the United States thereby had to give up
many of its other goals. It was important to maintain lines of
communication with the Kremlin. To take Moynihan's position
would have been childish and foolish. Kennedy could afford to be
magnanimous.

The two most frequently used descriptions of Kennedy's handling of the entire crisis have been "firmness" and "restraint." One
reads a great deal about his coolness under pressure during those
two weeks. In fact, of course, he was hardly cool throughout. He
often became irritated, even enraged, especially as he began to
lose tight control over the secret. On various occasions he also
showed tension, nervousness, exhaustion, or exhilaration. Bobby
saw this, and Kenneth O'Donnell, but most of the others did not.
None of them apparently ever saw him frightened or gloomy—the
kinds of emotions which could have become contagious and could
have destroyed the group's morale. His *relative* self-control was
therefore important. As to his "firmness," one can argue that
perhaps he overreacted, that the threat from either Cuba or the
Soviet Union was not that great, particularly since, as he well
knew, the Russians throughout these two weeks refused to
mobilize their forces. But given the political temper of the time
and John Kennedy's own personality and needs, one could not
have expected him to have taken a more moderate, more yielding
stand. In the abstract one can question his belligerence, but not
within its context.

All in all, one is struck, not by his "firmness"—which was after
all an easy position for him to take—but by his restraint, especially
at the end when he refused to humiliate Khrushchev.

Democrats did rather well in the November elections. Accord-

ing to polls taken in California just before the crisis, Richard Nixon
had almost drawn even with Governor Edward Brown. In the last
days of the campaign he suddenly fell back and lost. In Indiana,
Birch Bayh defeated Homer Capehart, the senator who had
wanted to invade Cuba. Kennedy believed some of the success of
the Democrats resulted from the missile crisis, but analyst Louis
Harris told him that the chief factors seemed to have been local
issues rather than international.

The Russians did dismantle the bases. They took everything
away and bulldozed the installations into rubble. Within a few days
an aerial photograph of one site showed only a single dump truck
driving slowly around the area, picking up the last remnants.
Rumors spread, especially within the Cuban exile community, that
the Russians had not taken all the missiles away from the island,
that they had hidden them in caves and had sent out dummies to
fool the Americans. This charge seems remotely possible but
improbable. Eventually the Russians would have suffered the
embarrassment of getting caught. They might thereby have even
forced the United States to invade the island. Besides, storing such
missiles for a long time would be technically inefficient, since
missiles require a certain amount of attention, especially rockets
obsolete to begin with. On the other hand it does seem likely, in
light of all the reports, that the Russians did store something in the
caves, probably some sort of military equipment.

It should be noted that three months after the crisis, the United
States removed all its missiles from Turkey and Italy, and sixty of
its Thors from Britain. Kennedy had apparently kept Bobby's
promise to Dobrynin.

Certain signs of a thaw appeared in the Cold War. A hot line,
discussed first under Eisenhower, was adopted in 1963. (Crises like
this one required instant communications. Traditional methods
were clumsy. A long Soviet written message required hours to
reach the Oval Office. This apparently had been one reason
Khrushchev had begun using Moscow Radio during the crisis.) The
two countries would also sign a test ban treaty. Most importantly
the two powers pulled back from nuclear confrontations. From this
time on both sides would be very chary of major provocative acts.

But a real détente had not occurred. Soviet Deputy Foreign
Minister Vasily Kuznetsov warned John J. McCloy, "Never will we

be caught like this again." The Soviet Union accelerated a major
overhaul of its military forces and a drastic increase in their size.
Moreover, a disturbing attitude remained in the United States. A
National Security Council memorandum, written on October 29,
1962, tried to sum up the significance of the Russian withdrawal.
"If we have learned anything from this experience," it said, "it is
that weakness, even only apparent weakness, invites Soviet trans-
gression. At the same time, firmness in the last analysis will force
the Soviets to back away from rash initiatives." The implication of
this memorandum was that the United States should henceforth
avoid even the *appearance* of weakness and should be forever *firm*.
One wonders whether such conclusions—internalized by these
men—would help to drag the United States deep into Southeast
Asia. Their desire to exude strength may have made them reject
any "defeat" in Vietnam. (One can also argue that because the crisis
had made both sides draw back from *nuclear* confrontations,
Washington felt more confident about involvement in Asia.)

John Kennedy himself and his brother Robert received most of
the praise that followed the crisis, perhaps rightly so. Yet what
made them succeed—in addition to Russia's own rationality—was
America's governmental machinery which in general ran smoothly.
The military, particularly the Navy, performed well. The CIA
seems to have done a fine job. But the part of the government
which worked best during this period was that much-maligned
department which John Kennedy had once compared to Jell-O: the
Department of State. Here was Dean Rusk supervising a remarkably complex series of diplomatic maneuvers. Here were Chip
Bohlen and Llewellyn Thompson, perceptive and prudent analyz-
ers of the Soviet Union. Here was Ed Martin's Latin American
desk; and the USIA which delivered a torrent of information to the
world; and Roger Hilsman, the brainy and literate intelligence
man; and George Ball, the organizer of peace; and Adlai Stevenson
at the UN. They were a terribly impressive lot.

At first Fidel Castro was furious. When he heard of the
Kremlin's surrender, he reportedly became so angry he kicked the
wall and broke a mirror. A few days later he contemptuously said
that Khrushchev lacked *cojones* (balls).

Castro personally was not so willing to back down. Pierre Salinger recalls that on Monday, October 29, Cuban anti-aircraft guns fired again at American reconnaissance planes. The Cuban leader also refused initially to give up the IL-28s which the Russians had turned over to him. But Kennedy kept the pressure on, threatening to invade the island, and on November 19 the Maximum Leader gave in and allowed the Russians to take them back to the Soviet Union.

One result of the crisis was the suspension of Pan American flights to Miami. Since January 1, 1959 these had carried 250,000 refugees to the United States. Now they were stopped. They would start again in 1965 but under severe restrictions. The exodus from the island was now abruptly ended—the deluge out of Cuba, swelling in the months just before the crisis, had halted. The effects of this on the Cuban population—both on the island and in the United States—are incalculable.

As for Cuban-American relations, they started to grow less volatile. The American government soon ended Operation MON-GOOSE and abolished the Special Group (Augmented). The National Security Council set up a committee called the Standing Group (to take the place of both ExCom and the SGA) whose membership consisted of Robert Kennedy, McNamara, Sorensen, McCone, and Bundy. This group gradually gave up the idea of either assassinating or overthrowing Castro, though in June 1963, with the President's approval, it reinstituted a program of sabotage by which it hoped to harass Castro's government and cause general unrest.

Gradually the Kennedy administration contemplated trying to improve relations with Cuba. Just before his death John Kennedy had decided to try to get along with Castro.

Khrushchev once told a story about a Russian peasant who became so poor he had to live in the same house with a goat. Although he grew used to the smell, he never liked the arrangement. He knew however he had no choice.

Cuba, Khrushchev said, was America's goat. "You are not happy about it, you won't like it, but you'll learn to live with it."

Perhaps understanding how to live with one's goats is the very foundation of diplomacy.

Notes

Prologue

The information in this chapter unless otherwise noted comes from the pages of the New York *Herald Tribune*, the *Daily News*, and most especially, the *New York Times*.

p. 1. On the matter of Castro's age most biographers have concluded that he was born in 1926. A letter found in the National Archives may well be from a young Fidel Castro to President Franklin Delano Roosevelt. In it the boy claims to be twelve years old. If so, and if it was the same Castro, he may conceivably have been born in 1928.

p. 7. On Khrushchev: Edward Crankshaw, *Khrushchev: A Career* (New York: Viking, 1966); Nikita Khrushchev, *Khrushchev Remembers* (Boston: Little, Brown, 1970).

p. 7. "I went about barefoot . . .": Quoted in Crankshaw, p. 3.

p. 7. "When I think back . . .": Khrushchev, p. 22. On his schooling, compare *ibid*, and Edward Crankshaw, *Khrushchev's Russia* (Baltimore: Penguin Books, 1959), p. 52.

p. 8. "Life is a . . .": Quoted in Crankshaw, *Khrushchev: A Career*, p. 13.

p. 12. CIA meeting with Roselli: U.S., Congress, Senate, Select Committee to Study Governmental Operations with Respect to Intelligence Activities, *Alleged Assassination Plots Involving Foreign Leaders* (New York: Norton, 1976), p. 76.

1. *Cuba*

There are, of course, many histories and descriptions of Cuba. Without question the best single-volume history is Hugh Thomas, *Cuba* (New York: Harper & Row, 1971). For a recent journalistic view, see the excellent book by Jose Yglesias, *In the Fist of the Revolution* (New York: Pantheon, 1968). Of the many books on Castro's revolution, see especially Theodore Draper, *Castroism: Theory and Practice* (New York: Praeger, 1965).

p. 15. "A Marine sergeant . . .": Quoted in W. Douglas Lansford, "Shoup of Tarawa," in *The Kennedy War Heroes*, edited by Phil Hirsch (New York: Pyramid Books, 1962), p. 157.

p. 15. The audio-visual demonstration: David Halberstam, *The Best and the Brightest* (New York: Random House, 1972), pp. 66–67.

p. 20. "Castro was one . . .": Richard Nixon, "Cuba, Castro and John F. Kennedy," *Reader's Digest*, November 1964, pp. 283–284. "In private conversation . . .": George McGovern, "A Talk with Castro," *The New York Times Magazine*, March 3, 1977, p. 20.

p. 20. On Castro's early life: Thomas pp. 802–891, is best. Among others, see also Herbert Matthews, *Castro, A Political Biography* (London: Penguin Press, 1969); Juana Castro, "My Brother, Fidel," *Life*, August 28, 1964, pp. 22–33.

p. 21. "never went to . . .": Quoted in Thomas, p. 810.

p. 21. "My desire to . . .": *Ibid.*, pp. 810–811.

p. 22. "I had no. . .": Oscar Lewis *et al.*, *Four Men* (Urbana: University of Illinois Press, 1977), p. 350.

p. 24. 2,000 died: *Ibid.*, p. 1044n.

p. 25. "A little while. . .": "Comparencia de Fidel en la 'Universidad Popular,' 1 December 1961," *Hoy*, December 2, 1961.

p. 27. "Never, not then . . .": Edmundo Desnoes, *Inconsolable Memories* (New York: New American Library, 1967), p. 18.

p. 27. Refugee center statistics: Richard Fagen *et al.*, *Cubans in Exile* (Stanford, Calif.: Stanford University Press, 1968), p. 113.

2. *America vs. Castro*

p. 30. Drunken sailors: told to author. "I am a . . .": Hugh Thomas, *Cuba*, (New York: Harper & Row, 1971), p. 796.

p. 32. Opinion of Eisenhower himself: C. L. Sulzberger, *The Last of the Giants* (New York: Macmillan, 1970), p. 678.

p. 32. "I would be . . .": Warren Miller, *90 Miles from Home* (Greenwich, Conn.: Fawcett, 1961), pp. 161–162. "We were hysterical . . .": U.S., Congress, Senate, Select Committee to Study Governmental Operations with Respect to Intelligence Activities, *Alleged Assassination Plots Involving Foreign Leaders* (New York: Norton, 1976), pp. 157–158.

p. 32. Reston on Kennedy: *New York Times*, January 18, 1966. "That son of. . .": Arthur Schlesinger, Jr., *A Thousand Days*, (Greenwich, Conn.: Crest Books, 1965), p. 363.

p. 33. "Let the record . . .": *New York Times*, April 21, 1961. JFK to Taylor: Select Committee, p. 135.

p. 33. SGA's memorandums: *Ibid.*, pp. 139, 147n, 161–163.

p. 34. JM WAVE: Taylor Branch and George Crile III, "The Kennedy Vendetta," *Harpers's*, August 1975, pp. 49–63.

p. 35. "We were doing. . .": *Ibid.*, p. 52. "I would return . . .": Interview with a "Mr. Lopez," Presidential Office Files, Kennedy Library.

p. 36. Alpha 66: Miami *Daily News*, October 10–11, 1962; Andrew St. George, "Hit and Run to Cuba with Alpha 66," *Life*, November 16, 1962, pp. 55ff.

p. 36. Havana (Miramar) raid: Branch and Crile, p. 60; James Bayard, *The Real Story on Cuba* (Derby, Conn.: Monarch Books, 1963), pp. 104–106.

p. 37. On assassination: Select Committee; Branch and Crile, pp. 60–61.

p. 37. "the Russians that. . .": Quoted in Thomas, p. 1391.

p. 37. Prospects of a coming invasion: *Ibid*, pp. 1386–1393. For a series of Castro's statements on this, see Claude Julien, *Le Monde*, March 22, 1963; Lee Lockwood, *Castro's Cuba, Cuba's Fidel* (New York: Macmillan, 1967), p. 200; Herbert L. Matthews, *Revolution in Cuba* (New York: Scribners, 1975). pp. 209–210.

3. *The Missiles*

Among the best analyses of Soviet motives during this period see especially Michel Tatu, *Power in the Kremlin* (New York: Viking, 1969); Graham T. Allison, *Essence of Decision* (Boston: Little, Brown, 1971); and Herbert S. Dinerstein, *The Making of a Missile Crisis* (Baltimore: The Johns Hopkins Press, 1976). On Soviet leadership, see particularly Carl A. Linden, *Khrushchev and the Soviet Leadership* (Baltimore: The Johns Hopkins Press, 1966); William Hyland and Richard Shyrock, *The Fall of Khrushchev* (New York: Funk & Wagnalls, 1968); Roman Kolkowitz, *Conflict in Soviet Party-Military Relations: 1962–63*, RM-3760-PR (RAND Corporation, August 1963). On Soviet strategic weapons, see the annual estimates compiled by the Institute for Strategic Studies in London.

p. 39. Khrushchev's promises and threats (emphasis added): "Soviet Public Statements with Respect to Cuban Security," September 14, 1962, Roger Hilsman MSS, Kennedy Library.

p. 40. Presidium discussions: Tatu, pp. 236–238; Malcolm Mackintosh, "The Soviet Military's Influence on Foreign Policy," in *Soviet Naval Policy: Objectives and Restraints*, edited by Michael MccGwire *et al.* (New York: Praeger, 1975).

p. 40. "I paced back . . .": Nikita Khrushchev, *Khrushchev Remembers* (Boston: Little, Brown, 1970), p. 494.

p. 41. "I realized that . . .": Ron Nessen, "Too Much Trivia, Too Little Substance,"*TV Guide*, March 12, 1977, p. 4.

p. 41. Nuclear power, missiles, and game theory: See Ralph E. Lapp, *Kill and Overkill* (New York: Basic Books, 1962); Herman Kahn, *On Thermonuclear War* (Princeton, N.J.: Princeton University Press, 1961); Joseph Kraft, *Profiles in Power* (New York: New American Library, 1966); Irving Louis Horowitz, "Deterrence Games: From Academic Casebook to Military Codebook," in *The Strategy of Conflict*, edited by Paul Swingle (New York: Academic Press, 1970); Edmund Beard, *Developing the ICBM* (New York: Columbia University Press, 1976).

p. 47. "Accidents and all . . .": Oleg Penkovskiy, *The Penkovskiy Papers* (New York: Avon, 1965), p. 328.

p. 51. Arnold Smith and Kremlin rumors: Robert W. Reford, *Canada and Three Crises* (Lindsay, Ont.: John Deyell, 1968), p. 170.

p. 52. Dobrynin to Sorensen: Theodore C. Sorensen, *Kennedy* (New York: Bantam Books, 1965), p. 752.

p. 52. "It would have . . .": Khrushchev, p. 493.

p. 53. "I suppose we . . .": *Congressional Record*, June 29, 1961, p. 11704. State Department statements: Joseph W. Neubert to Dean Rusk, October 17, 1962, Hilsman MSS, Kennedy Library.

4. *The Kremlin Enterprise*

p. 55. A group of . . .": Edmundo Desnoes, *Inconsolable Memories* (New York: New American Library, 1967), pp. 55–56. The CIA estimates that the probable cost of Russia's 1962 Cuban venture ran upwards to $1 billion: CIA, "Memorandum: THE CRISIS," October 26, 1962, Kennedy Library.

p. 57. "machine tools, wheat . . .": State Department Press Briefing, August 24, 1962, pp. 23–24, Hilsman MSS, Kennedy Library,

p. 57. "I could see . . .": U.S., Congress, Senate, Preparedness Investigating Subcommittee of the Committee on Armed Services, "Investigation of the Preparedness Program: On the Cuban Military Buildup," Washington, 1962, (henceforth referred to as IOTPP), pp. 10–11. (Mimeographed.)

p. 57. "You have two . . .": James Bayard, *The Real Story on Cuba* (Derby, Conn.: Monarch Books, 1963), pp. 95–104. Increase in shipping: IOTPP, p. 10; (Admiral) George Dennison, Oral History Interview, p. 406, Naval History Division, U.S. Navy, Washington, D.C. Forty-seven locations: James Daniel and John G. Hubbell, *Strike in the West* (New York: Holt, Rinehart and Winston, 1963), p. 60. Boys' reformatory: Tetlow, pp. 143–144.

p. 58. 40,000 troops: There is some disagreement about this number, but see IOTPP, pp. 6, 14; Hanson Baldwin, "A Military Perspective," in *Cuba and the United States*, edited by John Plank (Washington: Brookings Institution, 1967), p. 205. Military equipment sent: Memorandum for McGeorge Bundy: Intelligence Information on Cuban Military Posture, December 24, 1962, National Security Council MSS, Kennedy Library. Roberta Wohlstetter's theory: Roberta Wohlstetter, "Cuba and Pearl Harbor. Hindsight and Foresight," *Foreign Affairs* 43 (July 1965), 691–707.

p. 59. Greek captain to Lincoln White: Memorandum for files, September 4, 1962, Hilsman MSS, Kennedy Library. McNamara on several thousand reports: U.S. Department of Defense, "Special Cuba Briefing (by Robert S. McNamara)," Washington, February 6, 1963, p. 47. (Mimeographed.)

p. 60. "I can remember . . .", Salvador Lew's report: Victor Marchetti and John D. Marks, *The CIA and the Cult of Intelligence* (New York: Knopf, 1974), p. 329.

p. 61. "large quantities of. . .": State Department Press Briefing, pp. 4, 14.

p. 62. McCone's gut feeling: Arthur Krock, *Memoirs* (New York: Funk & Wagnalls, 1968), pp. 378–379; IOTPP, p. 17; Arthur Schlesinger, Jr., *A Thousand Days* (Greenwich, Conn.: Crest Books, 1965), p. 730; Elie Abel, *The Missile Crisis* (Philadelphia: Lippincott, 1966), pp. 17–18.

p. 65. Keating's twenty-five speeches. NBC, Monitor, November 4, 1962.

p. 66. JFK's September 4th statement: Norbert A. Schlei, Oral History Interview, pp. 7–12, Kennedy Library; Schlei to Abram Chayes, in Abram Chayes, *The Cuban Missile Crisis* (New York: Oxford University Press, 1974), pp. 132–134; cf. Abel, pp. 19–20.

5. Pumping Steel

p. 69. COMOR meeting: Elie Abel, *The Missile Crisis* (Philadelphia: Lippincott, 1966), pp. 25–26.

p. 70. Intelligence reports: Roger Hilsman, *To Move a Nation* (Garden City, N.Y.: Doubleday, 1967), pp. 174–175; Abel, p. 24; U.S., Congress, House, Subcommittee of the Committee on Appropriations, *Department of Defense Appropriations for 1964: Hearings*, 88th Cong., 1st sess., 1963, pp. 27, 64–65, 68; Robert F. Kennedy, *Thirteen Days* (New York: Norton, 1969), p. 29; Thyraud de Vosjoli, " A Head That Holds Some Sinister Secrets," *Life*, April 26, 1968, p. 35; Andrew Tully, *The Super Spies* (New York: Pocket Books, 1969), p. 166.

p. 72. "low level photograph . . .": CIA, "Memorandum: THE CRISIS," October 26, 1962, Kennedy Library.

p. 72. Questions about the missiles: Robert Hotz, "What Was the Threat?" *Aviation Week and Space Technology*, November 12, 1962, p. 21; Bernard H. Ross, "American Government in Crisis: An Analysis of the Executive Branch of Government During the Cuban Missile Crisis" (unpublished Ph.D. dissertation, New York University, 1971), p. 118n; James Trainor, "Cuba Missile Threat Detailed," *Missiles and Rockets*, October 29, 1962, pp. 12–14, 47; U.S. Department of Defense, "Special Cuba Briefing (by Robert S. McNamara)," Washington, February 6, 1963, p. 7. (Mimeographed.); U.S., Congress, House, Committee on Armed Services, *Hearings on Military Posture*, 88th Cong., 1st sess., 1963, p. 8; *Jane's All the World's Aircraft, 1963–64* (New York:

McGraw-Hill, 1963), pp. 421–423; John W. R. Taylor (editor of *Jane's*) to the author, September 15, 1977; Warren Rogers, Jr., "Reflections on the Bob and John Show," *The New Republic*, February 23, 1963, pp. 10–11; Richard Rovere, "Letter from Washington," *The New Yorker*, March 2, 1963, pp. 125–131.

p. 74. Board of Estimates: Abel, pp. 23–24; *DOD Appropriations*, p. 51; David Wise and Thomas B. Ross, *The Invisible Government* (New York: Bantam Books, 1964), pp. 311–312.

p. 74. Castro's pilot: Abel, p. 24.

p. 74. Conversation between the Cuban and the American: Henry Brandon, Oral History Interview, p. 14, Kennedy Library. Brandon's "bearded Cuban" may have been Castro's pilot, and Brandon may have been the one who sent this report to Washington. Note that the Cuban did not say they could hit Washington or New York—a much strong rejoinder and the kind of thing an angry man would say if the missiles really *could* go that far. This seems to reinforce the theory that the MRBMs were of limited range.

p. 75. The *Aviation Week* article: Larry Booda, "U.S. Watches for Possible Cuban IRBMs," *Aviation Week and Space Technology*, October 1, 1962, pp. 20–21.

p. 76. Keating's October 2 speech: *Congressional Record*, October 2, 1962, p. 20467. October 3rd: Hilsman, p. 175; Graham T. Allison, *Essence of Decision* (Boston: Little, Brown, 1971), p. 192.

p. 76. COMOR meeting: Abel, p. 26. On Truman's Korean decision: David Detzer, *Thunder of the Captains* (New York: Crowell, 1977).

p. 78. U-2 controversy: Abel, pp. 25–27; Allison, p. 123.

p. 79. IL-28s: *DOD Appropriations*, p. 12; Committee on Armed Services, *Military Posture*, p. 249; Nikita Khrushchev, *Khrushchev Remembers* (Boston: Little, Brown, 1970), p. 495; DOD, "Special Briefing," p. 42. Keating's October 10 speech: *Congressional Record*, October 10, 1962, p. 21728; NBC, Monitor, November 4, 1962; Memorandum, T. L. Hughes to McGeorge Bundy, January 2, 1963, National Security Council MSS, Kennedy Library.

6. *Discovery*

p. 83. "With peace hanging . . ." (emphasis added): *New York Times*, October 22, 1962.

p. 84. Rapid City: *Ibid.*

p. 84. Students: Miami *News*, October 9–11, 1962.

p. 86. "The embassy community . . .": Letter, John C. Shea to the author, August 14, 1977.

p. 87. On Guantanamo: See Edwin Tetlow, *Eye on Cuba* (New York: Harcourt, Brace & World, 1966), pp. 209–222; Tampa *Tribune*, October 25, 1962.

p. 88. Cubans: Interviews by author.

p. 91. Rudolf Anderson: Greenville (S.C.) *News*, October 28–November 5, 1962; James Daniel and John G. Hubbell, *Strike in the West* (New York: Holt, Rinehart and Winston, 1963), pp. 24–25, 172–173.

p. 92. U-2 flight over Cuba: There is a mystery about this flight. All sources agree that Anderson had another pilot with him that day, Major Richard S. Heyser. See *Air Force and Space Digest*, December 1962, p. 21. But McNamara later stated that the U.S. only sent one U-2 that day: U.S., Congress, House, Subcommittee of the Committee on Appropriations, *Department of Defense Appropriations for 1964: Hearings*, 88th Cong., 1st sess., 1963, p. 4. Possibly the two men were flying the U-2D, a two-seater. The Air Force has refused to clear up this mystery, though they have told the author that they doubted that Anderson and Heyser were flying a U-2D.

p. 94. JM WAVE: Taylor Branch and George Crile III, "The Kennedy Vendetta," *Harper's*, August 1975, p. 62.

p. 95. "Hey, take a. . . .": Daniel and Hubbell, p. 29.

p. 96. Hilsman's call to Martin: Roger Hilsman, *To Move a Nation* (Garden City, N.Y.: Doubleday, 1967), pp. 193–194.

7. How Tojo Felt

p. 100. Bundy's call to Hilsman: Robert Hurwitch, Oral History Interview, pp. 139–140, Kennedy Library.

p. 102. "World opinion? . . .": Arthur Schlesinger, Jr., *A Thousand Days* (Greenwich, Conn.: Crest Books, 1965), p. 445.

p. 103. "You still think . . .": Kenneth P. O'Donnell and David F. Powers, *"Johnny, We Hardly Knew Ye"* (New York: Pocket Books, 1972), p. 378.

p. 104. Rumor about JFK's first reaction: Alexander L. George, "The Cuban Missile Crisis, 1962," in *The Limits of Coercive Diplomacy*, edited by Alexander L. George *et al.* (Boston: Little, Brown, 1971), p. 89n. "soft on communism . . .": Theodore Sorensen, Oral History Interview, p. 64, Kennedy Library. "If I don't. . .": O'Donnell and Powers, p. 355.

p. 104. Rusk's thoughts on the matter: Cited in William Gustaf Skillern, "An Analysis of the Decision-Making Process in the Cuban Missile Crisis" (unpublished Ph.D. dissertation, University of Idaho, 1971), pp. 245–246.

p. 105. U.S. military superiority: Memorandum, Theodore Sorensen, October 17, 1962, Sorensen MSS, Kennedy Library. "politically changed the . . .": Interview, December 17, 1962, in *Public Papers of the Presidents, John F. Kennedy* (Washington: G.P.O., 1963), p. 898.

p. 106. "I keep thinking. . .": O'Donnell and Powers, 329.

p. 106. Salinger's meeting: Pierre Salinger, *With Kennedy* (New York: Avon, 1965), pp. 312–313.

p. 107. "I for one . . .": Robert Kennedy, *Thirteen Days* (New York: Norton, 1969), p. 24.

p. 109. "I now know. . .": *Ibid.*, p. 31.

p. 109. General Adams' plan: P. D. Adams, Oral History Interview, pp. 9–11, Military History Institute, Carlisle Barracks, Pa.

p. 110. "My assignment from . . .": O'Donnell and Powers, p. 361. On the meetings that day: Maxwell D. Taylor, *Swords and Plowshares* (New York:

Norton, 1972), pp. 264–265; Gilpatric, Daily Diary; Elie Abel, *The Missile Crisis* (Philadelphia: Lippincott, 1966), pp. 43–44; Dean Rusk, Daily Diary, October 16, 1962, and Telephone Log, October 16, 1962, Hilsman MSS, Kennedy Library; Theodore Sorensen, *Kennedy* (New York: Bantam Books, 1965), pp. 761–762.

p. 112. "considered that just . . .": Skillern, p. 193. "We'll have to . . .": Abel, p. 49.

p. 112. "Let's not go . . .": Letter, Stevenson to JFK, October 17, 1962, Presidential Office Files, Kennedy Library. "Adlai's not soft . . .": Quoted in Bert Cochran, *Adlai Stevenson* (New York: Funk & Wagnalls, 1969), p. 326.

p. 113. "It seems in . . .": Quoted in Henry M. Pachter, *Collision Course* (New York: Praeger, 1967), p. 30n.

p. 116. Kennedy at Alsop's: Abel, p. 54.

p. 116. Yarmolinsky at movies: Adam Yarmolinsky, Diary, October 16, 1962, Yarmolinsky MSS, Kennedy Library.

8. *Nations Make Love Like Porcupines*

p. 126. "We're going in . . .": Kenneth P. O'Donnell and David F. Powers, *"Johnny, We Hardly Knew Ye"* (New York: Pocket Books, 1972), pp. 366–367.

p. 127. Conversation with Bartlett: Charles Bartlett, Oral History Interview, pp. 126–127, Kennedy Library.

p. 128. "Are you saying . . .": Theodore Sorensen, *Kennedy* (New York: Bantam Books, 1965), pp. 768–769.

p. 128. "I didn't leave . . .": David A. Burchinal, Oral History Interview, p. 113, Military History Institute, Carlisle Barracks, Pa.

p. 128. Military planning: Maxwell D. Taylor, *Swords and Plowshares* (New York: Norton, 1972), pp. 268–269; Theodore Sorensen, Oral History Interview, p. 58, Kennedy Library; Theodore Sorensen, Memorandum, October 17, 1962, Sorensen MSS, Kennedy Library. *New York Times*, October 26, 1968; Robert Hurwitch, Oral History Interview, pp. 141–143, Kennedy Library.

p. 130. McNamara and LeMay: Burchinal, p. 114. McNamara, in a letter to the author, has absolutely denied this story. I have included it because, despite the secretary's recollections, many high officials that week were frantically searching out alternatives which in calmer retrospect seem implausible, and it would have been understandable for McNamara to hope for the impossible.

p. 131. "repetitive, leaderless, and . . .": Dean Acheson, "Dean Acheson's Version of Robert Kennedy's Version of the Cuban Missile Crisis," *Esquire*, February 1969, p. 77.

p. 131. "I am on . . .": Sorensen to Robert C. Sorensen, October 12, 1962, Sorensen MSS, Kennedy Library. "It was an . . .": Sorensen, *Kennedy*, p. 767. Mac Bundy and Shoup proposing no action at all: Sorensen, Oral History Interview, p. 53.

p. 132. "the question was . . .": Dean Acheson, Oral History Interview, pp. 22–23, Kennedy Library.

p. 133. "We would be . . .": Robert Lovett, Oral History Interview, p. 49, Kennedy Library.

p. 133. "Ted—Have you . . .": Sorensen, *Kennedy*, p. 775.

p. 134. Illegality of the quarantine: See Quincy Wright, "The Cuban Quarantine of 1962," in *Power and Order*, edited by John G. Stoessinger and Alan F. Westin (New York: Harcourt, Brace & World, 1964), pp. 199–212.

p. 134. "impart a sense . . .": Walter W. Rostow, "The Possible Role of a Progressive Economic Blockade Against Cuba," Memorandum, October 25, 1962, NSC MSS, Kennedy Library.

p. 135. "quick, and hopefully . . .": U. Alexis Johnson, Oral History Interview, p. 42, Kennedy Library. "the group across . . .": Burchinal, p. 114. "worried about the . . .": C. L. Sulzberger, *The Last of the Giants* (New York: Macmillan, 1970), p. 920. "He was a . . .": Barksdale Hamlett, Oral History Interview, VI, 10, Military History Institute, Carlisle Barracks, Pa.

p. 136. "It could happen . . .": Paul B. Fay, Jr., *The Pleasure of His Company* (New York: Dell Books, 1966), pp. 162–163. Dean Acheson believed that one of the main reasons Kennedy pulled away from bombing was the Air Force's insistence on increasing the targets: Acheson, "Dean Acheson's Version . . ." pp. 76–77.

p. 136. JFK and LeMay: Robert Kennedy, *Thirteen Days* (New York: Norton, 1969), pp. 36–37; O'Donnell and Powers, pp. 368–369. "The first advice . . .": Benjamin Bradlee, *Conversations with Kennedy* (New York: Norton, 1975), p. 122.

p. 137. Thompson's advice: Llewellyn Thompson, Oral History Interview, p. 11, Kennedy Library.

p. 195 "He always wants . . .": Joseph Kraft, *Profiles in Power* (New York: New American Library, 1966), p. 106.

p. 138. Schlei's plan: Letter, Schlei to Abram Chayes, May 22, 1968, in Abram Chayes, *The Cuban Missile Crisis* (New York: Oxford University Press, 1974), pp. 132–134.

p. 139. Other proposals: *New York Times*, September 16, 19, 1962. "emotional or intuitive": Acheson, "Dean Acheson's Version . . .," p. 76.

p. 139. "courage and sensitivity": Jack Newfield, *Robert Kennedy: A Memoir* (New York: Bantam Books, 1970), p. 21. "I think Bobby . . .": *Ibid.*, p. 38.

p. 140. "a Pearl Harbor . . .": Sorensen, *Kennedy*, p. 772. "My brother is . . .": Elie Abel, *The Missile Crisis* (Philadelphia: Lippincott, 1966) p. 64.

p. 141. "It had never . . .": Elie Abel, "A Working Reporter Looks at Oral History," in *The Fourth National Colloquium on Oral History*, edited by Gould P. Colman (New York: The Oral History Association, 1970), p. 32.

p. 141. JFK and Acheson: Acheson, Oral History Interview, p. 24.

p. 142. Meeting with Gromyko: *New York Times*, October 27, 1962; Abel, pp. 76–77; Sorensen, *Kennedy*, pp. 778–778; Pierre Salinger, *With Kennedy* (New York: Avon, 1966), p. 369; JFK, Daily Diary, October 18, 1962; Lovett's recollections about "low-level photographs" were in error; the government did not have these yet.

p. 144. "I know there . . .": Abel, p. 79.

p. 144. Straw vote: Arthur Schlesinger, Jr., *A Thousand Days* (Greenwich, Conn.: Crest Books, 1965), p. 739.

p. 144. "What if we . . .": *Ibid.*, p. 81. "It would be . . .": Sorensen, *Kennedy*, p. 779.

p. 145. Martinez: Taylor Branch and George Crile III, "The Kennedy Vendetta," *Harper's*, August 1975, p. 62.

9. The Decision

p. 147. Rusk to Schoenbrun: CBS Reports, November 28, 1962. "Are you going . . .": Summary of activities, October 18, 1962, NSC MSS, Kennedy Library.

p. 147. Bundy's questionnaire: Hugh Sidey, *John F. Kennedy, President* (Greenwich, Conn.: Crest Books, 1963), p. 308.

p. 147. Intelligence experts: Elie Abel, *The Missile Crisis* (Philadelphia: Lippincott, 1966), pp. 65–66, 73–74; Robert W. Reford, *Canada and Three Crises* (Lindsay, Ont.: John Deyell, 1968), pp. 172–173. "AP report": Miami *News*, October 17, 1962. Hal Hendrix and CIA: Victor Marchetti and John D. Marks, *The CIA and the Cult of Intelligence* (New York: Knopf, 1974), p. 366. In a letter to the author (August 28, 1978) Hendrix has categorically denied my hypothesis. The word "quarantine": Abram Chayes, *The Cuban Missile Crisis* (New York: Oxford University Press, 1974), pp. 14–15n. In fact the *final* decision about using "quarantine" was not made until next Monday morning.

p. 148. JFK asked Theodore Sorensen to push for consensus: Sorensen, *Kennedy* (New York: Bantam Books, 1965), p. 780. He did not stipulate which of the two choices he wanted. On the other hand he told O'Donnell he definitely wanted the blockade: Kenneth P. O'Donnell and David F. Powers, *"Johnny, We Hardly Knew Ye"* (New York: Pocket Books, 1972), pp. 369–370. If so, why did not JFK tell ExCom that fact, rather than make them go through the agony? Also, why was he so much in favor of a consensus: Was he gun-shy from the Bay of Pigs? Most likely O'Donnell was merely incorrect in his recollections; it probably only *seemed* to him in retrospect that that is what the President wished.

p. 151. I have pieced together the events in Chicago from: O'Donnell and Powers, pp. 369–372; Pierre Salinger, *With Kennedy* (New York: Avon, 1966), pp. 314–316; John F. Kennedy, Daily Diary, October 19–20, 1962, Kennedy Library.

p. 153. "If the President . . .": Abel, pp. 92–93. JFK Returns: Sorensen, p. 781; Robert Kennedy, *Thirteen Days* (New York: Norton, 1969), p. 47. The two sources here are almost totally contradictory.

p. 154. McCone's briefing: CIA, "Memorandum: THE CRISIS," October 21, 1962, Kennedy Library. Dean Rusk's summary: Abel, p. 93. Presumably Abel got this information from Rusk who no doubt consulted the two-page summary which Abel describes. But none of the other participants mentions Rusk's presentation or the two-page document. All other sources state clearly that it was McNamara who argued that day for the blockade. Probably Rusk only said a few sentences and *handed* his opinion to the President who glanced at it, and returned it. "Berlin is the . . .": C. L. Sulzberger, *The Last of the Giants* (New York: Macmillan, 1970), p. 860.

p. 154. RFK on nuclear strike: Kennedy, p. 48.

p. 154. JFK's reaction: Sorensen, *Kennedy*, pp. 782–783; Sorensen, Oral History Interview, p. 61, Kennedy Library.

p. 155. Stevenson proposals: Letter, Adlai Stevenson to Arthur M. Schlesinger, Jr., n.d. (probably late December 1962), Schlesinger MSS, Kennedy Library.

p. 156. "Well, everyone knows . . .": Sorensen, Oral History Interview, p. 65.

p. 156. Harriman on Turkish missiles: Averell Harriman, "Memorandum on Kremlin Reactions," October 22, 1962, Kennedy Library.

p. 157. The March 20, 1961, NSC memorandum; Kennedy's demand for a review; and the June 22, 1961 memorandum are all in the NSC records, Kennedy Library.

p. 157. JFK on "American payrolls": Abel, p. 190. The October 21 meeting: Chayes, pp. 81–82.

p. 158. JFK to Bradlee: Benjamin Bradlee, *Conversations with Kennedy* (New York: Norton, 1975), p. 132.

p. 159. *Post* article: Stewart Alsop and Charles Bartlett, "In Time of Crisis," *Saturday Evening Post*, December 8, 1962, pp. 15–21.

p. 159. JFK to Bartlett: Charles Bartlett, Oral History Interview, pp. 130–131, Kennedy Library.

p. 159. "I guess Homer . . .": Sorensen, Oral History Interview, p. 60. The balcony scene: O'Donnell and Powers, pp. 373–375.

p. 160. Rusk's call to Acheson: Acheson, Oral History Interview, pp. 24–25, Kennedy Library.

p. 161. Salinger's calls: Salinger, pp. 316–17.

p. 162. There are several contradictions in the accounts about the government's requests to the newsmen not to print their findings: O'Donnell and Powers, pp. 377–378; Abel, p. 99; Max Frankel, "A Washington Education," *The Columbia Forum*, Winter 1973, p. 10.

p. 162. Marines: Mel Jones, "Crisis Report," *Leatherneck* 46 (April 1963), 19; John H. Johnstone, "A Brief History of the 1st Marines," (Washington; Historical Branch, USMC, 1968), p. 25.

p. 163. Naval planning; Alfred G. Ward, Oral History Interview, pp. 187–189, Naval History Division; Ward, "Cuban Quarantine: Personal History," pp. 3–5, Naval History Division (Typewritten); James Daniel and John G. Hubbell, *Strike in the West* (New York: Holt, Rinehart and Winston, 1963), pp. 100–103. Lippmann's comment: Salinger, p. 317.

10. *Preparations*

p. 164. Missiles: AF, Staff Message Division, Action information, JCS/J3(4–10); cf. *Newsweek*, November 28, 1963, p. 25, which uses different figures.

p. 165. "When I went . . .": *Newsweek*, November 28, 1963, p. 24. Fort Hood: Joseph R. Wisnack, "Old Ironsides' Response to the Cuban Crisis," *Army*, April 1963, pp. 26–30.

p. 165. On gathering Navy: Alfred G. Ward, "Cuban Quarantine: Personal History," p. 7, Naval History Division (Typewritten).

p. 166. *Essex*: "Essex and the Navy: Ready and Responsive," mimeographed account, forwarded to the Navy Department by J. M. West; L. J. Johnson, personal account of Cuban quarantine (forwarded with above).

p. 166. Guantanamo evacuation: "1494–1964" (privately published; Naval History Division, n.d.), pp. 61–64; J. D. Ferguson, "Historical Diary of Fleet Training Group, Guantanamo Bay, Cuba" (Mimeographed; Naval History Institute, n.d.); *New York Times*, October 24, 1962, Miami *Herald*, October 26, 1962.

p. 166. Account of Navy wife: Miami *Herald*, October 27, 1962.

p. 169. "You always go . . .": Pierre Salinger, *With Kennedy* (New York: Avon, 1966), p. 323.

p. 169. "How long do . . .": Elie Abel, *The Missile Crisis* (Philadelphia: Lippincott, 1966), p. 102. Newsmen in Roosevelt Roads: James Daniel and John G. Hubbell, *Strike in the West* (New York: Holt, Rinehart and Winston, 1963), pp. 96–97.

p. 170. Acheson story: Dean Acheson, Oral History Interview, p. 25, Kennedy Library.

p. 171. Lovett story: Robert Lovett, Oral History Interview, pp. 53–54, Kennedy Library.

p. 172. Lunch with Ormsby-Gore: Abel, pp. 105–106. "Maybe it's because . . .": Kenneth P. O'Donnell and David F. Powers, *"Johnny, We Hardly Knew Ye"* (New York: Pocket Books, 1972), p. 402.

p. 172. Message for Macmillan: Harold Macmillan, *At the End of the Day* (New York: Macmillan, 1973), pp. 182–183.

p. 172. ExCom meeting: There is some question whether or not this was a formal convocation of the NSC. Abel, p. 107, says it was; so does Theodore Sorensen, *Kennedy* (New York: Bantam Books, 1965), p. 787; and Dean Rusk's Daily Diary, October 21, 1962, Lyndon Baines Johnson Library. On the other hand there was no mention of it, as there normally would be, in the President's Daily Log; and a hand-written note in the Roger Hilsman papers, Kennedy Library, says it was "really Excom & Hilsman."

p. 173. "Well, Admiral, it . . .": George W. Anderson, Jr., "The Cuban Crisis," *Proceedings: Naval History Symposium* (United States Naval Academy, 1973), p. 81.

11. *A Television Event*

p. 174. Acheson in Paris: Dean Acheson, Oral History Interview, pp. 26–29, Kennedy Library,; C. L. Sulzberger, *The Last of the Giants* (New York: Macmillan, 1973), pp. 930–931. (One wonders why Acheson did not know that Kennedy planned to invade Cuba if the blockade did not work. Had not Rusk and Ball informed him when they briefed him Sunday morning? If not, why not? President Kennedy himself told Macmillan that the United States would attack almost precisely at the same moment Acheson was talking to De Gaulle [see below]. Were there some differences of interpretation between the people from State and the White House? The evidence is unclear. It seems possible that Acheson was merely mistaken, either in his presentation to De Gaulle or in his later recollections. This, however, seems unlikely; he was quite definite about the incident.)

p. 176. Macmillan's reaction: Harold Macmillan, *At the End of the Day* (New York: Macmillan, 1973), pp. 187–194.

p. 177. Ottawa: Robert W. Reford, *Canada and Three Crises* (Lindsay, Ont.: John Deyell, 1968), pp. 174–185.

p. 177. Caroline: Evelyn Lincoln, *My Twelve Years with John F. Kennedy* (New York: McKay, 1965), p. 325.

p. 178. Salinger: Pierre Salinger, *With Kennedy* (New York: Avon, 1966), pp. 327–328.

p. 178. Call to Meany; George Meany, Oral History Interview, p. 25, Kennedy Library. Calls to Sorensen: Theodore Sorensen, *Kennedy* (New York; Bantam Books, 1965), p. 790.

p. 179. Mansfield: Mike Mansfield, Oral History Interview, pp. 18–19, Kennedy Library.

p. 180. Fulbright; J. W. Fulbright, Oral History Interview, pp. 66–68, Kennedy Library.

p. 180. Kennedy to Dirksen: Kenneth P. O'Donnell and David F. Powers, *"Johnny, We hardly Knew Ye"* (New York: Pocket Books, 1972), p. 378.

p. 181. JFK exchange with Russell and Fulbright: Fulbright, Oral History Interview, pp. 70–73; "Fulbright's Role in the Cuban Missile Crisis," *Inter-American Economic Affairs*, 27 (Spring 1974), 86–94 (originally printed in *Congressional Record*, December 10, 1973). (Possibly Fulbright and Russell had discussed an invasion on their plane ride to Washington.)

p. 181. "Last Tuesday I . . ." and "Oh, sure, . . .": O'Donnell and Powers, p. 380. Humphrey's call to his wife: *Newsweek*, November 12, 1962, p. 17. Kennedy and Humphrey: James Daniel and John G. Hubbell, *Strike in the West* (New York: Holt, Rinehart and Winston, 1963), p. 94.

p. 182. "If they want. . . .": Sorensen, p. 372.

p. 182. Wilson and Minow: Donald M. Wilson, Oral History Interview, pp. 19–20, Kennedy Library.

p. 183. Savings and loan commercial; Elie Abel, *The Missile Crisis* (Philadelphia: Lippincott, 1966), pp. 120–121.

p. 184. "I wish to . . .": *Department of State Bulletin*, November 19, 1973, p. 636.

p. 184. "When we saw . . .": "Conversation with Fidel Castro," *Oui*, January 1975, p. 156.

p. 186. Martinez: Taylor Branch and George Crile III, "The Kennedy Vendetta," *Harper's*, August 1975, p. 62.

p. 186. Among the various accounts of the immediate reaction to Kennedy's speech, see *New York Times*, October 23, 1962; Miami *Herald*, October 23, 1962.

p. 188. Dean Rusk quotation: Peter Lisagor, Oral History Interview. p. 75, Kennedy Library.

12. *A Spectrum of Reaction*

p. 192. Lubell: Miami *Herald*, October 27, 1962. Gallup: St. Louis *Post-Dispatch*, October 24, 1962. See also *Wall Street Journal*, October 24, 1962.

p. 192. Various other reactions: Interviews with author; *New York Times*, October 23–26, 1962.

p. 194. Camouflaging the missiles: Why did not the Russians do so before? Graham T. Allison, *Essence of Decision* (Boston: Little, Brown, 1971), p. 111, has perceptively suggested that the missilemen failed to do so because such an action would not have been a part of their standard operating procedures.

p. 195. Most Cuban reactions: Interviews with author.

p. 196. Gabriel Capote Pacheco; Oscar Lewis *et al.*, *Four Men* (Urbana: University of Illinois Press, 1977), pp. 486–487.

p. 197. "We have won . . .": Elie Abel, *The Missile Crisis* (Philadelphia: Lippincott, 1966), p. 127. JFK smiling: Kenneth P. O'Donnell and David F. Powers, *"Johnny, We Hardly Knew Ye"* (New York: Pocket Books, 1972), p. 382. "a certain spirit . . .": Robert Kennedy, *Thirteen Days* (New York: Norton, 1969), p. 57.

p. 197. Conversation about Tuchman's book: Robert Kennedy, p. 62; O'Donnell and Powers, p. 383.

p. 198. Latin American reactions: "Intelligence Note: US Moves Catch Latin Communists Off Balance," October 26, 1962, Hilsman MSS, Kennedy Library; CIA, "Memorandum: THE CRISIS," October 26, 27, 1962, Kennedy Library.

p. 199. The quarantine: According to Robert Kennedy, p. 67, Ormsby Gore suggested to the President that he order the quarantine line to pull back from 800 miles away from Cuba to 500 miles, in order to give the Kremlin that much extra time (before their ships reached the quarantine line) to decide what to do. This dubious tale is backed by Harold Macmillan, *At the End of the Day* (New York: Macmillan, 1973), p. 197. This story creates a mystery. The historian, Graham T. Allison, pp. 129–130, 309, has perceived a White House-military conflict here, for he has calculated that the Navy's line never changed from its original 500 miles. See also Alexander L. George, "The Cuban Missile Crisis, 1962," in *The Limits of Coercive Diplomacy*, edited by Alexander L. George *et al.* (Boston: Little, Brown, 1971), pp. 108–110. If Robert Kennedy's (and Macmillan's) recollections were accurate, then the President may have been confused when he told Ormsby-Gore about the Navy's quarantine design. According to the *original* blockade plans, drawn up by Admiral Anderson on Saturday, concurred in by Maxwell Taylor and Admirals Dennison and Ward, and approved by ExCom and the President on Sunday, the quarantine line was to be 500 miles out from Cuba's eastern tip. The reason for choosing this distance was that some military planners were worried that Cuban planes might fly out and attack the ships. Taylor and Ward, among others, thought the line was set too far out, requiring too many ships to cover the waterways. Taylor wanted the line set at 180 miles and Ward agreed. As the orders were actually written, all they said was that the line should be beyond the range of all Cuban weapons. This was so vague that Ward and the Navy decided to use the 500-mile figure to be on the safe side. But by Saturday, October 27, it was clear that the Cubans either did not intend to fly out or their planes did not have the capacity, and the line was reduced to 180 miles. Alfred G. Ward, "Cuban Quarantine: Personal History," pp. 4–6, Naval History Institute (Typewritten); George Dennison, Oral History Interview, p. 424, Naval History Division, U.S. Navy. Perhaps JFK had forgotten the details of Anderson's plan when he explained it to Ormsby Gore; or maybe he calculated 800 miles, mistakenly using Havana as his axis. At any rate there was no White House-military disagreement on the quarantine line, or at least none evident in naval archives.

13. The Quarantine

p. 200. Russian reactions: *New York Times*, October 25, 28, 1962; Stewart Alsop and Charles Bartlett, "In Time of Crisis," *Saturday Evening Post*, December 8, 1962, p. 17.

p. 201. Kremlin divisions: Michel Tatu, *Power in the Kremlin* (New York: Viking, 1969), pp. 272–276.

p. 201. Conversation with Knox: William E. Knox, "Close-up of Khrushchev During a Crisis," *The New York Times Magazine*, November 18, 1962, pp. 32ff; *New York Times*, October 27, 1962.

p. 202. Zorin at the UN: CIA, "Memorandum: THE CRISIS," October 27, 1962.

p. 203. Bertrand Russell and the crisis: Bertrand Russell, *Unarmed Victory* (New York: Simon & Schuster, 1963).

p. 204. Gene Miller's flight: Miami *Herald*, October 25, 1962.

p. 205. *J. R. Perry:* James Daniel and John G. Hubbell, *Strike in the West* (New York: Holt, Rinehart and Winston, 1963), pp. 163–165.

p. 206. African airfields: William Attwood, Oral History Interview, p. 7, Kennedy Library; William Attwood, *The Reds and the Blacks* (New York: Harper & Row, 1967), p. 109; Elie Abel, *The Missile Crisis* (Philadelphia: Lippincott, 1966), pp. 136–138; Department of State, Bureau of Intelligence and Research, Research Memorandum, INR-92, October 26, 1962. CIA shipping estimates: CIA, "Memorandum: THE CRISIS," October 23–24, November 3, 1962.

p. 207. "we think it . . .": Department of State: Director of Intelligence and Research, "Intelligence Note: Soviets Soft-Pedal Direct US-Soviet Confrontation," October 24, 1962, Hilsman MSS, Kennedy Library. "Our ships will . . .": Abel, p. 134. "It looks really . . .": Robert Kennedy, *Thirteen Days* (New York: Norton, 1969), p. 67. "There wasn't one . . .": Alsop and Bartlett, p. 16. "it seemed highly . . .": Abel, p. 153.

p. 208. "While you're safe . . .": Kenneth P. O'Donnell and David F. Powers, *"Johnny, We Hardly Knew Ye"* (New York: Pocket Books, 1972), p. 376.

p. 208. New instructions: Tazewell Shepard, Memorandum for Evelyn Lincoln, October 26, 1962, Presidential Office Files, Kennedy Library.

p. 208. David Powers' neighbors: O'Donnell and Powers, p. 389.

p. 208. Department of Agriculture preparations: Robert Reed, Oral History Interview, p. 6, Kennedy Library; Arthur Thompson, Oral History Interview, p. 28, Kennedy Library. Poker club: Tang Sri Ong Yoke Lin, Oral History Interview, pp. 16–17, Kennedy Library. "I may not . . .": Elie Abel, "A Working Reporter Looks at Oral History," *The Fourth National Colloquium on Oral History*, edited by Gould P. Colman (New York: The Oral History Association, 1970), p. 31. "This could well. . .": Abel, p. 133.

p. 209. Canadian nervousness: Robert W. Reford, *Canada and Three Crises* (Lindsay, Ont.: John Deyell, 1968), p. 196.

p. 209. "For a few . . .": Kennedy, pp. 69–70. The psychological analysis: Irving L. Janis, *Victims of Groupthink* (Boston: Houghton Mifflin, 1967), p. 156.

p. 210. The Russian ships stop Tuesday: CIA, "Memorandum: THE CRISIS," October 23–27, 1962, Kennedy Library.

p. 211. The decision not to harrass the Soviet ships: Alsop and Bartlett, p. 16; Kennedy, pp. 71–72; Arthur Schlesinger, Jr., *A Thousand Days* (Greenwich, Conn.: Crest Books, 1965), p. 108.

p. 211. On ASW: Alfred G. Ward, Oral History Interview, pp. 193–194, 204, and George Dennison, Oral History Interview, pp. 434–437, Naval History Division; P. Eleson, "Underwater Ordnance," *Ordnance*, 47 (January–February, 1963), p. 384.

p. 212. Anderson-McNamara exchange: Abel, pp. 154–156; O'Donnell and Powers, p. 385; Ward, p. 199; Dennison, pp. 435–436; letter, McNamara to author, August 18, 1978; an interview (name withheld) with the author.

p. 211. JFK and Luce: Henry Luce, Oral History Interview, pp. 32–37, Kennedy Library.

p. 214. Both conversations with Bartlett: Charles Bartlett, Oral History Interview, pp. 124–125, Kennedy Library. Message from Khrushchev: *Department of State Bulletin*, November 19, 1973, pp. 637–639.

14. *The Ends of the Rope*

p. 226. Stevenson thinking he had "gone too far": Quoted in Kenneth S. Davis, *The Politics of Honor* (New York: Putnam, 1967), p. 484.

p. 226. "Stevenson, we don't . . .": Kenneth P. O'Donnell and David F. Powers, *"Johnny, We Hardly Knew Ye"* (New York: Pocket Books, 1972), p. 387.

p. 227. "I never knew . . .": *Ibid.*

p. 227. The quarantine: CIA, "Memorandum: THE CRISIS," October 24–27, 1962.

p. 228. "We don't want . . .": Robert Kennedy, *Thirteen Days* (New York: Norton, 1969), p. 77.

p. 229. *Marucla* incident: Reports by Nicholas Mikhalevsky and K. C. Reynolds, October 26, 1962, Naval History Division; Alfred G. Ward, "Cuban Quarantine: Personal History," p. 13, Naval History Division.

p. 230. "I suppose everybody . . .": O'Donnell and Powers, p. 386.

p. 232. ExCom's morning meeting: McGeorge Bundy, NSC Executive Committee Record of Action, October 26, 1962, 10:00 A.M., Meeting No. 6, NSC MSS, Kennedy Library.

p. 233. "very bloody fight": Kennedy, p. 85.

p. 233. Leaflets: Donald M. Wilson, Oral History Interview, pp. 22–23; Richard Mayhew Brown, "United States Propaganda in Crisis, 1960–1965" (unpublished Ph.D. dissertation, University of North Carolina, 1970), pp. 109–110.

p. 234. SGA meeting: Roswell Gilpatric, Daily Diary, October 26, 1962, Gilpatric MSS, Kennedy Library. "Any further delay . . .": Quoted in Arthur Schlesinger, Jr., Memorandum for the President, November 5, 1962, Presidential Office Files, Kennedy Library.

p. 235. Message for Castro: U. Alexis Johnson, Memorandum for McGeorge Bundy, October 26, 1962, NSC MSS, Kennedy Library.

p. 235. I have intermixed the Scali/Fomin conversations with the Khrushchev letters in order to show how the decision makers received the two proposals. Scali's story: John Scali, "I Was the Secret Go-Between in the Cuban Crisis," *Family Weekly*, October 25, 1964, pp. 4–14; a seven-page memorandum among the Hilsman papers at the Kennedy Library, called, "Expurgated Version of Events Which Will Be Basis for ABC News Handling of Story"; Scali's actual memo for Excom, in Pierre Salinger, *With Kennedy* (New York: Avon, 1966), pp. 341–344. Scali at White House: *Ibid.*, p. 342; O'Donnell and Powers, pp. 387–388. (Rusk's diary indicates he was still at a meeting at this time, so Salinger and O'Donnell may have seen *Hilsman* with Scali and later gotten them confused: Daily Diary, October 26, 1962, Lyndon Baines Johnson Library.) Khrushchev's message for Kennedy: *Department of State Bulletin*, November 19, 1973, pp. 640–645; original is in the Kennedy Library. See also Roger Hilsman, *To Move a Nation* (Garden City, N.Y.: Doubleday, 1967), pp. 218–219; Abel, pp. 175–184; Roger Hilsman, Daily Diary, Hilsman MSS, Kennedy Library; and Hilsman, Telephone Log, Hilsman MSS, Kennedy Library. Also, letter, Scali to author, August 10, 1978; and letter, Hilsman to author, September 6, 1978.

15. At the Brink

p. 241. "a greater willingness . . .": W. W. Rostow to McGeorge Bundy, October 27, 1962, "Report Number Four of the Planning Subcommittee," NSC MSS, Kennedy Library.

p. 242. FBI report: Robert Kennedy, *Thirteen Days* (New York: Norton, 1969), p. 93.

p. 242. *Grozny:* Roger Hilsman, *To Move a Nation* (Garden City, N.Y.: Doubleday, 1967), p. 220, writes: "a single Soviet ship had detached itself from the others outside the quarantine line and was headed for Cuba. It looked very much as if the Soviets had decided to test our determination." Hilsman was wrong on two counts. There is no evidence that Soviet ships formed themselves into a group. According to the CIA daily memorandums, every Soviet ship bound for the Caribbean slowed or stopped on Tuesday; some like the *Grozny* came on again almost right away. The CIA noted its progress every morning. It continued moving at the same speed—all by itself—throughout the remainder of the week. The Soviets, therefore, were not making a sudden test of America's determination with the *Grozny*. Given the new situation as of Saturday morning's meeting, obviously the real question in the minds of ExCom's members was whether the United States should stop the Russian ship and thereby test the *Kremlin's* determination.

p. 243. Khrushchev's message: *Department of State Bulletin*, November 19, 1973, pp. 646–649. There has been much speculation—still unresolved—about which of the two Kremlin messages was written first and why a change occurred. See Herbert S. Dinerstein, *The Making of a Missile Crisis* (Baltimore: The Johns Hopkins Press, 1976), especially p. 229. An ironic note to this apparently new demand: On October 3, 1977, Marcelo Fernández Font, Cuba's minister for foreign trade, said that America's economic sanctions should be lifted without reference to any deal. "It was a unilateral measure," he said, "and it should be lifted unilaterally. You cannot take a unilateral action and then expect to get something for lifting that action—this defies all logic." *New York Times*, October 4, 1977. This, in 1962, seemed precisely what the Soviet Union was attempting to do by demanding the dismantling of the Turkish bases.

p. 243. State Department exchange of notes about Turkey: (1) Ball telegram: Department of State, telegram, Ankara 445/Paris for USRO 2355, October 24, 1962; (2) Response from Turkey: No. 587, October 26, 1962; (3) Response from Finletter: No. POLTO 506, October 25, 1962.

p. 244. JFK's anger: Kenneth P. O'Donnell and David F. Powers, *"Johnny, We Hardly Knew Ye"* (New York: Pocket Books, 1972), p. 390. "Get those frigging . . .": Graham T. Allison, *Essence of Decision* (Boston: Little, Brown, 1971), p. 142. Thompson's suggestion: O'Donnell and Powers, p. 392. ExCom's decisions: NSC Executive Committee Record of Action, October 27, 1962, 10:00 A.M. Meeting No. 7, National Security Council MSS, Kennedy Library. This document, drawn up by Bundy, raises an interesting question. Listing the decisions sequentially, Bundy makes no mention of news of Anderson's U-2 crash. His Record of Meeting No. 8, the 4 o'clock meeting discussed below, does mention the crash. Elie Abel, *The Missile Crisis* (Philadelphia: Lippincott, 1966), pp. 188–189, *implies* that ExCom's morning session found out about Anderson's crash. Theodore Sorensen, *Kennedy* (New York: Bantam Books, 1965), pp. 803–804, and Kennedy, p. 97, merely state that they found out that day. Only O'Donnell and Powers, p. 390, of the actual participants, assert unequivocally that the morning meeting was told about Anderson. Bundy's note shows that the morning session focused on Khrushchev's message. The afternoon meeting, according to Bundy's Report No. 8, dwelled almost solely on military matters, especially questions of reconnaissance. The matter is important because it helps to explain the day's *growing* tensions, the result of a series of hammer blows, with their sequence moving inexorably toward military action. I am here assuming that the tenor of Bundy's sketchy notes, taken down just after the meeting, are a more accurate barometer of important matters than O'Donnell's recollections written almost a decade later. The matter, however, is still open to question. A preliminary report on the crash might possibly have come in during the morning meeting and been confirmed later.

p. 245. Kennedy's order to Gilpatric: Abel, p. 195. Once again, O'Donnell's recollections are substantially different. He says he and Robert Kennedy overheard the President's idea, discussed it over lunch, then, agreeing it would be a bad plan, had rushed back to offer the President their objections. According to O'Donnell, John Kennedy laughed and said that he never really planned doing such a thing; he was merely wondering what NATO would think about it. O'Donnell and Powers, p. 392. O'Donnell's story seems untrue for two reasons: (1) George Ball had already asked NATO about it; (2) JFK did agree only a few hours later to take the missiles out. YAF demonstration: *New York Times*, October 28, 1962.

p. 245. U-2 over USSR: Hilsman, p. 221; Henry Brandon, "An Untold Story of the Cuban Crisis," *Saturday Review*, March 9, 1963, pp. 56–57.

p. 246. McNamara's excitement: David A. Burchinal, Oral History Interview, pp. 114–115, Military History Institute, Carlisle Barracks, Pa.

p. 247. Yarmolinsky at football: Yarmolinsky Diary, October 27, 1962, Yarmolinsky MSS, Kennedy Library.

p. 247. T-29 incident: CIA, "Memorandum: THE CRISIS," October 28, 1962, Kennedy Library.

p. 247. The SAMs shooting down Anderson: In addition to the sources listed above under ExCom's morning discussion, see CIA, "Memorandum: THE CRISIS," October 28 and November 1, 1962. Although all other sources declare that the SAMs were being controlled by Russians, it should be noted that Castro later told U Thant that Cubans had shot down Anderson. U Thant, *View from the UN* (Garden City, N.Y.: Doubleday, 1978), p. 188.

p. 248. "He had a . . .": O'Donnell and Powers, p. 393. Tuesday's agreement: Kennedy, p. 58. Stevenson: *New York Times*, October 28, 1962.

p. 248. Castro: Herbert L. Matthews, *Revolution in Cuba* (New York: Scribners, 1975), pp. 212–213. McNamara: Kennedy, p. 13.

p. 249. Scali: Pierre Salinger, *With Kennedy* (New York: Avon, 1966), pp. 344–346; "Expurgated Version of Events Which Will Be Basis for ABC News Handling of Story," NSC MSS, Kennedy Library; John Scali, "I Was the Secret Go-Between in the Cuban Crisis," *Family Weekly*, October 25, 1964, pp. 4–14.

p. 250. ExCom meeting: "NSC Executive Committee Record of Action, October 27, 1962, 4:00 P.M., Meeting No. 8," NSC MSS, Kennedy Library; Kennedy, pp. 96–102.

p. 251. Pentagon shock: Allison, pp. 142, 225. Allison does not footnote this rather startling statement. Missiles of October: Kennedy, p. 127. JFK and Sweeney: Abel, p. 200.

p. 252. "If you disagree . . .": *Ibid.*, p. 197. An odd point should be mentioned.

Whereas all the published sources by ExCom's members agree that Robert Kennedy first made the proposal to ignore Saturday morning's message from Moscow, Evelyn Lincoln, *My Twelve Years with John F. Kennedy* (New York: McKay, 1965), p. 329, states that during that afternoon the President had dictated the rough draft of a message for Khrushchev. She quotes the entire note. It is remarkably like the message Kennedy did eventually send that night, presumably the one "independently" arrived at by Bobby and Sorensen. The Lincoln-JFK draft, like the Sorensen-RFK letter, ignores the October 27th Moscow message, and simply agrees with the one of October 26. Mrs. Lincoln's book is filled with small, technical lapses and perhaps this is one of them. But if the note she quotes was not a preliminary message from the President, what was it? It is possible but improbable that it was the Sorensen-RFK draft. But assuming that her recollections were accurate on this subject, John Kennedy *himself* originally considered the so-called "Trollope ploy" of ignoring that morning's message. It is even possible that he mentioned his idea to Robert Kennedy before the evening's session, and that the attorney general was—as he often did—speaking for his brother. It is a significant if academic point, for a part of Robert Kennedy's later reputation for rationality and cleverness derives from the belief that he was the one who first thought of this compromise position.

p. 252. Khrushchev on RFK: Nikita Khrushchev, *Khrushchev Remembers* (Boston: Little, Brown, 1970), pp. 497–498.

p. 253. RFK's meeting with Dobrynin: Kennedy, pp. 107–109.

p. 254. Nine o'clock meeting: "NSC Executive Committee Record of Action, October 27, 1962, 9:00 P.M., Meeting No. 9," NSC MSS, Kennedy Library.

p. 255. State message: Department of State to Amembassy Paris TOPOL 578, 12:12 A.M., October 28, 1962, NSC MSS, Kennedy Library.

16. To Live with Goats

p. 256. RFK: Robert Kennedy, *Thirteen Days* (New York: Norton, 1969), pp. 109–110.

p. 256. "All of a . . . .": Donald Wilson, Oral History Interview, p. 30, Kennedy Library.

p. 257. "There was great . . .": Andrew J. Goodpaster, Oral History Interview, p. 20, Military History Institute, Carlisle Barracks, Pa. "This is the . . .": Kennedy, p. 110.

p. 257. "leadership, fairness, and . . .": Letter, Acheson to JFK, October 29, 1962, Presidential Office Files, Kennedy Library. Moynihan, "defeat": "Daniel Moynihan: Interview," *Playboy*, March 1977, p. 70. Presidential orders: "NSC Executive Committee Record of Action, October 28, 1962, 11:00 A.M., Meeting No. 10," NSC MSS, Kennedy Library; JFK, Daily Diary, October 28, 1962.

p. 257. SGA: U.S., Congress, Senate, Select Committee to Study Governmental Operations with Respect to Intelligence Activities, *Alleged Assassinations Plots Involving Foreign Leaders* (New York: Norton, 1976), hereafter called Church Committee, pp. 147–148.

p. 258. Example of "firmness" and "restraint": Letter, Chester Bowles to Bundy, November 3, 1962, Bowles MSS, Sterling Library, Yale University.

p. 258. The elections of 1962: Sorensen, Oral History Interview, p. 66, Kennedy Library.

p. 259. Dump truck: U.S., Congress, House, Committee on Armed Services, *Hearings on Military Posture*, 88th Cong., 1st sess., 1963, p. 246.

p. 259. Kuznetsor to McCloy: *Newsweek*, June 12, 1978, p. 31. NSC memorandum: "Significance of the Soviet Backdown for Future US Policy," October 29, 1962, NSC MSS, Kennedy Library.

p. 260. Castro's anger: Herbert L. Matthews, *Revolution in Cuba* (New York: Scribners, 1975), p. 213. Cuba's attack on planes: Pierre Salinger, *With Kennedy* (New York: Avon, 1966), pp. 348–349.

p. 261. SGA: Church Committee, pp. 170–174.

p. 261. Story of the goat: William E. Knox, "Close-Up of Khrushchev During a Crisis," *The New York Times Magazine*, November 18, 1962, p. 128.

Bibliography

In addition to the many published works on this topic, I have primarily depended on two types of sources: (1) the unpublished materials at the John F. Kennedy Library; and (2) the recollections of over a hundred individuals whom I interviewed in the United States and Cuba. The Kennedy Library offers a magnificent storehouse of information and a remarkably able staff with it. I and two researchers—Sheilah Millman and Joseph Becker—spent many enjoyable hours there. I also had considerable success at the military research libraries at Carlisle Barracks, Pennsylvania and the various facilities in Washington, D.C. Many of those I interviewed (especially those still living in Cuba) asked me not to use their names. I can only thank them. I would also like to thank those with whom I corresponded and those who were kind enough to read parts of the manuscript. These include: John C. Shea, Roger Hilsman, John Scali, and Gaddis Smith.

Among the manuscript collections I found helpful were those of Hanson Baldwin and Chester Bowles at the Sterling Library, Yale University; Dean Rusk in the Lyndon Baines Johnson Library, Austin, Texas; and Roswell Gilpatric, Roger Hilsman, John F. Kennedy, Robert F. Kennedy, Godfrey McHugh, Arthur Schlesinger, Jr., Theodore Sorensen, and Adam Yarmolinsky at the Kennedy Library, Waltham, Massachusetts.

There is a vast and growing treasure of oral histories on this era. I found especially useful those of Paul Dewitt Adams, David A. Burchinal, Andrew J. Goodpaster, Barksdale Hamlett, and Arthur Gilbert Trudeau (Military History Institute, Carlisle Barracks, Pennsylvania); George Dennison and Alfred G. Ward (Naval History Division, U.S. Navy, Washington, D.C.); Dean Acheson, William Attwood, Charles Bartlett, Hale Boggs, Bernard Boutin, Henry Brandon, John Cogley, Charles W. Cole, Leroy Collins, J. William Fulbright, Gilbert Harrison, August Heckscher, Roger Hilsman, Robert Hurwitch, U. Alexis Johnson, William Lawrence, Peter Lisagor, Robert Lovett, Henry Luce, Edward McDermitt, Mike Mansfield, George Meany, Tang Sri Ong Yoke Lin, Francis Plimpton, Robert

Reed, Leonard Reinsch, Chalmers Roberts, Leverett Saltonstall, Norbert Schlei, Theodore Sorensen, Arthur Thompson, Llewellyn Thompson, and Donald M. Wilson (Kennedy Library).

I found two types of documents fruitful. There were the extensive collections of memorandums, notes, and analyses in the files of the National Security Council, the CIA, and the Naval Department. (Most of their documents have recently been declassified.) There were also the more formal, public documents of various branches of the government. From Congress comes of course the *Congressional Record*. Also, the House of Representatives committees: Committee on Armed Services, *Hearings on Military Posture*, 88th Cong., 1st sess., 1963; Subcommittee of the Committee on Appropriations, *Department of Defense Appropriations for 1964: Hearings*, 88th Cong., 1st sess., 1963. Senate committees: Committee on Armed Services, *Military Procurement Authorization, Fiscal Year 1964: Hearings*, 88th Cong., 1st sess., 1963; Preparedness Investigating Subcommittee of the Committee on Armed Services, "Investigation of the Preparedness Program: On the Cuban Military Buildup" (Mimeographed), 1963; Select Committee to Study Governmental Operations with Respect to Intelligence Activities, *Alleged Assassination Plots Involving Foreign Leaders*, New York: Norton, 1976. The Department of Defense: "Actions of Military Services in Cuban Crisis Outlined," November 29, 1962; *Annual Report (for Fiscal Year 1963)*, 1964; "Special Cuba Briefing (by Robert S. McNamara)" (Mimeographed), February 6, 1963. Department of State: Press Briefing (Mimeographed), August 24, 1962. Marine Crops: John H. Johnstone, "A Brief History of the 1st Marines," 2d ed., rev., 1968; "Report of the Commandant of the Marine Crops, 1963"; James S. Santelli, "A Brief History of the 8th Marines," 1976. Navy: "Essex and the Navy: Ready and Responsive" (Mimeographed), 1962; J. D. Ferguson, "Historical Diary of Fleet Training Group, Guantanamo Bay, Cuba," 1962; "1949–1964: United States Naval Base: Guantánamo Bay, Cuba"; Alfred G. Ward, "Committee of One Hundred of Miami Beach: Address at Surf Club, February 16, 1963"; Ward, "Cuban Quarantine: Personal History."

I checked through the following magazines: *Aviation Week and Space Technology*, *Bohemia* (Havana), *Le Monde*, *Life*, *Newsweek*, *The New Republic*, *The New Yorker*, *Time*, *U.S. News and World Report*, and *Verde Olivo* (Havana). Also, the following newspapers: *Diario de las Americas* (Miami), *El Mundo* (Havana), *Granma* (Havana), Greenville (South Carolina) *News*, *Hoy* (Havana), St. Louis *Post-Dispatch*, Tampa *Tribune*, *Times of Havana* (Americas Edition), *Ultimas Noticias* (Mexico City).

I found four doctoral dissertations helpful: Richard Mayhew Brown, "United States Propaganda in Crisis, 1960–1965," University of North Carolina, 1970; Jerrold Jackson Merchant, "Kennedy-Khrushchev Strategies of Persuasion During the Missile Crisis," University of Southern California, 1971; Bernard H. Ross, "American Government in Crisis: An Analysis of the Executive Branch of Government During the Cuban Missile Crisis," New York University, 1971; and William Gustaf Skillern, "An Analysis of the Decision-Making Process in the Cuban Missile Crisis," University of Idaho, 1971.

I have listed below many of the books and articles that are particularly useful on this subject.

Books

Abel, Elie. *The Missile Crisis.* Philadelphia: Lippincott, 1966.
Allison, Graham T. *Essence of Decision.* Boston: Little, Brown, 1971.
Alsop, Stewart. *The Center.* New York: Popular Library, 1968.
Attwood, William. *The Reds and the Blacks.* New York: Harper & Row, 1967.
Baldridge, Letitia. *Of Diamonds and Diplomats.* New York: Ballantine Books, 1968.
Bayard, James. *The Real Story on Cuba.* Derby, Conn.: Arlington House, 1969.
Bradlee, Benjamin. *Conversations with Kennedy.* New York: Norton, 1975.
Chayes, Abram. *The Cuban Missile Crisis.* New York: Oxford University Press, 1974.
Cline, Ray S. *Secrets, Spies and Scholars.* Washington: Acropolis Books, 1976.
Cochran, Bert. *Adlai Stevenson.* New York: Funk & Wagnalls, 1969.
Crankshaw, Edward. *Khrushchev: A Career.* New York: Viking, 1966.
————. *Khrushchev's Russia.* Baltimore: Penguin Books, 1959.
Daniel, James, and John G. Hubbell. *Strike in the West.* New York: Holt, Rinehart and Winston, 1963.
Davis, Kenneth S. *The Politics of Honor.* New York: Putnam, 1967.
Desnoes, Edmundo. *Inconsolable Memories.* New York: New American Library, 1967.
Dinerstein, Herbert S. *The Making of a Missile Crisis.* Baltimore; The Johns Hopkins University Press, 1976.
Fagen, Richard R., *et al. Cubans in Exile.* Stanford, Calif.: Stanford University Press, 1968.
Fay, Paul B., Jr. *The Pleasure of His Company.* New York: Dell Books, 1966.
Gallagher, Mary Barelli. *My Life with Jacqueline Kennedy.* New York: Paperback Library, 1969.
Gilly, Adolfo. *Cuba: Coexistencia o Revolucion.* Buenos Aires: Editorial Perspectives (ediciones monthly review), 1965.
Halberstam, David. *The Best and the Brightest.* New York: Random House, 1972.
Halperin, Maurice. *The Rise and Decline of Fidel Castro.* Berkeley: University of California Press, 1972.
Harris, Patricia. *Adlai: The Stevenson Years.* Nashville: Aurora Publishers, 1975.
Hilsman, Roger. *To Move a Nation.* Garden City, N.Y.: Doubleday, 1967.
Hirsch, Phil (ed.). *The Kennedy War Heroes.* New York: Pyramid Books, 1962.
Hoopes, Townsend. *The Devil and John Foster Dulles.* Boston: Little, Brown, 1973.
Janis, Ward. *Military Men.* New York: Knopf, 1970.
Kennedy, Robert F. *Thirteen Days.* New York: Norton, 1969.
Khrushchev, Nikita. *Khrushchev Remembers.* Boston: Little, Brown, 1970.
Kraft, Joseph. *Profiles in Power.* New York: New American Library, 1966.

Krock, Arthur. *Memoirs*. New York: Funk & Wagnalls, 1968.

Lapp, Ralph E. *Kill and Overkill*. New York: Basic Books, 1962.

Lazo, Mario. *Dagger in the Heart*. New York: Funk & Wagnalls, 1968.

Lewis, Oscar, *et al. Four Men*. Urbana: University of Illinois Press, 1977.

Lincoln, Evelyn. *My Twelve Years with John F. Kennedy*. New York: McKay, 1965.

Lockwood, Lee. *Castro's Cuba, Cuba's Fidel*. New York: Macmillan, 1967.

MccGwire, Michael (ed.). *Soviet Naval Developments: Capability and Context*. New York: Praeger, 1973.

Macmillan, Harold. *At the End of the Day*. New York: Macmillan, 1973.

Mankiewicz, Frank, and Kirby Jones. *With Fidel*. New York: Playboy Press, 1975.

Manrara, Luis V. *Betrayal, Opened the Door to Russian Missiles in Red Cuba*. Miami: Truth About Cuba Committee, 1968.

Marchetti, Victor, and John D. Marks. *The CIA and the Cult of Intelligence*. New York: Knopf, 1974.

Martin, John Bartlow. *Adlai Stevenson of Illinois*. Garden City, N.Y.: Doubleday, 1976.

Matthews, Herbert L. *Revolution in Cuba*. New York: Scribners, 1975.

Miller, Warren. *90 Miles from Home*. Greenwich, Conn.: Fawcett Publications, 1961.

Monahan, James, and Kenneth O. Gilmore. *The Great Deception*. New York: Farrar, Straus, 1963.

Morrow, Robert D. *Betrayal*. Chicago: Regnery, 1976.

Newfield, Jack. *Robert Kennedy: A Memoir*. New York: Bantam Books, 1970.

O'Donnell, Kenneth P., and David F. Powers. *"Johnny, We Hardly Knew Ye."* New York: Pocket Books, 1972.

Pachter, Henry M. *Collision Course*. New York: Praeger, 1967.

Penkovskiy, Oleg. *The Penkovskiy Papers*. New York: Avon, 1965.

Plank, John (ed.). *Cuba and the United States*. Washington: Brookings Institution, 1967.

Powers, Francis Gary. *Operation Overflight*. New York: Holt, Rinehart and Winston, 1970.

Reford, Robert W. *Canada and Three Crises*. Lindsay, Ont.: John Deyell, 1968.

Resnick, Marvin D. *The Black Beret: The Life and Meaning of Che Guevara*. New York: Ballantine Books, 1969.

Rostow, W. W. *View from the Seventh Floor*. New York: Harper & Row, 1964.

Russell, Bertrand. *Unarmed Victory*. New York: Simon & Schuster, 1963.

Salinger, Pierre. *With Kennedy*. New York: Avon, 1966.

Schlesinger, Arthur, Jr. *A Thousand Days*. Greenwich, Conn.: Crest Books, 1965.

————. *The Imperial Presidency*. Boston: Houghton Mifflin, 1973.

Sidey, Hugh. *John F. Kennedy, President*. Greenwich, Conn., Crest Books, 1963.

Sorensen, Theodore. *Kennedy*. New York: Bantam Books, 1965.

Stevenson, Adlai E. *Looking Outward*. New York: Harper & Row, 1963.

Stone, I. F. *Time of Torment*. New York: Random House, 1967.

Suárez, Andrés. *Cuba: Castroism and Communism, 1959–1966.* Cambridge, Mass.: M.I.T. Press, 1967.

Sulzberger, C. L. *The Last of the Giants.* New York: Macmillan, 1970.

Sutherland, Elizabeth. *The Youngest Revolution.* New York: Dial Press, 1969.

Tatu, Michel. *Power in the Kremlin.* New York: Viking, 1969.

Taylor, Maxwell D. *Swords and Plowshares.* New York: Norton, 1972.

Tetlow, Edwin. *Eye on Cuba.* New York: Harcourt, Brace & World, 1966.

Thant, U. *View from the UN.* Garden City, N.Y.: Doubleday, 1978.

Theberge, James D. *Soviet Seapower in the Caribbean.* New York: Praeger, 1972.

Thomas, Hugh. *Cuba.* New York: Harper & Row, 1971.

Trewhitt, Henry L. *McNamara.* New York: Harper & Row, 1971.

Tully, Andrew. *The Super Spies.* New York: Pocket Books, 1969.

Vosjoli, P. L. Thyraud de. *Lamia.* Boston: Little, Brown, 1970.

Walton, Richard J. *Cold War and Counterrevolution.* Baltimore: Penguin Books, 1972.

Weintal, Edward, and Charles Bartlett. *Facing the Brink.* New York: Scribners, 1967.

West, J. B. *Upstairs at the White House.* New York: Coward, McCann & Geoghegan, 1973.

Wise, David, and Thomas B. Ross. *The Invisible Government.* New York: Bantam Books, 1964.

———. *The U-2 Affair.* New York: Random House, 1962.

Yarmolinsky, Adam. *The Military Establishment.* New York: Harper & Row, 1971.

Articles

Abel, Elie. "A Working Reporter Looks at Oral History." *The Fourth National Colloquium on Oral History.* Edited by Gould P. Colman. New York: The Oral History Association, 1970.

Acheson, Dean. "Dean Acheson's Version of Robert Kennedy's Version of the Cuban Missile Crisis." *Esquire,* February 1969, pp. 76ff.

Allison, Graham T. "Conceptual Models and the Cuban Missile Crisis." *American Political Science Review* 63 (September 1969), 689–718.

Alsop, Stewart, and Charles Bartlett. "In Time of Crisis." *Saturday Evening Post,* December 8, 1962, pp. 15–21.

Anderson, George W., Jr. "The Cuban Crisis." *Proceedings: Naval History Symposium.* United States Naval Academy, April 27–28, 1973.

Asprey, Robert B. "FMLANT: Profile of Readiness." *Marine Corps Gazette* 47 (January 1963), 20–27.

Bonsal, Philip W. "Cuba, Castro and the United States." *Foreign Affairs* 45 (January 1967), 260–276.

Booda, Larry. "U.S. Watches for Possible Cuban IRBMs." *Aviation Week and Space Technology,* October 1, 1962, pp. 20–21.

Branch, Taylor, and George Crile III. "The Kennedy Vendetta." *Harper's,* August 1975, pp. 49–63.

Brandon, Henry. "An Untold Story of the Cuban Crisis." *Saturday Review*, March 9, 1963, pp. 56–57.

Brzezinski, Zbigniew. "Cuba in Soviet Strategy." *The New Republic*, November 3, 1962, pp. 7–8.

Castro, Juana. "My Brother Fidel." *Life*, August 28, 1964, pp. 22–33.

Chesler, Mark, and Richard Schmuck. "Student Reactions to the Cuban Crisis and Public Dissent." *Public Opinion Quarterly* 28 (Fall 1964), 467–482.

"Conversation with Fidel Castro." *Oui*, January 1975, pp. 113ff.

"Cuba and Berlin." *The New Republic*, November 3, 1962, pp. 1–5.

Daniel, Jean. "Further Clarification." *The New Republic*, December 21, 1963, pp. 6–7.

Eleson, P. "Underwater Ordnance." *Ordnance* 47 (January–February 1963), 384f.

Francis, Michael J. "The U.S. Press and Castro: A Study in Declining Relations." *Journalism Quarterly* 44 (Summer 1967), 257–266.

Frankel, Max. "A Washington Education." *The Columbia Forum*, Winter 1973, pp. 9–14.

Fulbright, J. William. "Fulbright's Role in the Cuban Missile Crisis." *Inter-American Economic Affairs* 27 (Spring 1975), 86–94.

George, Alexander L. "The Cuban Missile Crisis, 1962." *The Limits of Coercive Diplomacy*. Edited by Alexander L. George *et al*. Boston: Little, Brown, 1971.

Hagen, Roger, and Bart Bernstein. "Military Value of Missiles in Cuba." *Bulletin of the Atomic Scientists*, February 1963, pp. 8–13.

Horelick, Arnold L. "The Cuban Missile Crisis: An Analysis of Soviet Calculations and Behavior." *World Politics* 16 (April 1964), 363–389.

Horowitz, Irving Louis. "Deterrence Games: From Academic Casebook to Military Codebook." *The Structure of Conflict*. Edited by Paul Swingle. New York: Academic Press, 1970.

"I Spied on Castro's Cuba." *Ebony*, April 1963, pp. 16ff.

Jones, Mel. "Crisis Report." *Leatherneck* 16 (April 1963), 18–27, 63.

———. "Key West." *Leatherneck* 15 (December 1962), 23ff.

Kahan, Jerome H., and Anne K. Long. "The Cuban Missile Crisis: A Study of Its Strategic Context." *Political Science Quarterly* 87 (December 1972), 564–590.

Kelley, Joe. W. "MATS Looks at the Cuban Crisis." *Air University Review* 14 (September–October 1963), 2–20.

Kester, Charles. "Guantánamo Bay." *Leatherneck* 46 (February 1963), 19–25.

Kissinger, Henry. "Reflections on Cuba." *The Reporter*, November 22, 1962, pp. 21–24.

Knorr, Klaus. "Failures in National Intelligence Estimates: The Case of the Cuban Missiles." *World Politics* 16 (April 1964), 455–467.

Knox, William E. "Close-Up of Khrushchev During a Crisis." *The New York Times Magazine*, November 18, 1962, pp. 32ff.

McDonnell, John. "The Soviet Defense Industry As a Pressure Group." *Soviet Naval Policy: Objectives and Constraints.* Edited by Michael MccGwire *et al.* New York: Praeger, 1975.

McDonough, Joseph A., Jr. "Crisis Diplomacy—Cuba, 1962." *Naval War College Review* 20 (Summer 1967), 3–23.

McGovern, George. "A Talk with Castro." *The New York Times Magazine*, March 13, 1977, pp. 20ff.

Mackintosh, Malcolm. "The Soviet Military's Influence on Foreign Policy." *Soviet Naval Policy: Objectives and Constraints.* Edited by Michael MccGwire *et al.* New York: Praeger, 1975.

"Major Rudolf Anderson, Jr., USAF." *Air Force and Space Digest*, December 1962, p. 21.

Matthews, Herbert. "Castro's Cuba." *The Sunday [London] Times*, October 22, 1972, p. 17.

MccGwire, Michael. "Soviety Naval Interests and Intentions in the Caribbean." *Soviet Naval Developments: Capability and Context.* Edited by Michael MccGwire. New York: Praeger, 1973.

"Messages Exchanged by President Kennedy and Chairman Khrushchev During the Cuban Missile Crisis of October 1962." *Department of State Bulletin*, November 19, 1973, pp. 635–655.

Mitchell, Donald W. "The Strategic Significance of Soviet Naval Power in Cuban Waters." *Soviet Naval Developments: Capability and Context.* Edited by Michael MccGwire. New York: Praeger, 1973.

Nathan, James A. "The Missile Crisis: His Finest Hour Now." *World Politics* 27 (January 1975), 256–281.

Nixon, Richard. "Cuba, Castro and John F. Kennedy." *Reader's Digest*, November 1964, pp. 282–300.

Piper, Don C. "The Cuban Missile Crisis and International Law: Precipitous Decline or Unilateral Development." *World Affairs* 138 (Summer 1975), 26–31.

Rabinowitch, Eugene. "After Cuba: Two Lessons." *Bulletin of Atomic Scientists*, February 1963, pp. 2–8.

Rogers, Warren, Jr. "Reflections on the Bob and John Show." *The New Republic*, February 23, 1963, pp. 10–11.

Rovere, Richard. "Letter from Washington." *The New Yorker* 39 (March 2, 1963), 125–131.

Scali, John. "I Was the Secret Go-Between in the Cuban Crisis." *Family Weekly*, October 25, 1964, pp. 4–14.

Scholin, Allan R. "Aerospace World." *Air Force Magazine*, December 1962, pp. 20–22.

Schulz, Donald E. "Kennedy and the Cuban Connection." *Foreign Policy* 26 (Spring 1977), 57–64, 121–139.

Sugden, G. Scott. "Public Diplomacy and the Missiles of October." *Naval War College Review* 24 (October 1971), 28–43.

"The Man Who Fights the Bull Knows." *Army*, January 1963, pp. 8–10.

Trainor, James. "Cuba Missile Threat Detailed." *Missiles and Rockets*, October 29, 1962, pp. 12ff.

Vosjoli, P. L. Thyraud de. "A Head That Holds Some Sinister Secrets." *Life*, April 26, 1968, p. 35.

Wisnack, Joseph R. "Old Ironsides' Response to the Cuban Crisis." *Army*, April 1963, pp. 26–30.

Witze, Claude. "Airpower in the News." *Air Force Magazine*, January 1963, pp. 13–17.

Wohlstetter, Albert and Roberta. "Notes on the Cuban Crisis (as of Sunday, October 28, 1962)." John F. Kennedy Library. Waltham, Massachusetts.

Wohlstetter, Roberta. "Cuba and Pearl Harbor: Hindsight and Foresight." *Foreign Affairs* 43 (July 1965), 691–707.

Wolfe, Thomas W. "Soviet Naval Interaction with the United States and Its Influence on Soviet Naval Developments." *Soviet Naval Developments: Capability and Context*. Edited by Michael MccGwire. New York: Praeger, 1973.

Wrong, Dennis H. "After the Cuban Crisis." *Commentary*, January 1963, pp. 28–33.

Index

293